DESTINS DE FEMMES

Destins de femmes

French Women Writers, 1750–1850

John Claiborne Isbell

https://www.openbookpublishers.com

© 2023 John Claiborne Isbell

This work is licensed under an Attribution-NonCommercial 4.0 International (CC BY-NC 4.0). This license allows you to share, copy, distribute and transmit the text; to adapt the text for non-commercial purposes of the text providing attribution is made to the authors (but not in any way that suggests that they endorse you or your use of the work). Attribution should include the following information:

John Claiborne Isbell, *Destins de femmes: French Women Writers*, 1750–1850. Cambridge, UK: Open Book Publishers, 2023, https://doi.org/10.11647/OBP.0346

Copyright and permissions for the reuse of many of the images included in this publication differ from the above. This information is provided in the captions and in the list of illustrations. Every effort has been made to identify and contact copyright holders and any omission or error will be corrected if notification is made to the publisher.

Further details about CC BY-NC licenses are available at
http://creativecommons.org/licenses/by-nc/4.0/

All external links were active at the time of publication unless otherwise stated and have been archived via the Internet Archive Wayback Machine at https://archive.org/web

Any digital material and resources associated with this volume will be available at https://doi.org/10.11647/OBP.0346#resources

ISBN Paperback: 978-1-80511-032-3
ISBN Hardback: 978-1-80511-033-0
ISBN Digital (PDF): 978-1-80511-034-7
ISBN Digital ebook (EPUB): 978-1-80511-035-4
ISBN XML: 978-1-80511-037-8
ISBN HTML: 978-1-80511-038-5
DOI: 10.11647/OBP.0346

Cover image: Nanine Vallain, *Freedom* (1794), https://commons.wikimedia.org/wiki/File:Nanine_Vallain_-_Libert%C3%A9.jpg

Cover design: Jeevanjot Kaur Nagpal

Table of Contents

Acknowledgements vii
Introduction ix
1. Marie de Vichy-Chamrond, Marquise du Deffand 1
2. Marie Jeanne Riccoboni 7
3. Louise Florence Pétronille Tardieu d'Esclavelles d'Épinay 13
4. Julie Jeanne Éléonore de Lespinasse 19
5. Suzanne Necker 23
6. Isabelle Agnès Élisabeth de Charrière 29
7. Stéphanie Félicité, Marquise de Sillery, Comtesse de Genlis 33
8. Marie Olympe Gouze [Olympe de Gouges] 39
9. Marie Jeanne 'Manon' Roland de la Platière 45
10. Marie Louise Élisabeth Vigée Le Brun 51
11. Adélaïde Marie Émilie de Souza-Botelho 57
12. Sophie de Grouchy or Sophie de Condorcet 63
13. Beate Barbara Juliane Freifrau von Krüdener 69
14. Anne Louise Germaine, Baronne de Staël-Holstein 75
15. Constance Marie Pipelet or Constance, Princesse de Salm 83
16. Henriette Lucie Dillon, Marquise de La Tour-du-Pin Gouvernet 87
17. Marie Sophie Risteau Cottin 91
18. Marie Françoise Sophie Gay 95
19. Claire Louisa Rose Bonne, Duchesse de Duras 101
20. Claire Élisabeth Jeanne, Comtesse de Rémusat 107

21. Adélaïde Charlotte Louise Éléonore, Comtesse de Boigne	111
22. Marceline Félicité Josèphe Desbordes-Valmore	117
23. Hortense Thérèse Sigismonde Sophie Alexandrine Allart de Méritens	123
24. Flore Célestine Thérèse Henriette Tristán y Moscoso [Flora Tristan]	129
25. Delphine Gay de Girardin [Vicomte de Launay]	137
26. Amantine Lucile Aurore Dupin, Baronne Dudevant [George Sand]	143
27. Louise Angélique Bertin	151
28. Marie Catherine Sophie de Flavigny, Comtesse d'Agoult [Daniel Stern]	155
29. Julienne Joséphine Gauvin [Juliette Drouet]	161
30. Louise Colet	167
Index	173

Acknowledgements

This book is the product of some decades of research focused on one woman writer in particular, Germaine de Staël, and it seems appropriate here to record the names of those members of the Staël community who most shaped my thought, notably Simone Balayé—to whom I owe half the book's title—Frank Paul Bowman, Avriel Goldberger, Madelyn Gutwirth, and Florence Lotterie. Staël research continues, and it is Stéphanie Genand who facilitated the academic year at Paris which has made concluding this project possible. In that vein, I would like to thank the LIS laboratory—*Lettres, Idées, Savoirs*—and its directors, Anne Raffarin and Pascal Sévérac. Various thinkers at Cambridge University helped along my thinking: Alison Fairlie, David Kelley (my Ph.D. thesis director), Rosemary Lloyd, and Roger Paulin. Isabelle Naginski advanced my thinking on George Sand over the years, as did many speakers on different women writers at the annual Nineteenth-Century French Studies and Eighteenth-Century Studies conferences, in email and conversation. Let their contribution be remembered here. Over the years, my students at Indiana University-Bloomington and the University of Texas—Rio Grande Valley directly shaped my thought, and I remember their input gladly. The lion's share of the research for this study was conducted at the splendid Bibliothèque nationale de France, and its librarians were unfailingly helpful. Let my grateful thanks to Kilho Lee and Eunsil Yim, Andrew Verschoyle and Clare Coull also find their place on this page.

Research on this book crystallized as I considered the shape of European and American Romanticism, and the relative occlusion of women writers in its story outside the British Isles. Many scholars shaped my thought, notably Anne K. Mellor via her work *Romanticism & Gender*. I would like here to thank Alessandra Tosi and the whole team at Open Book Publishers for shepherding this project from conception to completion. Lastly, I would like to thank my wife Margarita, without whom this book would not have been written.

Introduction

This modest anthology collects thirty women writers in French for the period 1750–1850, a period for which no such anthology yet exists. While there are excellent monographs focused on either side of the 1800 century divide, and while some individual authors are much-studied—Germaine de Staël or George Sand in particular—for many others that are presented, secondary literature is sparse; France's national library lists none for the memoirist Claire de Rémusat, nor have I identified any elsewhere. All however form the rich loam on which some in this period came to lasting fame, and all have their place in this narrative. Some major Enlightenment names are absent from this collection: Marguerite de Staal-Delaunay, Claudine de Tencin, and Émilie du Châtelet had all died by 1750; Marie Thérèse Geoffrin it seems wrote little. Françoise de Graffigny's correspondence fills fourteen large volumes in the critical edition, but her epochal *Lettres d'une Péruvienne* appeared in 1747, and she died in 1758. We open instead with du Deffand, the great prose stylist and *salonnière* who lost her sight in later years, and we end with Colet, born in 1810. Juliette Adam, born in 1836, made her name after 1850 and under the Second Empire, as did Louise Ackermann, born in 1813. Non-French writers are included: thus, Charrière and Krüdener, who wrote in French but lived outside France, feature in these pages.

The intention is to provide a brief outline for interested students of women's writing in French over the eventful century from 1750 to 1850, a time of three linked French revolutions and of Romantic art across the West, a time when French armies marched on Moscow bringing revolution with them. An extract of each author's writing is given. This is often an extract from the author's best-known work, as seems appropriate in an introductory survey. More specifically, extracts are chosen in the hope of being characteristic and interesting: for du Deffand, it is the last long letter in her correspondence; for Staël, the opening of her short fiction *Zulma* (1794); for Drouet, her first long letter to Hugo. For fictions, rather than cite random passages from within the plot, the opening is given, since openings to fictions are interesting things. Many of these authors worked in several genres, including poetry, prose, and drama, as laid out in the biographies and bibliographies, but this anthology in the end contains less verse than it does prose—fiction, feuilleton, memoir, diary, declaration, treatise, correspondence—and drama does not appear. It proved difficult to extract a short, characteristic passage from a play. Gay, a prolific dramatist, is however represented by the dialogue that opens her fiction *Anatole* (1815). I have freely translated each extract in its accompanying footnote.

The anthology's one-paragraph biographies, which follow each extract and precede each section's commentary and bibliography, contain no revelations to scholarship, their function is simply to give readers a brief consensus overview of the major life events of each author listed. This volume is called *Destins de femmes*, and certainly that is reflected in the biographies cited here. An author is referred to by their pen name— d'Épinay, Cottin, Desbordes-Valmore, Tristan—only as and when it is adopted within the chronology of their biography, a method both true to their lives and feminist in reflecting their lived experience. Prior to this, first names or maiden names are used. Author pseudonyms—George Sand, Daniel Stern—are first given in square brackets; "Mme de" on the other hand is eschewed. Sources include notably the unfinished *Dictionnaire de biographie française*, the *Encyclopedia of the Enlightenment*, the *Dictionnaire universel des créatrices*, the *Grand dictionnaire universel Larousse du XIXe siècle*, and the *Encyclopedia Britannica*. A final point: full author names in each section heading follow the format they receive in the seven-volume *Index biographique français*.

Commentary in this anthology focuses on each author extract, with some contextualization, the whole intended to briefly situate that author's art within the history of French literature and European civilization. The latter clearly embraces both public and private spheres, and the commentaries reflect that truism. New thoughts regarding our featured writers will tend to appear here.

For the closing bibliographies—divided into 'works', citing writers' first or critical editions, and such modern 'sources' as we could identify— our method was to review each author entry in the catalogue of the Bibliothèque nationale de France (repository of all that is published in France) and cite each monograph or conference proceeding listed. This was possible for every author except Staël and Sand, who have too many entries to make that feasible; in their case, a selection of material is offered. Those writers who published extensively, such as Gay, Genlis, and Sand, are similarly represented by a selection of their works.

Does any single event define the period 1750–1850? Almost exactly halfway through this period, in 1789, the French Revolution began, marking a turning point both in the history of women in France and in world history. It was followed by further French revolutions in 1830 and 1848. Asked in 1972 what he thought of the French Revolution, Chou En-Lai responded, "It's too early to tell." Revolution and Empire dominate our middle section, and there does seem to be a gulf between the prose of du Deffand in 1780 and that of Drouet in 1833. A revolution in French women's writing may indeed have occurred, a watershed of sorts. Let us look then at the event itself more closely for a moment.

People do not write in a vacuum, and patriarchy has its role here as elsewhere. "Il suffit que je sois bien malheureuse," says the paper held in Marat's cold hand, "pour avoir droit à votre bienveillance." This blood-stained letter from Charlotte Corday has engineered his death. The scene is David's *The Death of Marat*, which hung in the Convention from its completion in 1793 until the fall of Robespierre: the days of the *Grande Terreur*, but also of a radical curtailing of Frenchwomen's newfound rights. The word *citoyenne* was banned, as was women's ability to wear the Revolutionary *cocarde* or trousers—a law in effect in France for another two hundred years. Hercules replaced Marianne in government documents. Charlotte Corday, Olympe de Gouges, Manon Roland, Marie Antoinette all went to the guillotine.

Corday stabbed to death in the bath Marat—a man whose own writing had caused the deaths of countless victims. But was he really found in his tub with Corday's letter in his hand? Or is this a fiction even more convenient for its play with old tropes about female authorship and what we might call public women? In France in 1793, writing was a gendered activity, and various 'private' genres, such as correspondence, translation, and memoir, were less problematic for women authors. David has done something remarkable in making Corday's villainy depend on her taking pen in hand to write a letter. She is, in a sense, the Terror's most famous *épistolière*.

It seems reasonable to ask, then, what this revolution meant for women's writing. Is the elegance of a du Deffand in 1780, a Charrière in 1784, possible in France by 1833? Or have the rules of art forever changed? Has there, for instance, been some sort of Romantic break with an enlightened or neoclassical past? The question is vast. One might look a moment at Girardin, elegant like du Deffand, in the text from 1835 presented in this volume. The text appears under a pseudonym, the Vicomte de Launay: in itself, this is interesting, as male pen names abound after 1800 and are rare in this anthology prior to that date. Girardin is witty, again like du Deffand; but she also talks of revolutions as if they are two a penny. Hers is very much a post-revolutionary text.

Out of these thirty extracts, the beginnings of a history may in short emerge, though complicated by the play between public and private that shapes them all: some extracts featured were intended for mass consumption, others for a single reader or even for the author alone, like perhaps Colet's memento. To an extent, this distinction is gendered; and it also shifted as the Old Regime gave way to Revolution, Empire, and a troubled Restoration. We are not here to define 'Romantic' art, but it seems fair to say that du Deffand's tone is courtly, like say d'Épinay's or Charrière's, in a way that Staël's, or Tristan's, or Drouet's, or Sand's is not. Beyond that, these various extracts may speak for themselves, in a sort of polyphony.

What, to conclude, is the shape of the field here? Where does women's writing stand in France during the period 1750–1850? Our thirty short bibliographies, drawn from the catalogue of the Bibliothèque nationale de France, suggest that it may be uneven, with a few authors earning more commentary than most—some indeed maintaining societies and journals—and a number of detailed studies presenting corpuses somewhat different than this one. The period 1750–1850, which might be called the Revolutionary or Romantic watershed, has, I believe, yet to be treated thus as a unit, though various studies group women authors within it; for instance, Michelle Perrot, *Des femmes rebelles—Olympe de Gouges, Flora Tristan, George Sand* (2014); Cécile Berly, *Trois femmes: Madame du Deffand, Madame Roland, Madame Vigée Le Brun* (2020); Whitney Walton, *Eve's Proud Descendants: Four Women Writers and Republican Politics in Nineteenth-century France* (2000); or Joyce Johnston, *Women Dramatists, Humor, and the French Stage: 1802–1855* (2014).

Several major overviews touching on the period confine themselves to particular centuries—notably, for the eighteenth century, Samia Spencer, ed. *French Women and the Age of Enlightenment* (1984); Laurence Vanoflen, ed., *Femmes et philosophie des Lumières: de l'imaginaire à la vie des idées* (2020); Ángeles Sirvent Ramos, María Isabel Corbi Sáez, and María Ángeles Llorca Tonda, eds, *Femmes auteurs du dix-huitième siècle: nouvelles approches critiques* (2016); Heidi Bostic, *The Fiction of Enlightenment: Women of Reason in the French Eighteenth Century* (2010); Annie K. Smart, *Citoyennes: Women and the Ideal of Citizenship in Eighteenth-century France* (2011); Anthony J. La Vopa, *The Labor of the Mind: Intellect and Gender in Enlightenment Cultures* (2017), and for the nineteenth century, Jeanne Pouget-Brunereau, *Presse féminine et critique littéraire: leurs rapports avec l'histoire des femmes de 1800 à 1830* (1994); Adrianna M. Paliyenko, *Genius Envy: Women Shaping French Poetic History, 1801–1900* (2016); Kathleen Hart, *Revolution and Women's Autobiography in Nineteenth-century France* (2004); and Alison Finch, *Women's Writing in Nineteenth-century France* (2006). Others focus on the Revolutionary decade: Jean and Marie-José Tulard, *Les égéries de la Révolution* (2019); Jacqueline Letzter and Robert G. Adelson, *Women Writing Opera: Creativity and Controversy in the Age of the French Revolution* (2001); and Huguette Krief, ed., *Vivre libre et écrire: anthologie des romancières de la période révolutionnaire (1789–1800)* (2005). Lastly, a smaller group of overviews cross the 1800 break to review works in both centuries: Henri Rossi, *Mémoires aristocratiques féminins 1789–1848* (2000); Anne Louis Anton Mooij, *Caractères principaux et tendances des romans psychologiques chez quelques femmes-auteurs, de Mme Riccoboni à Mme de Souza, 1757–1826* (1949); Steven Kale, *French Salons: High Society and Political Sociability from the Old Regime to the Revolution of 1848* (2004); Stephanie M. Hilger, *Women Write Back: Strategies of Response and the Dynamics of European Literary Culture, 1790–1805* (2009); and Julia Effertz, *Songbirds on the Literary Stage: The Woman Singer and Her Song in French and German Prose Fiction, from Goethe to Berlioz* (2015). All of these works, be they monographs or anthologies, appear in this volume's bibliographies and may usefully be consulted in understanding the field; however, they do not entirely replace this current global overview of the Romantic and Revolutionary period 1750–1850.

This chosen period is indeed marked both by revolution—the French Revolution and the Industrial Revolution, in particular—and by the emergence of Romantic art, reflecting a 'Romantic triangle' consisting of new means of production, with stereotype printing and then wood-pulp paper making mass production possible; a new, greatly increased, non-courtly reading market; and a certain concomitant thickening of line in art: Hugo is not Voltaire. It seems reasonable to ask what these various synchronous watersheds mean for women's writing in French. For the British Isles, that task has been largely accomplished, beginning perhaps with Anne K. Mellor's *Romanticism and Gender* (1993). The task seems not yet to have been carried out for production in French in the period, and that thought is where this anthology started. Is there a female tradition, in short, to govern the period 1750–1850 in French writing—the Romantic era, writ large—corresponding to the one recent scholarship has revealed in the United Kingdom? Perhaps. These thirty sections speak necessarily about women's choices in that age—*Destins de femmes*, as our title stresses—and about the field of power in which such choices were made. I would argue that while codes of sentiment are much in evidence, even under the Terror, and a variety of Romantic topoi do preponderate as the anthology continues—as noted in the extracts—nevertheless, a clear pattern and agenda for women's Romantic writing to match what Mellor and others trace in the British Isles is at first glance less apparent. This seems a worthwhile question for future scholarship.

Finally, there is perhaps another way to consider the Romantic question that inhabits this book. My monograph *An Outline of Romanticism in the West* (Cambridge: Open Book Publishers, 2022), which covers about thirty national traditions from Moscow to Buenos Aires, argues that the Romantic movement in the West is characterized by compassion for the voiceless and the oppressed, from Quasimodo to Jane Eyre to Hester Prynne. "Femme, réveille-toi!" writes Gouges in 1791. And here, one may see a pattern emerge after all in this anthology. Because from *Zulma* to *Ourika* via Gouges's *Déclaration des droits de la femme*, our authors increasingly return to the wretched of the Earth. They linger. They make marginal figures their narrators, in a strikingly modern gesture; they are engaged writers, and more than one text here is a political act, from Gouges to Tristan and beyond. They are ready for outsiders to be heard, be it Zulma on the Orinoco or Ourika in Paris, be it Saadi in medieval Persia or the peasants of the Berry. They are open to seeing the world find its voice.

1. Marie de Vichy-Chamrond, Marquise du Deffand
25 September 1696–23 August 1780

Fig. 1. Marie de Vichy-Chamrond, marquise du Deffand, by J. Encina. Photo by Pyb (2018). Wikimedia, https://upload.wikimedia.org/wikipedia/commons/archive/c/c3/20181021101003%21Mme_du_Deffant_CIPA0635.jpg, CC BY 4.0.

Correspondance complète de la marquise du Deffand

De Madame du Deffand à la Duchesse de Choiseul

Ce 18 août 1780

J'aime madame de Grammont à la folie. Ah ! je n'en suis point surprise, direz-vous ; mais ce n'est point pour ceci, pour cela, qui sont les raisons de tout le monde, c'est pour une toute particulière. Elle vint passer la soirée hier chez moi ; elle se fit un plaisir de m'apprendre que vous viendriez l'hiver prochain à Paris, comme à l'ordinaire. Si vous aviez vu ma joie, vous connaîtriez à quel point je suis sensible. Si vous n'étiez pas l'objet de cette sensibilité, j'en serais honteuse. N'est-elle pas déplacée et ridicule à un tel âge que le mien ? Aussi ne s'étend-elle pas plus loin que pour vous. Vous êtes une personne si singulière, si rare, que tout ce que vous inspirez doit être du même genre.

Je ne suis pas si bien avec l'abbé, et j'ai peut-être tort ; il me débite souvent des lieux communs. J'exige qu'ils soient bannis dans l'amitié. Il faut bien les tolérer dans l'usage du monde ; mais avec son amie, il faut se taire ou parler à cœur ouvert.

Que vous a-t-il donc dit ? me demandez-vous. Je lui ai parlé de l'Académie : il y a deux places vacantes, il y en aura bientôt quatre ... « Ah ! je n'en suis pas digne, je ne le désire point, et pourquoi moi ? Qu'ai-je fait ? ... » Cela n'est-il pas insupportable ? Voilà notre querelle. Je lui trouvai l'air de se bien porter.

Vous ne voulez donc jamais me parler de votre santé ; en vérité, cela n'est pas bien ; y a-t-il quelque chose au monde qui m'intéresse autant ? Et cette règle de ne point parler de soi est encore un lieu commun bien désagréable dans l'amitié.

M. de Beauvau va tant soit peu mieux ; il est entouré de tout ce qu'il aime ; femme, fille, sœurs ; par-ci, par-là, quelques académiciens.

Nous verrons, je crois la semaine prochaine, la nouvelle opération de M. Necker, c'est-à-dire sur la bouche. Vous savez les nouveaux établissements sur les prisons. Ceux-ci, vraisemblablement, seront durables. Il serait à souhaiter que les autres le fussent aussi ; mais tout est sujet au changement dans ce monde, excepté les vertus de la grand'maman [sic] et les sentiments de la petite-fille.

C'est par effort que je ne parle pas du grand-papa.[1]

---

1 Marie de Vichy-Chamrond, *Correspondance complète de la marquise du Deffand* [...], ed. M. de Lescure, 3 vols (Genève: Slatkine, 1971), III pp. 371–372.

Translation: This 18th of August 1780

I love Madame de Grammont madly. Ah! I am not at all surprised, you will say; but it is not for this thing, for that thing, which are everybody's reasons, it is for a quite particular one. Yesterday she came to spend the evening with me; she gave herself pleasure in informing me that you would come next winter to Paris, as usual. If you had seen my joy, you would know to what degree I am sensitive. If you were not the object of this sensibility, I would be ashamed of it. Is it not misplaced and ridiculous at such an age as mine? Thus, it extends no further than for you. You are so singular a person, so rare, that all you inspire must be of the same type.

I am not so well with the abbé, and perhaps I am at fault; he often pronounces commonplaces to me. I demand that they be banished from friendship. One really must tolerate them in the ways of the world; but with one's friend, one must either be silent or speak with open heart.

What then did he say to you? you ask me. I spoke to him of the Académie: there are two vacant places, there will soon be four ... "Ah! I am not worthy of it, I do not desire it,

1. Marie de Vichy-Chamrond, Marquise du Deffand

Marie de Vichy-Chamrond, Marquise du Deffand was born in the family château in Burgundy and raised in a convent in Paris. At twenty-two, she married the older Marquis du Deffand: her wit and beauty earned her admirers in Regency Paris, where she frequented libertine circles and met Voltaire, who became a lifelong friend. In 1742 she began her voluminous correspondence with the great names of the age: Voltaire, Walpole, d'Alembert, Lespinasse, the Duchesse de Luynes and others. At the death of her husband, she moved into Madame de Montespan's old apartments in Paris, rue Saint-Dominique, and she opened her salon in 1749. Her Mondays drew an intellectual elite, her fascination undiminished by the blindness which struck at the age of fifty-six. She then took her niece Julie de Lespinasse as a reader, separating from her vehemently nine years later after discovering that Lespinassse was meeting salon guests independently. In Sainte-Beuve's words, "Mme du Deffand est avec Voltaire, dans la prose, le classique le plus pur de cette époque, sans même en excepter aucun des grands écrivains."[2] Friend of Voltaire, d'Alembert, Fontenelle, Marivaux, Helvétius, of painters, sculptors, and architects, du Deffand brought a world of grace and intelligence to her salon. She died in Paris in 1780. From her deathbed, hearing her secretary of twenty years weeping, she said her last words: "Vous m'aimez donc?"[3]

Du Deffand was over eighty when she wrote this letter—our oldest author—and had been blind for almost thirty years. What strikes one perhaps the most here is the letter's grace: each subject is made new by her angle of attack, from the opening line, where rather than say how

---

and why me? What have I done? ..." Is that not unbearable? There is our quarrel. I found that he seemed in good health.

So, you never want to speak to me of your health; in truth, that is not good; is there anything in the world that interests me as much? And this rule of not speaking of oneself is another commonplace that is quite disagreeable in friendship.

M. de Beauvau is doing a little better; he is surrounded by all he loves; wife, daughter, sisters; here and there, some academicians.

We will see, I think next week, the new operation of M. Necker, that is to say on the mouth. You know the new establishments on prisons. These, apparently, will be lasting. One might wish that others were as well; but all is subject to change in this world, except the virtues of the grandmother and the feelings of the granddaughter.

It is by an effort that I do not speak of the grandfather.

2   Charles-Augustin Sainte-Beuve, *Causeries du lundi*, 16 vols (Paris: Garnier, 1857–1862), I, p. 413.
3   Benedetta Craveri, *Madame du Deffand et son monde* (Paris: Seuil, 1987), p. 356.

glad she was to hear the news from Madame de Grammont, she flips her premise, saying she loves Grammont "à la folie" and leaving her correspondent to guess why. This is the simple made interesting—in Pope's words, "What oft was thought, but ne'er so well expressed." Wit, charm, and grace characterize this prose: M. de Beauvau thus has all he loves around him—wife, daughter, sisters, and "par-ci, par-là, quelques académiciens." One might say this grace is quintessentially eighteenth-century in nature; a focus on wit, on avoiding tedium and the commonplace, does not distinguish Romantic thought, whereas it is fundamental to a Voltaire. It is elegant, and behind it lies a whole philosophy of lightness. It is the tone of refined conversation, in which the over-passionate, the monotonous, the false, risk being *insupportable*, if not ridiculous; in which whole regions of discourse are to be avoided for that reason—one's health, for instance—and anything worth saying is worth saying wittily. It is a discourse which requires agility and imagination, built on shared premises and conclusions (much as Mozart's glorious music is built on shared norms) in a way that will cease to be the case thirty years on. The discourse is, perhaps, epicurean: it regards pleasure as a central good, and therefore treats what is weighty lightly, rather than stir the depths that, say, prisons might evoke. "Tout est sujet au changement dans ce monde," writes du Deffand then, much as jesting Pilate in Bacon's famous essay said "What is truth?" and would not stay for an answer. Just so, the author pirouettes to family and closes with a *bon mot*. One guesses here at the skill with which du Deffand might have foregrounded any inelegance in du Châtelet, that brilliant mind, when Voltaire somewhat thoughtlessly brought her as a guest to his friend's salon. Wit and charm do not exclude cruelty, and that is a fundamental Romantic *aperçu*.

It is perhaps worth mentioning that the Beauvau family here mentioned were the very family that gave a home to Ourika—the subject of Duras's novel—when she was brought from enslavement in Senegal in 1786 by the chevalier de Boufflers. Around the elderly du Deffand, the world was changing. This is the last long letter in her correspondence, and she died the same year. Like Voltaire, she did not live to see 1789, which may after all have been a good thing.

Works

[du Deffand, Marie] *Correspondance complète de la marquise du Deffand* [...], ed. M. de Lescure, 3 vols (Genève: Slatkine, 1971)

Sources

Craveri, Benedetta, *Madame du Deffand et son monde*, trans. Sibylle Zavriew (Paris: Seuil, 1999)

Perey, Lucien, *Le Président Hénault et Madame Du Deffand, la cour du régent, la cour de Louis XV et de Marie Leczinska* (Paris: Calmann-Lévy, 1893)

Ségur, Pierre de, *Esquisses et récits* (Paris: Calmann-Lévy, 1908)

Sirvent Ramos, Ángeles, María Isabel Corbi Sáez, and María Ángeles Llorca Tonda, eds, *Femmes auteurs du dix-huitième siècle: nouvelles approches critiques* (Paris: Champion, 2016)

Vanoflen, Laurence, ed., *Femmes et philosophie des Lumières: de l'imaginaire à la vie des idées* (Paris: Garnier, 2020)

2. Marie Jeanne Riccoboni
25 October 1713–7 December 1792

Fig. 2. Marie Jeanne Riccoboni, by F.L. Couché. Photo by LeDeuxiemeTexte (2019). Wikimedia, https://upload.wikimedia.org/wikipedia/commons/8/8c/Marie-Jeanne_Riccoboni.png, CC BY 4.0.

Lettres de Mistriss Fanni Butlerd

Mss. Fanni, à un seul lecteur.

Si le naturel & la vérité, qui font tout le mérite de ces lettres, leur attirent l'approbation du public ; si le hasard vous les fait lire ; si vous reconnaissez les expressions d'un cœur qui fut à vous ; si quelque trait rappelle à votre mémoire un sentiment que vous avez payé de la plus basse ingratitude ; que la vanité d'avoir été l'objet d'un amour si tendre, si délicat, ne vous fasse jamais nommer celle qui prit en vous tant de confiance. Montrez-lui du moins, en gardant son secret, que vous n'êtes pas indigne à tous égards du sincère attachement qu'elle eut pour vous. Le désir de faire admirer son esprit ne l'engage point à publier ces lettres ; mais celui d'immortaliser, s'il est possible, une passion qui fit son bonheur, dont les premières douceurs sont encore présentes à son idée, et dont le souvenir lui sera toujours cher. Non, ce n'est point cette passion qui fit couler ses pleurs, qui porta la douleur & l'amertume dans son âme. Elle n'accuse que vous des maux qu'elle a soufferts ; elle ne connaît que vous pour l'auteur de ses peines. Son amour était en elle la source de tous les biens ; vous l'empoisonnâtes cruellement ! Elle ne hait point l'amour, elle ne hait que vous.[1]

Marie Jeanne Riccoboni was born in the parish of Saint Eustache in Paris, where she was later married and eventually buried. Her father, condemned in 1719 for bigamy, abandoned mother and daughter, who were thenceforth declared illegitimate. Housed in a convent and destined to stay there, Marie-Jeanne persuaded her mother to take her back at fourteen. In 1734, she married Antoine François Riccoboni, son of the director of the Comédie italienne. Her destitute mother lived with the couple until her death; the unhappy marriage continued until her husband's death in 1772, though they separated in 1761. Riccoboni seems to have loved other men without acting on it, including the Comte de Maillebois and the young Robert Liston. She first performed in the Comédie italienne in 1734, continuing until 1760, though Diderot calls her "l'une des plus mauvaises actrices de son temps."[2] He preferred her writing. For a time, Riccoboni frequented the salon of d'Holbach and possibly of Helvétius, befriending Marivaux, Adam Smith and David Hume, but she later withdrew from salon life and what she saw as its sectarianism and intolerance. After 1757, Riccoboni wrote ten novels, contributing to the fashion for the Richardsonian epistolary genre. The

---

1   Marie Jeanne Riccoboni, *Lettres de Mistriss Fanni Butlerd*, ed. Joan Hinde Stewart (Genève: Droz, 1979), pp. 3–4. Spelling modernized.

   Translation: Mistriss Fanny, to a single reader.

   If the naturalness and truth, which make up all the merit of these letters, earn them the approval of the public; if chance makes you read them; if you recognize the expressions of a heart which was yours; if some trait recalls to your memory a sentiment you repaid with the basest ingratitude; may the vanity of having been the object of a love so tender, so delicate, never make you name she who put so much trust in you. Show her at least, in keeping her secret, that you are not unworthy in every point of the sincere attachment she had for you. The desire to make her wit admired does not engage her to publish these letters; but rather that of immortalizing, if it is possible, a passion which made up her happiness, whose first sweetnesses are still present to her idea, and whose memory will always be dear to her. No, it is not this passion which made her tears flow, which brought pain and bitterness into her soul. She accuses only you of the pains she has suffered; she knows you alone as the author of her sorrows. Her love was the source of every good in her; you cruelly poisoned it! She does not hate love, she hates only you.

2   Denis Diderot, *Paradoxe sur le comédien*, *Œuvres complètes*, 25 vols (Paris: Hermann, 1975–1986), XX, p. 114.

Lettres de Mistriss Fanni Butlerd of 1757, her first success, is often thought to relate her unhappy passion for the Comte de Maillebois. In 1761, she imitated Marivaux well enough in her *Suite de la vie de Marianne* that disclaimers were needed, and she freely adapted Fielding's *Amelia* in 1762. She translated five English plays and wrote one herself, along with some lyric pieces. She died in poverty in 1792, after the Revolution suppressed the royal pension on which she had depended.

Va, je ne te hais point, says Chimène to Rodrigue in Pierre Corneille's *Le Cid* (1636). It is a moment famous enough for Riccoboni to nod to it in ending this prefatory letter to her first novel. This reminds us both that Riccoboni was an actress and that the eighteenth century valued the common coin of shared cultural referents over passion or authenticity in discourse. Contrast Juliette Drouet, another actress writing a century later, to Victor Hugo: "Je t'aime, je t'aime, je t'aime." In 1757, Rousseau's vogue was just beginning; the fashion remained for Richardsonian bourgeoises suffering at the hands of the aristocracy, a European fashion extending to the contemporary German *bürgerliches Trauerspiel*—Gotthold Ephraim Lessing, for instance—and opening a window on authenticity contrasting with the elegance of, say, a Valmont in Choderlos de Laclos's 1782 *Liaisons dangereuses*.

The sincerity is evident in Fanni's opening words on "le naturel et la verité." Indeed, the whole extract shows a seismic shift taking place in French, if not European thought, as Fanni struggles between "a spontaneous outpouring of powerful emotion," to use William Wordsworth's words from 1798, and a focus on the gap between *l'être* and *le paraître* which would not have been alien to Corneille himself. Fanni may be hurt, but her aim now is "l'approbation du public." Rather oddly, Fanni asks her "seul lecteur" not to name her, though she is doing just that on her title page; the furniture of lived emotion is present—*coeur, vanité, ingratitude*—but this is a far cry from Juliette Drouet. It seems fair to say that mid-eighteenth-century French society found the spontaneity of a Drouet a challenge, much though its participants began to desire it. "Le désir de faire admirer son esprit," writes Fanni in a construction quite alien to a Romantic mind, "ne l'engage point à publier ces lettres."

Let us remember that this novel was a great success in 1757. In the salon world that Riccoboni had abandoned, and in the interstices of that world's elegance, tact, grace and charm—the world of du

Deffand—something new and alien was rearing its head, resembling both authenticity and passion. That salon world was making room for Rousseau.

Nor should we dismiss Samuel Richardson too easily: his novels may seem slow going to a modern reader, but they were devoured in the decades before Rousseau's triumph. Much has been said of the role of the bourgeoisie in Europe between Enlightenment and Revolution, and the subject is in some ways inexhaustible. One might simply note that the bourgeoisie was a locus of authenticity for Riccoboni, as it would be for Staël a generation later. What could be more authentic than bourgeois letters? And from England, at that. There is a frisson to reading other people's mail, even if the writer says that was her intention; mail belongs to the private sphere, and in the very public world of eighteenth-century France, that private sphere was sometimes not easy to access.

Works

[Riccoboni, Marie Jeanne] *Lettres de Mistriss Fanni Butlerd*, ed. Joan Hinde Stewart (Genève: Droz, 1979)

Les Caquets, comédie en 3 actes en prose [imitation of « I Pettegolezzi », by Goldoni] (Paris: Ballard, 1761)

Le Nouveau Théâtre anglois, trans. Madame Riccoboni, 2 vols (Paris: Humblot, 1769)

Histoire de M. le marquis de Cressy (Amsterdam [Paris]: M.M. Rey, 1758)

Lettres d'Élisabeth-Sophie de Vallière à Louise Hortense de Canteleu, son amie, par Madame Riccoboni (Paris: A. Desrez, 1835)

Lettres de Milord Rivers à Sir Charles Cardigan (Paris: A. Desrez, 1835)

Lettres d'Adélaïde de Dammartin, Cesse de Sancerre, à M. le Cte de Nancé son ami (Paris: Belin, 1786)

Œuvres de Madame Riccoboni. Histoire du marquis de Cressy. Lettres de la comtesse de Sancerre. Histoire de deux jeunes amies. Histoire d'Ernestine. Lettres de Milady Catesby. Histoire d'Aloïse de Livarot. Histoire d'Enguerrand (Paris: Garnier frères, 1865)

Madame Riccoboni's letters to David Hume, David Garrick and Sir Robert Liston: 1764–1783, ed. James C. Nicholls (Oxford: Voltaire Foundation, 1976)

Sources

Bostic, Heidi, *The Fiction of Enlightenment: Women of Reason in the French Eighteenth Century* (Newark: University of Delaware Press, 2010)

Demay, Andrée, *Marie-Jeanne Riccoboni ou de la Pensée féministe chez une romancière du XVIIIe siècle* (Paris: la Pensée universelle, 1977)

Doucette, Wendy Carvalho, *Illusion and the Absent Other in Madame Riccoboni's "Lettres de mistriss Fanni Butlerd"* (New York; Bern; Paris: P. Lang, 1997)

Herman, Jan, Peeters, Kris and Pelckmans, Paul, eds, *Mme Riccoboni, romancière, épistolière, traductrice: actes du colloque international, Leuven-Anvers, 18–20 mai 2006* (Louvain ; Paris: Peeters, 2007)

Kaplan, Marijn S., *Marie Jeanne Riccoboni's Epistolary Feminism: Fact, Fiction, and Voice* (New York: Routledge, Taylor & Francis, 2020)

Kaplan, Marijn S., ed., *Translations and Continuations: Riccoboni and Brooke, Graffigny and Roberts* (London: Pickering & Chatto, 2011)

3. Louise Florence Pétronille Tardieu d'Esclavelles d'Épinay
11 March 1726–17 April 1783

Fig. 3. Louise Florence Pétronille Tardieu d'Esclavelles d'Épinay, by J.-É. Liotard. Photo by Adamvs (2023). Wikimedia, https://upload.wikimedia.org/wikipedia/commons/e/e6/Liotard_-_Portrait_de_Madame_Denis-Joseph_La_Live_d%27Epinay%2C_n%C3%A9e_Louise-Florence-P%C3%A9tronille_de_Tardieu_d%27Esclavelles%2C_dite_Madame_d%27Epinay%2C_vers_1759%2C_1826-0007.jpeg, CC BY 4.0.

Histoire de Madame de Montbrillant

Madame la Marquise de Beaufort à M. le Marquis de Lisieux

Décembre 1735

Ce que j'ai toujours craint est arrivé, Monsieur. Le nom de Gondrecourt va s'éteindre ; mon neveu touche à sa fin. Il est sans espérance et ne laisse point d'enfant mâle. J'ai souvent dit à la marquise de Gondrecourt que l'amour qu'elle portait à sa fille lui faisait oublier ce qu'elle devait à notre maison. Elle n'a cultivé personne. Qu'est-ce qu'un nom à la Cour, sans fortune et sans protection ? Vous nous avez toujours témoigné de l'attachement ; voilà le moment de nous en donner les preuves. Il faut nous emparer de ma petite nièce. Consentez à vous faire nommer son tuteur, servez-lui de père. Ou je me trompe fort, ou l'enfant est heureusement née. Il faut lui inspirer des sentiments dignes de sa naissance ; la douceur et la faiblesse du caractère de sa mère ne lui feront que trop rabattre de nos avis. Il faut étudier et suivre cet enfant sans relâche. Nous en tirerons parti, nous en ferons un grand sujet, et nous la marierons à quelque gentilhomme qui tiendra encore à l'honneur de prendre ses armes et son nom.

Partez, Monsieur, aussitôt ma lettre reçue, je vous en conjure. Tout de ma petite nièce va me devenir précieux et intéressant. Je veux recueillir exactement tout ce qu'elle dira, tout ce qu'elle fera ; à son âge les détails les plus minutieux indiquent souvent le caractère et ce qu'on a à en attendre. Bonjour, Monsieur, j'espère que vous seconderez mes projets. Venez essuyer les larmes de ma nièce qui se laisse abattre au lieu d'agir ; venez la guider. Que pourrais-je sans vous ? Reléguée dans un couvent par ma mauvaise fortune, irai-je traîner mon nom à la Cour et décliner les torts de ceux qui y brillent à mes dépens ? C'est à nos amis à faire valoir nos droits et je compte sur vous.[1]

---

[1] Louise d'Épinay, *Histoire de Madame de Montbrillant*, ed. Georges Roth and Elisabeth Badinter (Paris: Mercure de France 1989), p. 7.

Translation: December 1735

What I always feared has occurred, Sir. The name Gondrecourt will die out; my nephew is nearing his end. His situation is without hope and he leaves no male child. I often said to the Marquise de Gondrecourt that the love she bore to her daughter made her forget what she owed to our house. She cultivated no one. What is a name at Court, without fortune and without protection? You have always demonstrated attachment to us; here is the moment to furnish us the proof of it. We must seize my little niece. Agree to be named her tutor, act as a father to her. Either I am much mistaken, or the child is happily born. She needs to be inspired with feelings worthy of her birth; the sweetness and weakness of character of her mother will only make her batten down all too much on our counsels. This child must be studied and followed without a pause. We will turn her to good account, we will make her a great subject, and we will marry her to some gentleman who will still value the honor of bearing her arms and her name.

Depart, Sir, as soon as you receive my letter, I urge you. Everything about my little niece will become precious and interesting to me. I want to collect exactly all she says and all she does; at her age the most minute details often indicate the character and what one has to expect of it. Good day, Sir, I hope you will second my projects. Come wipe away the tears of my niece who allows herself to be brought down instead of acting; come guide her. What could I do without you? Relegated to a convent by my misfortune, will I go drag my name at Court and count out the faults of those who shine there at my expense? It is for our friends to make our rights heard and I count on you.

3. Louise Florence Pétronille Tardieu d'Esclavelles d'Épinay

Louise Florence Pétronille Tardieu d'Esclavelles d'Épinay was the daughter of the Baron d'Esclavelles, an officer of Louis XIV, governor of Valenciennes, and his much younger wife. He died when she was ten, and her education was neglected. In 1737–1739, she was put in a convent awaiting marriage, then married off at nineteen to her young first cousin, the Marquis d'Épinay. The marriage began happily enough, with two children, but d'Épinay suffered from her husband's prodigality and adultery and obtained a separation of property in 1749. Around 1747, a lover introduced her to Rousseau, for whom she prepared the little house known to history as l'Hermitage. She also met Grimm, who became a lifelong friend, unlike Rousseau who broke with her when thinking she had publicly criticized his passion for Sophie d'Houdetot. He moved out in December 1757, writing in his *Confessions* that she had got in her head the need to write "des romans, des lettres, des comédies, des contes, et d'autres fadaises comme cela."[2] Whatever the circumstances of their split, the two had a marked influence on each other. Soon after the rupture, d'Épinay retired from public life, remaining at home for a select company: Friedrich Melchior von Grimm, Denis Diderot, Jean le Rond d'Alembert, Pierre de Marivaux, Jean-François Marmontel, Jean François de Saint-Lambert, Jean Baptiste Antoine Suard, Guillaume Raynal, Paul-Henri d'Holbach, Ferdinando Galiani. Voltaire was another friend. She has an extensive and interesting correspondence and also took the reins of Grimm's *Correspondance littéraire* during his absence. In 1778, she hosted the young Mozart in Paris. Dialogues she wrote resemble works of Diderot and Rousseau, and one may wonder today who influenced whom. She died, likely of cancer, in 1783.

This extract opens another epistolary novel, one with a complex publishing history: the *Histoire de Madame de Montbrillant*. By 1757, d'Épinay had begun an epistolary novel in manuscript in response to Rousseau's *La Nouvelle Héloïse* (1761), whose opening pages he had shown her. Its focus is on women's existence: pregnancy, maternity, caring for children. It is a *roman à clé*, in which Rousseau, Grimm, Diderot and others figure under assumed names. D'Épinay left the manuscript to Grimm, and it appeared in 1818 minus start and finish as *Mémoires*

---

2   Jean-Jacques Rousseau, *Les Confessions. Autres textes autobiographiques*, ed. Bernand Gagnebin and Marcel Raymond (Paris: Gallimard, 1959), p. 411.

et correspondance de Madame d'Épinay. Later editions followed, with alleged actual names—Rousseau—replacing d'Épinay's pseudonyms or fictions, until a restored edition at last appeared in 1951.

As to the text, we begin *in medias res,* with the looming death of the speaker's nephew. Various factors are in play: a long friendship between the correspondents, for instance, on which the speaker relies in her sudden appeal. At issue are the family name and honor, two aristocratic preoccupations common in eighteenth-century fictions and rarer thereafter. This is not the bourgeois world of the jilted Mistress Fanni Butlerd. And yet, just as Fanni's destiny is shaped by her gender, so too is that of Madame la Marquise de Beaufort. To begin with, she is unable to pass on the family name, which will die with her childless nephew: a detail still topical today, when children and married names still go hand in hand. Moreover, she needs her male friend to act on her behalf as tutor to her niece, a person *in loco parentis.* Old Regime France placed obstacles in the way of women acting in such a capacity, but the marquise faces one in particular: she is "Reléguée dans un couvent par ma mauvaise fortune;" perhaps as a widow, perhaps owing to family politics. She writes her letters from inside a convent, which adds spice to her intrigue: "Il faut nous emparer de ma petite nièce."

The letter twice mentions the Court. Louis XIV created Versailles both to break the regional power of his nobility and to gather it where he could keep an eye on it; this worked for the remaining century and a half of the Old Regime, before Louis XVI was brought back to Paris in 1789. As the marquise remarks: "Qu'est-ce qu'un nom à la Cour, sans fortune et sans protection?" Freedom of action at Versailles required money and it required powerful friends, just as the Sun King had planned it. Court, more than anywhere, is the home of *l'être* and *le paraître*—a world where passion is a dangerous thing, and where interest plays out beneath a mask of civility. Thus, the marquise, who feels passionately about the loss of her family name, will seize her niece and educate her; the child will be "précieux et intéressant" to her, she writes, as she plots to salvage her family name from catastrophe. Interest, passion, and appearance will coincide. Again, these are aristocratic concerns, belonging to the noble world of the Old Regime novel. It is perhaps the very nakedness of this intrigue, as in Laclos, that marks a change of mood from the early eighteenth century.

Works

d'Épinay, Louise, *Histoire de Madame de Montbrillant*, ed. Georges Roth and Elisabeth Badinter (Paris: Mercure de France, 1989)

Les Conversations d'Émilie (Leipzig: S. L. Crusius, 1774)

Correspondence

Dulac, Georges and Maggetti, Daniel, eds, *Ferdinando Galiani, Louise d'Épinay: Correspondance (1769–1782)*, 5 vols (Paris: Desjonquères, 1992–1997)

Sources

Badinter, Élisabeth, *Mme du Châtelet, Mme d'Épinay ou L'ambition féminine au XVIIIe siècle* (Paris: Flammarion, 2006)

Deschanel, Paul, *Figures de femmes: Madame Du Deffand, Madame d'Épinay, Madame Necker, Madame de Beaumont, Madame Récamier, etc., etc* (Paris: G. Lévy, 1889)

David, Odette, *Autobiographie de convenance de Madame d'Epinay: écrivain-philosophe des Lumières: subversion idéologique et formelle de l'écriture de soi* (Paris: L'Harmattan, 2007)

Domenech, Jacques, ed., *Œuvre de madame d'Epinay, écrivain-philosophe des Lumières: actes du premier colloque international consacré à madame d'Epinay* (Paris: Harmattan, 2010)

Grangé, Jérémie, *Destruction des genres: Jane Austen et Madame d'Épinay* (Paris: Honoré Champion, 2014)

Mohr, Annette, *Madame d'Epinays Konzeption der Mädchenerziehung im Umfeld von frauenspezifischen Erziehungstraktaten des 18. Jahrhunderts in Frankreich*. Saarländische Schriftenreihe zur Frauenforschung; 7 (Röhrig: St. Ingbert, 1997)

Perey, Lucien and Maugras, Gaston, *Une femme du monde au XVIIIe siècle. La jeunesse de Madame d'Épinay: d'après des lettres et documents inédits* (Paris: C. Lévy, 1883)

Perey, Lucien and Maugras, Gaston, *Une femme du monde au XVIIIe siècle: dernières années de Madame d'Épinay, son salon et ses amis, d'après des lettres et des documents inédits* (Paris: C. Lévy, 1883)

Spencer, Samia, ed., *French Women and the Age of Enlightenment* (Bloomington, IN: Indiana University Press, 1984)

Steegmuller, Francis, *A Woman, a Man, and Two Kingdoms: The Story of Madame d'Epinay and the Abbé Galiani* (Princeton: Princeton University Press, 1993)

Valentino, Henri, *Madame d'Épinay, 1726–1783, une femme d'esprit sous Louis XV* (Paris: Librairie académique Perrin, 1952)

4. Julie Jeanne Éléonore de Lespinasse
9 November 1732–23 May 1776

Fig. 4. Julie Jeanne Éléonore de Lespinasse, by L.C. Carmontelle. Photo by Shonagon (2020). Wikimedia, https://upload.wikimedia.org/wikipedia/commons/4/4a/Mademoiselle_de_Lespinasse_-_Carmontelle.jpg, CC BY 4.0.

Lettres suivies de ses autres œuvres

Mlle de Lespinasse à Nicolas de Condorcet

Ce vendredi, 27 juillet 1770.

Venez à mon secours, Monsieur, j'implore tout à la fois votre amitié et votre vertu. Notre ami, M. d'Alembert est dans un état le plus alarmant ; il dépérit d'une manière effrayante ; il ne dort plus, et ne mange que par raison ; mais ce qui est pis que tout cela encore, c'est qu'il est tombé dans la plus profonde mélancolie ; son âme ne se nourrit que de tristesse et de douleur ; il n'a plus d'activité ni de volonté pour rien ; en un mot, il périt si on ne le tire par un effort de la vie qu'il mène. Ce pays-ci ne lui présente plus aucune dissipation ; mon amitié, celle de ses autres amis ne suffisent pas pour faire la diversion qui lui est nécessaire. Enfin, nous nous réunissons tous pour le conjurer de changer de lieu et de faire le voyage d'Italie ; il ne s'y refuse pas tout à fait ; mais jamais il ne se déterminera à faire ce voyage seul, et moi-même je ne le voudrais pas ; il a besoin des secours et des soins de l'amitié, et il faut qu'il trouve tout cela dans un ami tel que vous, Monsieur, vous êtes selon son goût et selon son cœur ; vous seul pouvez nous l'arracher à un état qui nous fait tout craindre. Voilà donc ce que je désirerais, et que je soumets bien plus à votre sentiment qu'à votre jugement ; c'est que vous lui écrivissiez qu'il serait assez dans vos arrangements de faire le voyage d'Italie cette année, parce qu'il vous est important de profiter du séjour qu'y doit faire M. le cardinal de Bernis. Vous partiriez de ce texte pour lui dire que vous désireriez qu'il voulût bien faire ce voyage avec vous, et que vous pensez que cette espèce de dissipation le remettrait en état de travailler, et par conséquent de jouir de la vie, ce qu'il ne fait point depuis qu'il est privé du plus grand intérêt qu'il y eût, qui est le travail, etc., etc. Vous sentez bien que cette tournure est nécessaire, parce que, quelque confiance qu'il ait en votre amitié, il craindrait d'en abuser en vous demandant de faire ce voyage dans ce moment-ci.[1]

---

1   Julie de Lespinasse, *Lettres suivies de ses autres œuvres* […], ed. Eugène Asse (Genève: Slatkine, 1971), pp. 317–318. Spelling modernized by John Claiborne Isbell.

Translation: This Friday, 27 July 1770.

Come to my aid, Sir, I implore at once your friendship and your virtue. Our friend, M. d'Alembert is in a most alarming state; he is fading away in frightening fashion; he no longer sleeps, and only eats because he should; but what is worse even than all that is that he has fallen into the most profound melancholy; his soul nourishes itself only on sadness and pain; he has no more activity nor desire for anything; in a word, he will perish if we cannot pull him by an effort from the life he is leading. This country no longer presents him any dissipation; my friendship, and that of his other friends are not enough to make the diversion that he needs. In short, we are all uniting to beg him to change his location and make a trip to Italy; he does not entirely refuse it; but he will never determine himself to make this journey alone, and I myself would not wish it; he needs the aid and care of friendship, and he needs to find all that in a friend such as you, Sir, you are to his taste and to his heart; you alone can pull him out for us from a state which makes us fear everything. Here then is what I would desire, and which I submit much more to your sentiment than your judgment; it is that you should write to him that it would be well in your arrangements to make a trip to Italy this year, because it is important to you to profit from the stay that M. the Cardinal de Bernis is to make there. You would move on from this text to tell him you would desire that he might wish to make this journey with you, and that you think this type of dissipation would put him back in condition to work, and consequently to enjoy life, a thing he does not do since being deprived of the greatest interest he had in it, which is work, etc., etc. You see

4. Julie Jeanne Éléonore de Lespinasse

Julie Jeanne Éléonore de Lespinasse was born in Lyon, the natural child of the Comtesse d'Albon and possibly the Comte de Vichy-Chamron, and she died young in Paris in 1776. Her alleged father later married the comtesse's daughter, and Julie was raised by her mother (until her mother's death) as governess to her nephews and nieces, who may also have been her half-siblings. Her natural aunt, du Deffand, then appointed her as reader in her salon when her sight began to fail: a great opportunity for Lespinasse, who shone. She inspired lifelong passion in d'Alembert. The arrangement with her aunt lasted from 1754 to 1763, until du Deffand discovered that Lespinasse was receiving salon guests early, as her aunt was still getting up. Du Deffand felt betrayed and never forgave Lespinasse, even after the latter's death. Lespinasse opened her own salon in 1764, receiving her aunt's regular guests alongside Étienne de Condillac, Nicolas de Condorcet, Denis Diderot, Anne Robert Jacques Turgot, and others: the *Encyclopédie* took shape here. Lespinasse fell in love with the Marquis de Mora, son of the Spanish ambassador, but his family worked hard to prevent a marriage and succeeded; she later fell in love with Guibert, despite his apparent indifference. She and Guibert became lovers as Mora returned to France, dying in Bordeaux in 1774; wracked by guilt at this news, Lespinasse considered suicide, and she did not long survive Guibert's marriage, dying in her turn at forty-three.

From the closed world of court and salon, as seen in the texts of du Deffand or d'Épinay, we seem to enter a new universe with this late letter of the young Lespinasse. Her prose lacks du Deffand's perfection; but its charm is different. This is the world of Franklin and Jefferson, those plain-spoken Americans in Paris, and of the early Roman paintings of David; it is the world of republican virtue, as the rococo period comes to an end. Lespinasse is writing about friendship—somewhat ironically, one might think, given how her time with her aunt ended. She is not a mocker, she is all enthusiasm as she writes to one brilliant mathematician, Condorcet, about another, d'Alembert, a man who corresponded with Euler. D'Alembert, then, is sick—"il ne mange que par raison"—and Lespinasse will do something about it. She will not travel to Italy with him; she will instead put people with people, because she is a facilitator.

---

clearly that this turn of phrase is necessary, because, whatever trust he has in your friendship, he would fear abusing it in asking you to make this journey at this time.

Her letter opens with an odd appeal to Condorcet's *amitié* and his *vertu* in equal measure. She describes d'Alembert's alarming condition, zeroing in on his melancholy, his state of mind: "son âme ne se nourrit que de tristesse et de douleur," she writes, rather beautifully. Lespinasse knows this territory, and she sees the solution—what she calls *dissipation*—in a trip with Condorcet to Italy, a project shared, she writes, by "nous tous". You are, she tells Condorcet, "selon son goût et selon son cœur." There is a certain authenticity to this language which is absent in our earlier texts: it is a willed authenticity, as when Lespinasse says she submits her project "bien plus à votre sentiment qu'à votre jugement." This again is a major break, a Rousseauist rejection of reason in favor of the heart. It is not a position that Voltaire would find welcome or even necessarily comprehensible, but it will soon be the bread and butter of Europe's Romantics.

Lespinasse ends with concern for d'Alembert's sensibility; to accommodate that, the trip must be proposed as born of pure self-interest, a position neatly inverting the seeming concern that disguises self-interest in d'Épinay's marquise. Interest and compassion have evidently flipped. Finally, Italy was of course a key stop on any Grand Tour, and those continued into the nineteenth century. But it is also the land to which Keats traveled in a failed bid for recovery; it is that land of sun and laughter "wo die Zitronen blühen," where the lemon trees bloom, as Goethe's Mignon sings.

Works

Lespinasse, Julie de, *Lettres suivies de ses autres œuvres* [...], ed. Eugène Asse (Genève: Slatkine, 1971)

Sources

d'Aragon, Marie-Christine and Lacouture, Jean, *Julie de Lespinasse: mourir d'amour* (Bruxelles; Paris: Éd. Complexe, 2006)

Bluteau, Jeanne, *Marie et Julie* (Quimper: Quadri signe-A. Bargain, 1995)

Bott, François, *La demoiselle des Lumières* (Paris: Gallimard, 1997)

Bouissounouse, Janine, *Julie de Lespinasse* (Paris: Hachette, 1958)

5. Suzanne Necker
2 June 1737–6 May 1794

Fig. 5. Suzanne Necker, by J.-S. Duplessis. Photo by Bonarov (2019). Wikimedia, https://upload.wikimedia.org/wikipedia/commons/7/7b/Duplessis_-_Suzanne_Curchod%2C_Madame_Necker.jpg, CC BY 4.0.

Réflexions sur le divorce

L'on vient donc de la publier cette loi dangereuse qui autorise et favorise le divorce ; ce n'était pas assez des divisions attachées à l'esprit de parti, il fallait encore disjoindre les époux, isoler les enfants, et combattre toutes les affections naturelles ; c'est cependant leur réunion qui forme la Patrie et qui la protège, ce sont les rameaux d'un arbre sacré, qu'on ne peut en séparer successivement sans laisser sa tige chauve et déshonorée.

Qu'il me soit permis de plaider la cause de l'indissolubilité du mariage, je sais quelle défaveur est attachée à cette opinion, je sais que le langage du sentiment s'affaiblit et plie en présence des passions, mais malgré ces obstacles, je m'abandonne à l'impulsion d'une âme tendre, inaccessible jusqu'à présent à nos secousses morales, et qui voudrait faire désirer et goûter le genre de bonheur dont elle jouit ; pour en jouir davantage encore.

Toute loi nouvelle suppose quelques nouvelles observations propres à perfectionner l'ordre public ou particulier ; il est donc à présumer, qu'en permettant le divorce, l'on a cru améliorer l'institution du mariage par tous les genres d'influences qu'elle peut avoir sur le bonheur des époux, pris individuellement, dans leur jeunesse et dans leur vieillesse ; sur celui de leurs enfants, et enfin sur le maintien des mœurs. Ces divers points de vue formeront la division naturelle des objections que j'entreprends de présenter contre le divorce; je livre ce projet sans rougir à toute la dérision de nos philosophes; car l'on sait qu'ils voudraient nous faire abandonner cinq mille ans de douces habitudes, pour introduire dans l'espèce humaine, dans sa nature intime, morale et sensible, des nouveautés bizarres ou funestes, et ils rappellent ce médecin impromptu de Molière, qui disait, en dénigrement des anatomistes, nous autres modernes, nous avons changé tout l'ordre du corps humain, qui n'était bon que pour nos ancêtres, nous ne plaçons plus le cœur du même côté qu'eux.[1]

Suzanne Necker, *née* Curchod, daughter of a pastor in the Pays de Vaud near Lausanne, was born poor but received a good education. She was

---

1 9 Suzanne Necker, *Réflexions sur le divorce* (Lausanne: Durand Ravanel, 1794), pp. 5–7. Spelling modernized by John Claiborne Isbell.

> Translation: So, this dangerous law has just been published, that favors and authorizes divorce; it was not enough to have the divisions attached to party spirit, but spouses needed to be disunited, children isolated, all natural affections combated; it is nevertheless their union which makes the Fatherland and protects it, they are the branches of a sacred tree, which one cannot separate from it successively without leaving the stem bald and dishonored.
>
> May it be allowed me to plead the cause of the indissolubility of marriage, I know what disfavor is attached to this opinion, I know that the language of sentiment weakens and bends in the presence of the passions, but despite these obstacles, I abandon myself to the impulse of a tender soul, inaccessible until now to our moral shocks, and which would wish to make others desire and enjoy the happiness that it enjoys; to enjoy it all the more.
>
> Each new law supposes some new observations suited to perfecting the public or private order; it is then to be presumed that in permitting divorce, one thought to improve the institution of marriage by all the types of influences it can have on the happiness of the spouses, taken individually, in their youth and their old age; on that of their children; and finally on the maintenance of morals. These diverse points of view will form the natural division of the objections I undertake to present against divorce; I deliver this project without blushing to all the derision of our philosophers; for one knows that they would like to make us abandon five thousand years of sweet habits, to introduce into the human species, in its intimate, moral, and sensitive nature, bizarre or fatal novelties, and they recall that impromptu doctor of Molière's, who said, denigrating anatomists, we moderns have changed the whole order of the human body, which was good only for our ancestors, we no longer place the heart on the same side as them.

courted by Edward Gibbon—"I sighed as a lover; I obeyed as a son," he wrote on abandoning her—but in 1764 married the Genevan Jacques Necker, already a successful banker and future finance minister of Louis XVI. Their daughter became famous under her married name: Germaine de Staël. As Jacques Necker became a minister, Suzanne Necker founded their salon, soon among the most famous in Paris—it was arguably the last great salon of the Old Regime, where both literature and politics were discussed, welcoming Jean-François Marmontel, Jean-François de La Harpe, Georges-Louis de Buffon, Friedrich Melchior von Grimm, Guillaume Raynal, Jacques-Henri Bernardin de Saint-Pierre; also Denis Diderot, Jean le Rond d'Alembert, Thérèse Geoffrin, Marie Anne du Deffand, and the Swiss visitors the Neckers both valued. A passionate writer, Necker barely published during her life, perhaps at her husband's urging, but at her death, he brought out her notes and reflections in five solid volumes. She is known primarily for her *Mémoire sur l'établissement des hospices* (1786) and for her *Réflexions sur le divorce* (1794), written during her daughter's somewhat high-profile affair with the Comte de Narbonne. Necker had worked to give her daughter an education far superior to what was typical of the age and the milieu; she is also remembered for having founded the *Hôpital Necker-enfants malades* in Paris. After the fall of her husband's ministry in September 1790, Necker retired to their château in Coppet outside Geneva. Having written instructions as to the erection of her tomb and the treatment of her remains—in 1790, she published her work *Des inhumations précipitées*—she died in 1794 in Lausanne, in the château of Beaulieu. Her body is interred with those of her husband and daughter in the grounds of Coppet.

Suzanne Necker, then, is a Swiss author, like Rousseau, like Isabelle de Charrière who follows here: born in the Pays de Vaud, Necker married a Genevan citizen and retired from Paris to Geneva; Charrière, born three years later in the Netherlands, settled in the Pays de Vaud and remained there. This is a reminder that France's cultural hegemony in Europe lasted well into the nineteenth century: Frederick the Great of Prussia wrote in French, not German, and Tolstoy's *War and Peace* (1869), like Thomas Mann's *Buddenbrooks* (1900), features dialogue in French. Given French censorship under the Old Regime, it was also typical for major French works to appear first abroad—in Amsterdam, or in Geneva. For the Neckers in 1794, a Lausanne publication was convenient—they were living near Geneva—and perhaps necessary since Paris was under the Reign of Terror. It may seem an odd time to focus on divorce, among all that the new French republic was up to, but Necker had the extra incentive of her daughter Staël's recent affair with Narbonne, Minister for War from 1791–1792. Necker died this same year, and her daughter was not admitted to her deathbed.

What of the text? Two things seem worth noting at once: first, that the author was Protestant, a branch of Christianity open to divorce since at least Henry VIII of England; and second, that she got her wish: divorce—made legal in 1792—was restricted in 1804, made illegal in 1816, and not reestablished until 1884. Tens of millions of Frenchwomen, Flora Tristan for one, faced the consequences of that decision. One might then suggest that the text represents a certain failure of imagination on the part of Necker, a woman who spent her married years happy. Her husband was not drunk or abusive, a gambler or a cheat. He was not violent. Did Necker indeed have no suspicion that such husbands existed? That seems unlikely. Perhaps it is fairer to treat her text as a dream of married happiness—her daughter Staël, after all, has a rather more generous chapter in *De l'Allemagne* (1810/1813) called "De l'amour dans le mariage," and who frankly has not similarly felt that love in marriage is to be celebrated, or said their vows with that belief in mind? Perhaps Necker, caught up in disappointment at her daughter's actions, simply allowed herself thus to imagine lasting marital concord and to look to publish that appeal to happiness on paper. Perhaps, caught up in argument as one sometimes can be, she laid out her personal principles with a certain amount of vigor while missing the real-world consequences of the arguments she was both proposing and providing.

Works

Necker, Suzanne, *Des inhumations précipitées* (Paris: Impr. royale, 1790)

Réflexions sur le divorce (Lausanne: Durand Ravanel, 1794)

Mélanges extraits des manuscrits de Mme. Necker, 3 vols (Paris: Charles Pougens, An VI/1798)

Nouveaux Mélanges extraits des manuscrits de Mme. Necker, 2 vols (Paris: Charles Pougens, An X/1801)

Sources

Boon, Sonja, *The Life of Madame Necker: Sin, Redemption and the Parisian Salon* (London: Pickering & Chatto, 2011)

Bredin, Jean-Denis, *Une singulière famille: Jacques Necker, Suzanne Necker et Germaine de Staël* (Paris: le Grand livre du mois, 1999)

Cahiers staëliens 57, «Madame de Staël et les études féminines; Autour de Madame Necker» (Paris: Champion, 2006)

Corbaz, André, *Madame Necker, humble vaudoise et grande dame...* (Lausanne: Payot, 1945)

Dubeau, Catherine, *La lettre et la mère: roman familial et écriture de la passion chez Suzanne Necker et Germaine de Staël* (Paris: Hermann, 2013)

Favre, Madline, *Suzanne Necker et son hospice de charité* (Genève: Slatkine, 2018)

Vopa, Anthony J. La, *The Labor of the Mind: Intellect and Gender in Enlightenment Cultures* (Philadelphia: University of Pennsylvania Press, 2017)

6. Isabelle Agnès Élisabeth de Charrière

20 October 1740–27 December 1805

Fig. 6. Isabelle Agnès Élisabeth de Charrière, attr. G. de Spinny. Photo by Jan Arkesteijn (2017). Wikimedia, https://upload.wikimedia.org/wikipedia/commons/5/59/Belle_van_Zuylen%2C_attributed_to_Guillaume_de_Spinny.jpg, CC BY 4.0.

Lettres écrites de Lausanne

Première Lettre

Le 30 Novembre 1784

Combien vous avez tort de vous plaindre ! Un gendre d'un mérite médiocre, mais que votre fille a épousé sans répugnance : un établissement que vous-même regardez comme avantageux, mais sur lequel vous avez été à peine consultée ! Qu'est-ce que cela fait ? que vous importe ? Votre mari, ses parents & des convenances de fortune ont tout fait. Tant mieux. Si votre fille est heureuse, en serez-vous moins sensible à son bonheur ?

> Si elle est malheureuse, ne sera-ce un chagrin de moins que de n'avoir pas fait son sort ? Que vous êtes romanesque ! Votre gendre est médiocre ; mais votre fille est-elle d'un caractère ou d'un esprit si distingué ? On la sépare de vous ; aviez-vous tant de plaisir à l'avoir auprès de vous ? Elle vivra à Paris ; est-elle fâchée d'y vivre ? Malgré vos déclamations sur les dangers, sur les séductions, les illusions, le prestige, le délire, &c. seriez-vous fâchée d'y vivre vous-même ? Vous êtes encore belle, vous serez toujours aimable ; je suis bien trompée, ou vous iriez de grand cœur vous charger *des chaînes de la Cour*, si elles vous étaient offertes. Je crois qu'elles vous seront offertes.[1]

Isabelle Agnès Élisabeth de Charrière, *née* van Tuyll van Serooskerken [Belle de Zuylen] was born in the château of Zuylen, near Utrecht, and died in the canton of Neuchâtel, which then belonged to Prussia. Belle van Zuylen spoke English, German, Italian, and Latin, and studied mathematics and physics, but it was in French, language of the European nobility in the eighteenth century, that she was to write, starting at twenty-two with *Le Noble* (1762), an anonymous satirical sketch. At thirty, she married the Swiss M. de Charrière, and from 1782, she began a career as a writer of letters, pamphlets, tales, and novels including the *Lettres neuchâteloises* (1784), *Lettres de Mistriss Henley publiées par son amie* (1784), *Lettres écrites de Lausanne* (1785), *Caliste* (1787), and *Trois femmes* (1796), along with plays, political tracts, and operas. Her production post-1789, a period when she hosted émigrés in Neuchâtel, is particularly rich. Her extensive list of correspondents includes James

---

1   Isabelle de Charrière, "Lettres écrites de Lausanne", in *Œuvres complètes*, 10 vols (Amsterdam: G.A. van Oorschot, 1980), VIII, p. 137. Spelling modernized by John Claiborne Isbell.

   Translation: This 30 November 1784
      How wrong you are to complain! A son-in-law of average merit, but whom your daughter married without repugnance: an establishment you yourself view as advantageous but about which you were barely consulted! What of it? what difference does it make to you? Your husband, his relatives and suitabilities of fortune did everything. So much the better. If your daughter is happy, will you be the less sensitive to her happiness? If she is unhappy, will it not be a grief the less to you not to have made her fate? How romantic you are! Your son-in-law is average; but is your daughter of so distinguished a character or wit? You are separated from her; did you have so much pleasure in having her near you? She will live in Paris; is she angry to be living there? Despite your declamations on the dangers, on the seductions, the illusions, the prestige, the whirlwind, &c. would you be angry to live there yourself? You are still quite beautiful, you will always be charming; I am sadly mistaken, or you would gladly go charge yourself with the *chains of the Court*, if they were offered to you. I believe they will be offered to you.

Boswell and Benjamin Constant, who was a great love of her life. She also composed music for piano, harpsichord, and string instruments. The asteroid (9604) Bellevanzuylen, discovered in 1991, bears her name.[2]

Isabelle de Charrière, a Dutch aristocrat living in what is now Switzerland, wrote this elegant text in French, like most of the ten volumes of her complete works. We are thus reminded that the national boundaries to which Europe has devoted such attention since about 1814, had much less weight just thirty years earlier. Thus, in Laurence Sterne's *Sentimental Journey* of 1767, he wanders happily through France for a good fraction of the book before noticing a) that France and his native England are at war and b) that he has no passport. Here then are a series of letters written from the Swiss Pays de Vaud which open with a review of Paris and the court—Versailles—and how our protagonists are to get admitted to it. Thus far did the impact of Louis XIV extend, in an age before nations as we know them existed. The Pays de Vaud, as it happened, owed suzerainty to German-speaking Bern, but it was to Paris that its aristocracy looked for guidance and meaning.

This is, as we have noted, an elegant text. It is *mondain*, not naïve, and at ease with the world's complexity. Thus, it admits at once that a disappointing son-in-law is just that, a disappointment—he is a man "d'un mérite médiocre," and the mother was not consulted—but it couches this *datum* in a broader review of the field: if things turn out badly, the mother will not feel responsible, while if they turn out well, she will not resent her lack of input. The argument provided has an almost metaphysical wit to it, pointedly avoiding cliché and the commonplace, and it is also Socratic, couched in a series of questions designed to elicit reasoned assent from the addressee. This is, in short, the play of reason at work for which the Enlightenment came into being. It is, moreover, an aristocratic text, starting with the focus on court; in this, too, it is typical of a century then already passing. It is not bourgeois. Lastly, these are letters, they are an example of the epistolary fictions so in vogue throughout the eighteenth century, and scarce in the nineteenth century. As such, the text offers a tight focus on speaker and listener, mouth and ear; as in Laclos, any epistolary novel quickly becomes a hall of mirrors, in which each short text echoes back to us a reflection both

---

[2] "JPL Small-Body Database Browser", *ssd.jpl.nasa.gov*.

of its author's agenda and of its designated reader's reaction to it. Each letter we read has a sender and recipient, acting and reacting precisely as Newton had defined the process in his Third Law of Motion of 1686: "For every action, there is an equal and opposite reaction." Reason, in Charrière's world, is a universal thing. It is a world that fundamentally makes sense.

Works

Charrière, Isabelle de, *Œuvres complètes,* 10 vols (Amsterdam: G.A. van Oorschot, 1979–1984)

Sources

Cahiers Isabelle de Charrière / Belle de Zuylen Papers (2006–2015)

Coüasnon, Marguerite de, *Écrire de soi: Madame de Genlis et Isabelle de Charrière au miroir de la fiction* (Rennes: Presses universitaires de Rennes, 2013)

Cossy, Valérie, *Isabelle de Charrière: écrire pour vivre autrement* (Lausanne: Presses polytechniques et universitaires romandes, 2012)

Godet, Philippe, *Bibliographie de Madame de Charrière* (Genève: A. Jullien, 1906)

Godet, Philippe, *Madame de Charrière et ses amis: d'après de nombreux documents inédits (1740–1805), avec portraits, vues, autographes, etc.* (Genève: Slatkine, 1973)

Solte-Gresser, Christiane, *Leben im Dialog: Wege der Selbstvergewisserung in den Briefen von Marie de Sévigné und Isabelle de Charrière* (Königstein: U. Helmer, 2000)

Trousson, Raymond, *Isabelle de Charrière: un destin de femme au XVIIIe siècle* (Paris: Hachette, 1995)

Van Luttervelt, Remmet, *Belle de Zuylen et son époque: Institut néerlandais, Paris, 3 mars-10 avril 1961, Rijksmuseum, Amsterdam, 21 avril-4 juin 1961* (Paris: Institut néerlandais, 1961)

7. Stéphanie Félicité, Marquise de Sillery, Comtesse de Genlis
25 January 1746–31 December 1830

Fig. 7. Stéphanie Félicité, marquise de Sillery, comtesse de Genlis, by P.-N. Violet. Photo by Ecummenic (2019). Wikimedia, https://upload.wikimedia.org/wikipedia/commons/b/be/Violet_-_Comtesse_de_Genlis.png, CC BY 4.0.

Adèle et Théodore ou Lettres sur l'éducation [...]

Cet ouvrage est le fruit de quinze ans de réflexions, d'observations, et de l'étude la plus suivie des inclinations, des défauts et des ruses des enfants. Je propose une méthode dont l'expérience m'a démontré les avantages ; mais je n'ai pas l'orgueil insensé de croire que ce faible traité d'éducation renferme tout ce qu'on peut dire d'utile sur cet important sujet.

J'ai cité beaucoup d'ouvrages relatifs à l'éducation, dans l'intention surtout de les faire connaître, et d'engager les pères de famille à les lire tous.

Plus on a médité et réfléchi sur ce sujet, plus on est éloigné de croire qu'il soit épuisé. Puisse-t-on ne jamais se lasser d'écrire sur une matière si intéressante ! Loin de regarder comme des rivaux les auteurs qui se distingueront dans cette carrière, personne ne s'intéressera plus sincèrement que moi à leurs succès, comme je crois déjà l'avoir prouvé par la manière dont j'ai parlé de tous les ouvrages modernes de ce genre.

Quelques partisans zélés de Rousseau, m'ont reproché de n'avoir pas assez loué Émile. Avant que ces lettres parussent, j'avais une opinion bien différente, je craignais qu'on ne m'accusât au contraire de n'avoir point assez critiqué un livre si répréhensible à tant d'égards ; et, en effet, je ne me sentais pas au fond du cœur entièrement exempte d'impartialité pour un homme, qui, malgré ses défauts, ses torts et ses égarements, possédait des talents si supérieurs et des qualités si attachantes. Rousseau aimait et connaissait parfaitement les enfants ; il méprisait sincèrement l'intrigue et la cabale ; il dédaignait les *prôneurs*, espèce de gens si facile à gagner quand on veut bien perdre beaucoup de temps, surmonter beaucoup d'ennui pour obtenir des succès qui n'ont qu'un seul avantage, celui de n'exciter l'envie de personne : Rousseau enfin, comme le grand Corneille, pouvait dire :

Je ne dois qu'à moi seul toute ma renommée.[1]

---

1 Stéphanie Félicité de Genlis, *Adèle et Théodore ou Lettres sur l'éducation contenant tous les principes relatifs aux trois différents plans d'éducation des Princes et des jeunes personnes de l'un et de l'autre sexe*, ed. Isabelle Brouard-Arends (Rennes: Presses universitaires de Rennes, 2006), pp. 49–50.

Translation: This work is the fruit of fifteen years of reflections, of observations, and of the most sustained study of the inclinations, the defects, and the tricks of children. I propose a method whose advantages experience has shown me; but I do not have the mad pride to believe that this paltry treatise on education contains all that one can usefully say on this important subject.

I have quoted many works relative to education, in the intention above all of making them known, and to engage fathers of families to read them all.

The more one has meditated and reflected on this subject, the more one is removed from believing that it is exhausted. May one never grow tired of writing on so interesting a matter! Far from seeing as rivals the authors who will distinguish themselves in this career, none is more sincerely interested than I in their successes, as I believe I have already shown by the manner in which I have spoken about all the modern works of this sort.

Some zealous partisans of Rousseau reproached me with not having praised Émile enough. Before these letters appeared, I had a very different opinion, I feared lest I be accused on the contrary of not having sufficiently criticized a book so reprehensible in so many ways; and in effect, I did not feel myself at heart's bottom entirely exempt of impartiality for a man who, despite his defects, his wrongs and his wanderings, possessed talents so superior and qualities so attaching. Rousseau loved and knew children perfectly; he sincerely despised intrigue and cabal; he disdained promoters, a species of people so easy to gain when one wants to lose a lot of time, overcome a lot of tedium to obtain successes which have just one advantage, that of exciting envy in nobody: Rousseau at the last, like the great Corneille, could say:

I owe all my fame to none but myself.

7. Stéphanie Félicité, Marquise de Sillery, Comtesse de Genlis

Stéphanie Félicité, Marquise de Sillery, Comtesse de Genlis was the daughter of the Marquis de Saint-Aubin, from a Burgundian noble family. She spent some time in a convent as a child, as was then common. Even before her somewhat dissolute father's death, his wife and two children faced straitened circumstances. Félicité's mother, the marquise, gained access to the salons of financiers of the time, in particular the Farmer General La Popelinière: her daughter shone as a harpist. Through her father, imprisoned by the British while returning from the Antilles, the teenaged Félicité met Charles Alexis Brûlart, Marquis de Sillery, Comte de Genlis, then aged thirty, and they married in 1763. She was presented at court and joined the Orléans household as a companion to the Duchesse de Chartres, with whose husband, the duke—the future Philippe Égalité—she seems to have begun an affair almost at once. She also took charge of educating the Chartres children, including the future Louis Philippe, a little awkwardly because royal princes traditionally were raised by men after the age of seven. Louis Philippe's memoirs express his youthful attachment to her. Genlis met Rousseau and Voltaire and was the friend of Buffon, Marmontel, Bernardin de Saint-Pierre, Talleyrand, of Juliette Récamier. Her works extend to 140 volumes, making her ensuing neglect somewhat puzzling. From 1789 to 1791, she held a salon, visited by the Duc d'Orléans, Talleyrand, David, and the young deputies Lameth, Barère, and Barnave. During the Terror, she fled to England: her husband and her lover Philippe Égalité were both guillotined. Her time in emigration, where royalist circles made her unwelcome, also made writing her primary source of income. She returned to France in 1801, becoming a paid spy for Bonaparte. Her complex life grew more difficult in 1815 with the return of the Bourbons, and she was reduced to living off her royalties. Throughout this time, she adopted and raised several children of all conditions, living just long enough to see her pupil become *Roi des Français*. Both confided in Victor Hugo their impression of the other: Louis Philippe recalled her 'férocité' as governess—no candy, sleeping on planks, learning manual trades. She said of him: "Il était prince, j'en ai fait un homme; il était lourd, j'en ai fait un homme habile; il était ennuyeux, j'en ai fait un homme amusant; il était poltron, j'en ai fait un homme brave; il était ladre, je n'ai pu en faire un homme généreux."[2]

---
2   Victor Hugo, *Choses vues* (Paris: Gallimard, 2002), pp. 439–440.

Genlis wrote several edifying works on raising children, starting in 1782 with *Adèle et Théodore*, an answer to Rousseau's *Émile* (1762). The work sold out in eight days, amid some controversy, including attacks from the *Encylopédistes* and songs about her in Paris. Rousseau had made the topic very much in vogue, and Genlis was not alone in reacting against his treatment of the girl Sophie in particular: Necker for instance gave her daughter a highly formalized education and regretted only that it had not been more so, while Genlis's Spartan program for her royal charges is outlined above. One might feel that Genlis's moral authority on the topic of raising royal children could be compromised by her ongoing affair with the children's father, but Genlis seems unperturbed by such questions, much as Rousseau in *Émile* seems unperturbed by the fact that he gave his four natural children up to the foundling hospital. Genlis notes that Rousseau "aimait et connaissait parfaitement les enfants," and one is reminded that praise for Rousseau was common coin around 1780 as a token of authenticity and virtue. Genlis was perhaps not a natural Romantic—more than once, she remarked on Staël's gushing style—but she found herself already on a Romantic playing field in pre-Revolutionary France, where engagement with Rousseau involved mentioning certain Romantic topoi to establish one's bona fides. Genlis, whose discomfort with Rousseau's "défauts, ses torts et ses égarements" is explicit from the outset, does exactly that.

Selected Works

Genlis, Félicité de, *Adèle et Théodore ou Lettres sur l'éducation contenant tous les principes relatifs aux trois différents plans d'éducation des Princes et des jeunes personnes de l'un et de l'autre sexe*, ed. Isabelle Brouard-Arends (Rennes: Presses universitaires de Rennes, 2006)

Mémoires de Mme la comtesse de Genlis (Paris: Albin Michel, 1925)

Théâtre à l'usage des jeunes personnes, 4 vols (Paris: Lambert & Baudouin, 1779–1780)

Théâtre pour servir à l'éducation, 4 vols (Paris: Lambert & Baudouin, 1780)

Théâtre de société, 2 vols (Paris: Lambert & Baudouin, 1781)

Le Club des dames, ou le retour de Descartes (Paris: Bibliothèque des romans, 1784)

La Religion considérée comme l'unique base du bonheur et de la véritable philosophie, (Orléans: Couret de Villeneuve, 1787)

Les Petits Émigrés, ou Correspondance de quelques enfans: ouvrage fait pour servir à l'éducation de la jeunesse, 4 vols (Hamburg: [s.n.], 1798)

Les Vœux téméraires, ou l'enthousiasme, 3 vols (Hamburg: [s.n.], 1799)

Nouveaux contes moraux, et Nouvelles historiques, 3 vols (Paris: Maradan, 1802)

Mademoiselle de Clermont (Paris: Maradan, 1802)

La Duchesse de La Vallière (Paris: Maradan, 1804)

Le Siège de La Rochelle, ou le Malheur et la conscience, 2 vols (Paris: Nicolle, 1808)

De l'influence des femmes sur la littérature française, comme protectrices des lettres et comme auteurs, ou Précis de l'histoire des femmes françaises les plus célèbres (Paris: Maradan, 1811)

Zuma, ou la Découverte du quinquina (Paris: Maradan, 1817)

Sources

Barthélémy, Jacques G., *Stéphanie Félicité, comtesse de Genlis* (Paris: Société des écrivains, 2005)

Bessire, François and Reid, Martine, eds., *Madame de Genlis. Littérature et éducation* (Rouen: Publications des Universités de Rouen et du Havre, 2008)

Broglie, Gabriel de, *Madame de Genlis* (Paris: Perrin, 1985)

Coüasnon, Marguerite de, *Écrire de soi: Madame de Genlis et Isabelle de Charrière au miroir de la fiction* (Rennes: Presses universitaires de Rennes, 2013)

De Poortere, Machteld, *Les idées philosophiques et littéraires de Mme de Staël et de Mme de Genlis* (New York: Peter Lang, 2004)

Deshayes, Olivier, *Le destin exceptionnel de Mme de Genlis, 1746–1830: une éducatrice et femme de lettres en marge du pouvoir* (Paris: L'Harmattan, 2014)

Gérard, Rosemonde, *La vie amoureuse de Madame de Genlis* (Paris: Ernest Flammarion, 1926)

Harmand, Jean, *Madame de Genlis, sa vie intime et politique, 1746–1830: d'après des documents inédits* (Paris: Perrin, 1912)

Navarro, Pascale, *La femme lettrée au XVIIIe siècle: fiction et théorie chez S. de Genlis* (Montréal: Université McGill, 1999)

Nikliborc, Anna, *L'œuvre de Madame de Genlis* (Wrocław: Wydawnictwa Uniwersytetu Wrocławskiego, 1969)

Plagnol-Diéval, Marie-Emmanuelle, *Madame de Genlis et le théâtre d'éducation au XVIIIe siècle* (Oxford: Voltaire Foundation, 1997)

Robb, Bonnie Arden, *Félicité de Genlis: Motherhood in the Margins* (Newark, University of Delaware Press, 2008)

Wyndham, Violet, *Madame de Genlis, a Biography* (London: A. Deutsch, 1958)

8. Marie Olympe Gouze [Olympe de Gouges]
7 May 1748–3 November 1793

Fig. 8. Marie Olympe Gouze [Olympe de Gouges]. Photo by PawełMM (2018). Wikimedia, https://upload.wikimedia.org/wikipedia/commons/0/05/Olympe_de_Gouges.png, CC BY 4.0.

Déclaration des droits de la femme et de la citoyenne

Article premier

La femme naît libre et demeure égale à l'homme en droits. Les distinctions sociales ne peuvent être fondées que sur l'utilité commune.

II

Le but de toute association politique est la conservation des droits naturels et imprescriptibles de la femme et de l'homme : ces droits sont la liberté, la propriété, la sûreté, et surtout la résistance à l'oppression.

III

Le principe de toute souveraineté réside essentiellement dans la nation, qui n'est que la réunion de la femme et de l'homme : nul corps, nul individu, ne peut exercer d'autorité qui n'en émane expressément.

IV

La liberté et la justice consistent à rendre tout ce qui appartient à autrui ; ainsi l'exercice des droits naturels de la femme n'a de bornes que la tyrannie perpétuelle que l'homme lui oppose ; ces bornes doivent être réformées par les lois de la nature et de la raison.

V

Les lois de la nature et de la raison défendent toutes actions nuisibles à la société : tout ce qui n'est pas défendu par ces lois, sages et divines, ne peut être empêché, et nul ne peut être contraint à faire ce qu'elles n'ordonnent pas.

VI

La loi doit être l'expression de la volonté générale ; toutes les citoyennes et citoyens doivent concourir personnellement, ou par leurs représentants, à sa formation ; elle doit être la même pour tous ; toutes les citoyennes et tous les citoyens, étant égaux à ses yeux, doivent être également admissibles à toutes dignités, places et emplois publics, selon leurs capacités, et sans autres distinctions que celles de leurs vertus et de leurs talents.[1]

---

1   Olympe de Gouges, *Déclaration des droits de la femme et de la citoyenne* (Paris: Gallimard, 2021), pp. 14–15.

Translation: Article One.

Woman is born free and remains equal to man in rights. Social distinctions can only be founded on common utility.

II

The goal of every political association is the conservation of the natural and imprescriptible rights of woman and man: these rights are liberty, property, safety, and especially resistance to oppression.

III

The principle of every sovereignty resides essentially in the nation, which is nothing but the union of woman and man: no body, no individual, can exert authority which does not derive expressly from it.

Marie Olympe Gouze [Olympe de Gouges] was born a butcher's daughter or bourgeoise in Montauban. Her mother's family was so closely tied to the Lefranc de Pompignan family that rumor considered Marie illegitimate. In 1765, at seventeen, she was married to a man thirty years her elder, Louis Yves Aubry; she later recalled her repugnance for this man "qui n'était ni riche ni bien né,"[2] who died after their first child was born around 1766. Marie reached Paris with her son in the early 1770s and took the name Olympe de Gouges, apparently depending on the kindness of men such as Jacques Biétrix de Rozières, who gave her 70,000 francs, and acquiring a certain reputation; but she gave no cause for scandal and lived freely on her own terms, featuring in the *Almanach de Paris* from 1774. Gouges began a course of study in the salons and the theaters of Paris to supplement the education she lacked, even founding a small troupe, purchased in 1787 by the Marquis de La Maisonfort. She wrote her play *Zamore et Mirza* in 1784, and it was produced at the Comédie-Française in December 1789 under the title *L'Esclavage des Noirs*. The play faced attacks from the right on its style and its content, and it folded after three performances. Gouges invoked the play at her trial to indicate her patriotism and her hatred of tyranny. A second abolitionist play and an abolitionist treatise followed. It seems possible that she met La Fayette and the abbé Grégoire at the *Amis des Noirs*; certainly, her abolitionist work was extensive and pioneering.

IV

Liberty and justice consist in returning all which belongs to others; thus, the exercise of the natural rights of woman is limited only by the perpetual tyranny that man opposes her; these limits must be reformed by the laws of nature and of reason.

V

The laws of nature and of reason forbid all actions harmful to society: everything which is not prohibited by these wise and divine laws cannot be restricted by them, and none can be constrained to do what they do not order.

VI

The law must be the expression of the general will; all citizens female and male must contribute personally or by their representatives in its formation; it must be the same for all; all citizens female and male being equal in its eyes, must be equally admissible to all dignities, places and public employments, according to their capacities, and with no distinctions other than their virtues and their talents.

2 Léopold Lacour, *Les origines du féminisme contemporain: trois femmes de la Révolution* (Paris: Plon-Nourrit, 1900), p. 13.

An admirer of Mirabeau, La Fayette, and Necker in 1788–1789, Gouges declared herself a monarchist, seeking parity between legislature and executive. She wanted universal suffrage, and became a republican after November 1792, charting a complex course between the Montagnards, party of Marat and Robespierre, and the Girondins whom they later sent to the guillotine. Almost all her writings call for women to participate in public debate. Her *Déclaration des droits de la femme et de la citoyenne* remarks, "La femme a le droit de monter sur l'échafaud; elle doit avoir également celui de monter à la Tribune." Gouges called also for the right to divorce and for freedom from religious vows in her revolutionary theater. In the spring of 1793, Gouges denounced Marat, Robespierre, and the September Massacres, and she denounced the charges leveled at the Girondins on 2 June 1793 in an appeal to Danton. Her suggestion that France might return to monarchy led to her arrest on 20 July 1793. Brought to the Tribunal on 2 November, forty-eight hours after her Girondin friends were guillotined, Gouges defended herself well. Condemned to death, she announced that she was pregnant. The doctors were unable to say, but the public prosecutor Fouquier-Tinville declared the statement false. Standing at the guillotine, she allegedly called out: "Enfants de la Patrie, vous vengerez ma mort."[3]

To date, the *Société des études robespierristes* has published not one study on Gouges; their first number on women appeared in 2006. Certainly, she has been the victim of a *légende noire*, calling into question her mental health, suggesting that she was unable to read or write. Writing after all is a fraught, if not dangerous activity. Gouges in her *Déclaration* argues that the forced inferiority of women has led them to use ruse and dissimulation, and certainly frank and honest dealing is easiest when one has the full weight of authority behind one. Transferring Gouges to the Panthéon remains a subject of controversy today.

This text is an extract from Gouges's *Déclaration* of 14 September 1791, which has seventeen articles (not six), and is prefaced with a dedication to Marie-Antoinette and a preamble and followed by a *postambule*. The whole is well worth reading, though less easily available in France than one might imagine—less available, for instance, than Wollstonecraft's echo of it the following year in England. That is not a problem faced

---

3   Nicole Pellegrin, "Les disparues de l'histoire," *Le Monde diplomatique*, 1 November 2008.

by the *Déclaration des droits de l'Homme* (1789). Two possible rationales present themselves: Gouges's text might be dull enough not to merit reading, or it might be outlandish enough that it fails to speak to any modern reader. Let us see if either of these is the case. To do so, let us focus for a moment on Article One: "La femme naît libre et demeure égale à l'homme en droits. Les distinctions sociales ne peuvent être fondées que sur l'utilité commune." It seems fair to say that sentence one here is not outlandish to a modern eye. Is it, then, unusually dull? That does not seem to be the case. It is, in fact, a mild tweak to Article One of the 1789 *Déclaration des droits de l'Homme*: "Les hommes naissent et demeurent libres et égaux en droits." Gouges has substituted *la femme* for *les hommes*, and moved *libre* to between *naît* and *demeure*: an interesting decision. Woman, says Gouges, is born free; thereafter, she remains equal in rights. This is an arresting observation, with its crisp inference that women do not remain free. It is also anchored elegantly in Rousseau, who was omnipresent in 1791: "L'homme est né libre, et partout il est dans les fers," he wrote in *Du contrat social*. One is tempted to conclude that more thought has gone into Gouges's 1791 declaration than into the 1789 version. And Gouges's second sentence, far from being outlandish, is identical to the original 1789 text; it simply applies to women now. In short, Gouges's first article, all two sentences of it, is neither dull nor outlandish; quite the contrary, it is crisp and pertinent. One is tempted to view Gouges's detractors as victims of a couple of cheap sexist tropes—Gouges was unstable, Gouges was illiterate—and to wonder, with some disappointment, at the French capacity to maintain a broad conspiracy of silence on this feminist manifesto for two centuries after its author climbed to the guillotine. To proceed here seems supererogatory. "Femme, réveille-toi," writes Gouges in the *postambule*, and the advice remains well taken.

Works

Gouges, Olympe de, *Œuvres complètes*, ed. Félix-Marcel Castan, 2 vols (Montauban: Cocagne, 1993)

L'Esclavage des Noirs, ou l'Heureux naufrage (Paris: veuve Duchesne, 1792), reworking Gouges's own *Zamore et Mirza, ou l'Heureux naufrage*, 1784

Réflexions sur les hommes nègres, 1788

Déclaration des droits de la femme et de la citoyenne, 1791 (Paris: Gallimard, 2021)

Sources

Bensaïd, Daniel, *Moi la Révolution* (Paris: Gallimard, 1989)

Blanc, Olivier, *Olympe de Gouges* (Paris: Éditions Syros, 1981)

Blanc, Olivier, *Marie-Olympe de Gouges: une humaniste à la fin du xviiie siècle* (Cahors: Éditions René Viénet, 2003)

Blanc, Olivier, *Marie-Olympe de Gouges: 1748–1793 des droits de la femme à la guillotine* (Paris: Tallandier, 2014)

Boggio, Maricla, *Olympe De Gouges al tempo della Rivoluzione* (Roma: Bulzoni, 2021)

Cole, John R., *Between the Queen and the Cabby: Olympe de Gouges's Rights of Woman* (Montréal: McGill-Queen's University Press, 2011)

Faucheux, Michel, *Olympe de Gouges* (Paris: Gallimard, 2018)

Lacour, Léopold, *Trois femmes de la Révolution: Olympe de Gouges, Théroigne de Méricourt, Rose Lacombe* (Paris: Plon, Nourrit et Cie, 1900)

Manzanera López, Laura, *Olympe de Gouges: la cronista maldita de la Revolución francesa* (Madrid: el Viejo topo, 2010)

Mensel, Isabelle, *Sprachliche Strategien der Überzeugung: Metaphern des revolutionären Diskurses, dargestellt am Beispiel Olympe de Gouges'* (Frankfurt am Main: Peter Lang, 2016)

Mousset, Sophie, *Olympe de Gouges et les droits de la femme* (Paris: Le Félin, 2003)

Perrot, Michelle, *Des femmes rebelles—Olympe de Gouges, Flora Tristan, George Sand* (Paris: Elyzad poche, 2014)

Peylet, Anne-Louise, *Olympe de Gouges: Le cri d'une humaniste dans la tourmente révolutionnaire* (Saint-Denis: Edilivre, 2021)

Ravera, Chiara, *Olympe de Gouges* (Roma: Elemento 115, 2019)

Sherman, Carol Lynn, *Reading Olympe de Gouges* (New York: Palgrave Macmillan, 2013)

Smart, Annie K., *Citoyennes: Women and the Ideal of Citizenship in Eighteenth-century France* (Newark: University of Delaware Press, 2011)

9. Marie Jeanne 'Manon' Roland de la Platière
17 March 1754–8 November 1793

Fig. 9. Marie Jeanne 'Manon' Roland de la Platière. Photo by Guise (2021). Wikimedia, https://upload.wikimedia.org/wikipedia/commons/0/09/Madame_Roland_-_mus%C3%A9e_Lambinet.jpg, CC BY 4.0.

Mémoires

Seconde Arrestation

De Sainte-Pélagie, le 20 août 1793

Le vingt-quatrième jour de ma détention à l'Abbaye commençait de s'écouler ; l'espace de cette détention avait été rempli par l'étude et le travail, je l'avais principalement employé à écrire des *Notes* dont la rédaction devait se ressentir de l'excellente disposition d'esprit dans laquelle je me trouvais. L'insurrection du 31 mai, les attentats du 2 juin m'avaient pénétrée d'indignation, mais j'étais persuadée que les départements ne les verraient pas d'un œil satisfait, et que leurs réclamations, soutenues des démarches nécessaires, feraient triompher la bonne cause. Peu m'importait avec cet espoir que, dans l'instant d'une crise ou les excès de la tyrannie expirante, je tombasse victime de la haine particulière ou de la rage de quelque forcené. Le succès de mes amis, le triomphe des vrais républicains me consolaient de tout à l'avance ; j'aurais subi un jugement inique ou succombé par quelque atrocité imprévue, avec le calme, la fierté, même la joie de l'innocence qui méprise la mort et sait que la sienne sera vengée. Je ne puis m'empêcher de répéter ici les regrets déjà exprimés de la perte de ces *Notes* qui peignaient si bien et les faits que j'avais connus, et les personnes dont j'avais été environnée, et les sentiments que j'éprouvais dans la succession des événements d'alors. J'apprends qu'il en est échappé quelques-unes à la destruction ; mais elles ne contiennent que les détails de ma première arrestation. Un jour peut-être la réunion de ces lambeaux offrira à quelque main amie de quoi ajouter de nouveaux traits au tableau de la vérité ...[1]

Marie Jeanne 'Manon' Roland de la Platière, *née* Phlipon was born and died in Paris. *Salonnière,* muse of the Girondins, and of the Romantics after her death, she helped put her husband at the forefront of politics from 1791 to 1793. Phlipon was born on the Île de la Cité in Paris, the daughter

---

1   Manon Roland, *Mémoires (Extraits)*, ed. Mlle Ch. Charrier (Paris: Hatier, n.d.), p. 40.

Translation: Second Arrest

From Sainte-Pélagie [prison], 20 August 1793

> The twenty-fourth day of my detention at the Abbaye was starting to end; the space of this detention had been filled by study and work, I had principally employed it to write these *Notes* whose writing should bear witness to the excellent disposition of spirit in which I found myself. The insurrection of 31 May, the lawlessness of 2 June had penetrated me with indignation, but I was persuaded that the departments would not see them with a satisfied eye, and that their demands, upheld by the necessary steps, would make the good cause triumph. With this hope, little was I concerned that in the instant of a crisis or the excesses of an expiring tyranny, I might fall victim to the particular hatred or the rage of some criminal. The success of my friends, the triumph of the true republicans consoled me of everything in advance; I would have undergone an unjust judgment or succumbed to some unforeseen atrocity, with the calm, the pride, even the joy of innocence which despises death and knows that its own will be avenged. I cannot prevent myself here from repeating the regrets already expressed at the loss of those *Notes* which painted so well both the facts I had known; and the persons I had been surrounded by; and the sentiments I felt in the succession of the events of that time. I learn that some of them have escaped destruction; but they contain only the details of my first arrest. One day perhaps the gathering of these shreds will offer some friendly hand the means to add new traits to the painting of truth ...

of a well-off engraver. Placed with a wet nurse until the age of two, she was the only one of seven children to survive. Intelligent and pious, she learned Latin and read Plutarch, the Bible, Bossuet, Montesquieu, and Voltaire. At eleven, she was put in a convent; at twenty, she lost her mother and found consolation in Rousseau's *La Nouvelle Héloïse* (1761). Rousseau remained a model. In 1774, she visited Versailles. She met the economist Jean Marie Roland de La Platière in 1776, twenty years her senior, who fell in love and asked for her hand. They married in 1780, working and writing together over the ensuing years: "Mariée dans tout le sérieux de la raison," she says in her *Mémoires*.[2] They returned to Paris in 1791, sleeping thenceforth in separate beds. Manon Roland joined the *club des Jacobins* that year, giving several speeches there, while her salon welcomed Brissot, Pétion, Robespierre, and others. Her husband became Minister of the Interior on 23 March 1792, her salon meeting twice a week. Roland played a major role in his ministry and helped write the letter that got her husband dismissed by the King on 13 June 1792, but at his reinstatement after the fall of the Tuileries on 10 August, she contributed ever more closely to his work. She hated Danton after the September Massacres. Attacks from the Montagne led her husband to resign his post on 23 January 1793. At the arrest of the Girondins on 31 May 1793, Roland did not flee like her husband; she was arrested and imprisoned in the Abbaye, writing unexpectedly to Buzot, "puis-je me plaindre de mon infortune, lorsque de telles délices me sont réservées?"[3] In prison, she had writing materials and could receive visits. She appeared before the Tribunal on 8 November 1793, six days after Gouges. Her alleged last words at the guillotine—"Ô Liberté, que de crimes on commet en ton nom!"—were an invention of the poet Lamartine.[4] Her husband learned of her death two days later and committed suicide, as did Buzot the following year.

"La tyrannie est une parvenue, le despotisme un grand seigneur," wrote Staël. It is perhaps fitting that the Bastille, on 14 July 1789, contained exactly seven prisoners, the Marquis de Sade having been transferred out the week before. Certainly, there were dungeons prior

---

2   *Mémoires de Madame Roland*, ed. C.A. Dauban (Paris: Plon, 1864), p. 172.
3   *Lettres de Madame Roland*, ed. Claude Perroud, 2 vols (Paris: Imprimerie nationale, 1902), II p.492.
4   Roger Bellet, *La Femme au xixe siècle: littérature et idéologie* (Lyon: Presses universitaires de Lyon, 1985), "Lamartine et Madame Roland," p. 60.

to the Revolution—*lettres de cachet* allowed aristocrats to imprison those they found troublesome with little judicial process, and they were abolished only in 1790—but the Revolution was not without its prisons, massacring some prisoners on the spot, in September 1792, while hauling others such as Manon Roland off to the guillotine after what might best be termed a show trial. What the Terror allowed, that France had not seen previously, was the emergence of a totalitarian state. Women were not executed often in Old Regime France: the regime which executed Roland, Gouges, Charlotte Corday, and Marie Antoinette counted one murderer among those four victims, and the charge against Gouges was her suggestion in print that a return to monarchy might constitute option three for the young republic. It was, in short, a thought police. "Brûler n'est pas répondre," said Desmoulins as his printing presses were smashed, and it is in these Romantic terms that we sense Roland's enduring appeal.

The year is 1793. Roland has been arrested with the Girondins, released, then rearrested twenty-four hours later. Her husband has fled; she has not. She is, like Condorcet in hiding writing a vision of human perfectibility, perhaps a starry-eyed optimist. Or perhaps she has read too much Plutarch. The fact is, her tone in this text is surprising: she had lived long enough to see kangaroo trials and the September Massacres, to see the Terror begin. And this is her second arrest. Where then does her hope lie? What is the source of her "excellente disposition d'esprit"? Her talk of the departments suggests that part of her hope lies in the rest of France; not, indeed, that France could intervene in time to save her own life, but that it might yet overthrow Robespierre and his henchmen and redeem the Revolution. This is a very Girondin hope; but it is not, I think, for personal salvation. Roland was no fool, she was an experienced political operative. As she says—and this text is not *post hoc*, it was written in prison awaiting her trial—"Peu m'importait [...] que je tombasse victime [...] Le succès de mes amis, le triomphe des vrais républicains me consolaient de tout à l'avance." That is an almost Roman sentiment.

Chateaubriand wrote *Les Martyrs* in 1809, and from Marat onward, the Terror produced its share of martyrs for France's various factions to celebrate—"Fils de saint Louis, montez au ciel!" were said to be the last words spoken to Louis XVI as he mounted to the guillotine. It is perhaps worth noting then how hard it was, working in the Bibliothèque nationale de France in 2022, to procure a copy of Roland's memoirs, memoirs which mattered so much to Lamartine. This voice from prison awaiting near-certain death, is it lacking in weight or intensity, a sort of *samizdat*? Is it not gripping, even poignant to see how the Girondins went to the guillotine *en masse*, women among them? Does it not say something about this revolution which perhaps deserves to be said and heard? "La Révolution est comme Saturne," proclaimed Desmoulins, "elle dévore ses propres enfants." In any case, holding a nineteenth-century school edition of the abridged memoirs in my hands, in the immense French national library, repository of all French knowledge, I wondered at the space devoted to Montagnards and *sans-culottes* across decades of twentieth-century scholarship, and the challenge of finding Roland in that copyright library in any modern edition.

Works

[Roland, Manon], *Lettres à une amie d'enfance. Madame Roland*, ed. Chantal Thomas (Paris: Mercure de France, 1996)

Mémoires de Madame Roland, ed. Claude Perroud and Paul de Roux (Paris: Mercure de France, 1986)

Sources

Perroud, Claude, *Études sur les Roland*, vol. I (Volonne: Bibliothèque du Bois-Menez, 2019)

Reynolds, Siân, *Marriage and Revolution: Monsieur and Madame Roland* (Oxford: Oxford University Press, 2012)

Tulard, Jean and Marie-José, *Les égéries de la Révolution* (Paris: Laffont, 2019)

10. Marie Louise Élisabeth Vigée Le Brun
16 April 1755–30 March 1842

Fig. 10. Marie Louise Élisabeth Vigée Le Brun, self portrait. Photo by Cybershot 800i (2012). Wikimedia, https://upload.wikimedia.org/wikipedia/commons/c/c9/Lebrun%2C_Self-portrait.jpg, CC BY 4.0.

Mémoires d'une portraitiste

Je ne puis vous dire ce que j'éprouvai en passant sur le pont Beauvoisin. Là seulement je commençais à respirer ; j'étais hors de France, et cette France qui pourtant était ma patrie, et que je me reprochais de quitter avec joie. L'aspect des monts parvint à me distraire de toutes mes tristes pensées, je n'avais jamais vu de hautes montagnes ; celles de la Savoie me parurent toucher au ciel avec lequel un épais brouillard les confondait. Mon premier sentiment fut celui de la peur, mais je m'accoutumai insensiblement à ce spectacle, et je finis par l'admirer.

Je montai le mont Cenis, comme plusieurs étrangers le montaient aussi ; un postillon s'approcha de moi : « Madame devrait prendre un mulet, me dit-il, car monter à pied, c'est trop fatigant pour une dame comme elle. » Je lui répondis que j'étais une ouvrière, bien accoutumée à marcher. « Ah ! reprit-il en riant, Madame n'est pas une ouvrière, on sait qui elle est. —Eh bien, qui suis-je donc ? demandai-je. — Vous êtes madame Le Brun, qui peint dans la perfection, et nous sommes tous très contents de vous savoir loin des méchants. »

Je n'ai jamais pu deviner comment cet homme avait pu savoir mon nom ; mais cela m'a prouvé combien les jacobins avaient d'émissaires. Heureusement je ne les craignais plus ; j'étais hors de leur exécrable puissance. À défaut de patrie, j'allais habiter des lieux où fleurissaient les arts, où régnait l'urbanité ; j'allais visiter Rome, Naples, Berlin, Vienne, Pétersbourg, et surtout, ce que j'ignorais alors, chère amie, j'allais vous trouver, vous connaître et vous aimer.

Toute à vous.[1]

Marie Louise Élisabeth Vigée Le Brun was born and died in Paris. An ardent royalist, she was in turn painter to the French court, to the Kingdom of Naples, to the court of the Austrian Emperor, to the Tsar, and to the Restoration. Her father and mother, a pastelist and a hairdresser, married in 1750. A younger brother, a successful dramatist, was born in

---

1   Marie Louise Élisabeth Vigée Le Brun, *Mémoires d'une portraitiste* (Paris: Scala, 2003), pp. 80–81.

> Translation: I cannot tell you what I felt in crossing the Beauvoisin bridge. There only did I begin to breathe; I was out of France, and that France which nevertheless was my fatherland, and which I reproached myself on leaving with joy. The aspect of the mountains succeeded in distracting me from all my sad thoughts, I had never seen high mountains; those of Savoy seemed to me to touch the sky with which a thick fog confounded them. My first sentiment was one of fear, but I insensibly accustomed myself to this spectacle, and I ended by admiring it.
>
> I climbed Mount Cenis, as many strangers were also climbing it; a coachman approached me: "Madame should take a mule, he told me, since to climb on foot is too tiring for a lady such as her." I replied to him that I was a worker well accustomed to walking. "Ah! he continued, laughing, Madame is not a worker, we know who she is. — Well then, who am I? I asked. — You are Madame Le Brun, who paints to perfection, and we are all very happy to know you are far from the wicked."
>
> I was never able to guess how this man could have known my name; but that proved to me how many emissaries the Jacobins had. Luckily, I no longer feared them; I was out of their execrable power. Lacking a fatherland, I was going to live in places where the arts flourished, where urbanity reigned; I was going to visit Rome, Naples, Berlin, Vienna, Petersburg and especially, what I did not then know, dear friend, I was going to find you, know you and love you.
>
> Entirely yours.

1757. The infant Élisabeth was given to a wet nurse, her father fetching her back to Paris six years later, where she entered a convent until 1766. Her father died the following year; her mother remarried, to a jeweler who later pocketed Élisabeth's earnings. In 1769, she introduced herself to Gabriel Briard, member of the Académie royale de peinture. At the Louvre, she met Horace Vernet and later Jean Baptiste Greuze, but as she later wrote, she never had a proper teacher. She kept a list of her paintings: twenty-seven in 1773. In 1776, she married Jean Baptiste Pierre Lebrun, a merchant and restorer of paintings, against advice; that same year, she was admitted to paint for the court of Louis XVI, then in 1778 for Marie-Antoinette. Her portraits sold for 12,000 francs, of which she saw just six, the rest pocketed by her husband. In 1785, a portrait of Calonne, her alleged lover, earned her 800,000 francs. Vigée Le Brun painted mainly portraits, though necessarily she entered the Académie as a history painter; in summer 1789, a *sans-culotte* crowd sacked her home and tried to set fire to it. On the night of 5 October 1789, as the royal family was brought back to Paris, Vigée le Brun fled the capital with her daughter and twenty francs, leaving a million to her husband who encouraged her departure. Added to the list of émigrés in 1792, Vigée Le Brun was unable to return from Italy to Paris. She instead left for Vienna. Her husband obtained a divorce in 1794, as his wife crossed Europe in triumph, reaching Saint Petersburg in 1795 and staying five years. In 1799, her husband petitioned for her removal from the list of émigrés, with 255 signatures, largely of artists. She returned in 1800, after her mother's death and her daughter's marriage, of which she disapproved. She found post-revolutionary France unpleasant and went to England for three years, meeting Byron, Benjamin West, and Lady Hamilton and staying with the court of Louis XVIII, whose return in 1814 she welcomed. Her daughter died in 1819, her brother in 1820. About two-thirds of her 900 paintings are portraits; that and her ties to Marie-Antoinette did not much help her posthumous reputation.

Vigée le Brun the artist is not our topic, though she has been enjoying rediscovery in recent years; our concern is with the memoirist. Here we are then at the outset of the Revolution, in 1789, and Vigée Le Brun is emigrating. Students of the Revolution will note that there were various emigrations: Staël, for instance, left Paris just after the storming of the Tuileries, late in 1792. The Comte d'Artois, future Charles X, left on 17

July 1789; Vigée Le Brun emigrated in October 1789, as seen here, amid the early royalist emigration, not the later monarchist one. This may be no surprise, given that a mob had attempted to burn down her Paris home that summer; but it is also worth noting her years spent painting absolutist royals from Marie-Antoinette to the King of Naples to the Habsburgs to the Tsar, not to mention her alleged affair with Calonne, among the most intransigent, if not incompetent, of Louis XVI's ministers. Vigée Le Brun then seems ready to condemn the Revolution lock, stock, and barrel: she describes the Jacobins as being in power in October 1789 (they were not), and notes, "j'étais hors de leur exécrable puissance." This is very much an émigré text.

It is interesting to see Vigée Le Brun twice use the word *patrie* in this short passage: the word was charged with revolutionary affect, as the opening of 1792's *Marseillaise* reminds us, but the author is unprepared to cede patriotism entirely to the Left. She tells us, first, not that it hurt to leave her *patrie*, but that she reproached herself for leaving with joy; later, she says she had no *patrie*. There is some conflict in her feelings here, in this age of emergent nationalism, but Vigée Le Brun, who spent years abroad, appears relatively at ease abandoning France, as other contemporaries were not. That is hardly unique in émigré literature, which includes memoirists who were prepared to make active war on the French Republic. It seems uncommon, though, among the women writers in this book: Vigée Le Brun, for instance, returned to France under Bonaparte and disliked it, departing for exile or at least emigration once again.

Works

Vigée Le Brun, Élisabeth, *Mémoires d'une portraitiste* (Paris: Scala, 2003)

Les femmes régnaient alors, la Révolution les a détrônées: souvenirs, 1755–1842, ed. Didier Masseau (Paris: Tallandier, 2009)

Geneviève Haroche-Bouzinac, *Élisabeth Vigée Le Brun—Souvenirs 1755–1842* (Paris: Champion, 2015)

Sources

Berly, Cécile, *Louise Élisabeth Vigée Le Brun* (Paris: Artlys, 2015)

Berly, Cécile, *Trois femmes: Madame du Deffand, Madame Roland, Madame Vigée Le Brun* (Paris: Passés/Composés, 2020)

Chauvel, Geneviève, *Le Peintre de la Reine. Élisabeth Vigée Le Brun* (Paris: Pygmalion, 2003)

Haroche-Bouzinac, Geneviève, *Louise Élisabeth Vigée Le Brun, histoire d'un regard* (Paris: Flammarion, 2011)

Kertanguy, Inès de, *Madame Vigée Le Brun* (Paris: Perrin, 1994)

Pitt-Rivers, Françoise, *Madame Vigée Le Brun* (Paris: Gallimard, 2001)

Robb Jr., David M., *Élisabeth Vigée Le Brun, 1755–1842: Catalogue of the Exhibition at the Kimbell Art Museum (Fort Worth, Texas)* (Seattle: University of Washington Press, 1982)

11. Adélaïde Marie Émilie de Souza-Botelho
14 May 1761–19 April 1836

Fig. 11. Adélaïde Marie Émilie de Souza-Botelho. Photo by Pbrks (2022). Wikimedia, https://commons.wikimedia.org/wiki/File:AdelaideSouza.jpg, CC BY 4.0.

Adèle de Sénange, ou Lettres de Lord Sydenham

Avant-Propos.

Cet ouvrage n'a point pour objet de peindre des caractères qui sortent des routes communes : mon ambition ne s'est pas élevée jusqu'à prétendre étonner par des situations nouvelles ; j'ai voulu seulement montrer, dans la vie, ce qu'on n'y regarde pas, et décrire ces mouvements ordinaires du cœur qui composent l'histoire de chaque jour. Si je réussis à faire arrêter un instant mes lecteurs sur eux-mêmes, et si, après avoir lu cet ouvrage, ils se disent : *Il n'y a rien là de nouveau* ; ils ne sauraient me flatter davantage.

J'ai pensé que l'on pouvait se rapprocher assez de la nature, et inspirer encore de l'intérêt, en se bornant à tracer ces détails fugitifs qui occupent l'espace entre les événements de la vie. Des jours, des années, dont le souvenir est effacé, ont été remplis d'émotions, de sentiments, de petits intérêts, de nuances fines et délicates. Chaque moment a son occupation, et chaque occupation a son ressort moral. Il est même bon de rapprocher sans cesse la vertu de ces circonstances obscures et inaperçues, parce que c'est la suite de ces sentiments journaliers qui forme essentiellement le fond de la vie. Ce sont ces ressorts que j'ai tâché de démêler.

Cet essai a été commencé dans un temps qui semblait imposer à une femme, à une mère, le besoin de s'éloigner de tout ce qui était réel, de ne guère réfléchir, et même d'écarter la prévoyance ; et il a été achevé dans les intervalles d'une longue maladie : mais, tel qu'il est, je le présente à l'indulgence de mes amis.

> ... A faint shadow of uncertain light,
> Such as a lamp whose light doth fade away,
> Doth lend to her who walks in fear and sad affright.

Seule dans une terre étrangère, avec un enfant qui a atteint l'âge où il n'est plus permis de retarder l'éducation, j'ai éprouvé une sorte de douceur à penser que ses premières études seraient le fruit de mon travail.

Mon cher enfant ! Si je succombe à la maladie qui me poursuit, qu'au moins mes amis excitent votre application, en vous rappelant qu'elle eût fait mon bonheur ! et ils peuvent vous l'attester, eux qui savent avec quelle tendresse je vous ai aimé ; eux qui si souvent ont détourné mes douleurs en me parlant de vous. Avec quelle ingénieuse bonté ils me faisaient raconter les petites joies de votre enfance, vos petits bons-mots, les premiers mouvements de votre bon cœur ! Combien je leur répétais la même histoire, et avec quelle patience ils se prêtaient à m'écouter ! Souvent à la fin d'un de mes contes, je m'apercevais que je l'avais dit bien des fois : alors, ils se moquaient doucement de moi, de ma crédule confiance, de ma tendre affection, et me parlaient encore de vous ! ... Je les remercie ... Je leur ai dû le plus grand plaisir qu'une mère puisse avoir.

A. de F ......
Londres, 1793.[1]

---

1 Adélaïde Marie Émilie de Souza-Botelho, *Adèle de Sénange* (Genève: Slatkine Reprints, 1995), pp. 1–3. Spelling modernized by John Claiborne Isbell.

11. Adélaïde Marie Émilie de Souza-Botelho

Adélaïde Marie Émilie de Souza-Botelho was born and died in Paris. Legend says that her mother was the mistress of Louis XV, then of a farmer general, Étienne Michel Bouret, one of whom was her father. At sixteen, Adélaïde's sister Julie married the brother of Madame de Pompadour; their mother died in 1767 and Julie took charge of her. Adélaïde was educated at a convent, leaving it in 1779 aged eighteen to marry Charles François, Comte de Flahaut de la Billarderie at the decision of her sister. He was thirty-six years older than her and both marshal and intendant of the King's gardens: according to her, the marriage was never consummated. They lived at the Louvre where Flahaut, as she then was, decided to write *Adèle de Sénange*, the story of a young girl married off to a much older man, living a passion resembling

---

Translation: Preface.

This work does not have the object of painting characters who leave the ordinary routes: my ambition has not climbed to wishing to astonish through new situations; I wanted only to show, in life, what one does not look at therein, and to describe those ordinary movements of the heart which compose the history of each day. If I succeed in making my readers pause a moment on themselves, and if, after having read this work, they say to themselves: *There's nothing new there*; they could not better flatter me.

I thought that one could approach nature enough, and still inspire interest, in limiting oneself to tracing those fugitive details which occupy the space between the events of life. Days, years, whose memory is erased, have been filled with emotions, with feelings, with little interests, with fine and delicate nuances. Each moment has its occupation, and each occupation has its moral spring. It is indeed good to bring to mind incessantly the virtue of these obscure and unnoticed circumstances, because it is the succession of these daily feelings which makes up in essence the basis of life. These are the springs I have tried to untangle.

This essay began in a time which seemed to impose on a woman, a mother, the need to distance oneself from all that was real, to reflect hardly at all, and even to push aside foresight; and it was finished in the intervals of a long illness; but such as it is, I present it to the indulgence of my friends.

[...] Alone in a foreign land, with a child who has reached the age where one may no longer delay his education, I felt a sort of sweetness in thinking that his first studies would be the fruit of my work.

My dear child! If I succumb to the illness which pursues me, let my friends at least excite your application, in reminding you that it would have caused me joy! and they can also bear witness to you, those who know with what tenderness I loved you; those who so often turned away my pains in speaking to me of you. With what ingenious goodness they made me tell of the little joys of your childhood, your little witticisms, the first movements of your good heart! How much I repeated to them the same story, and with what patience they lent themselves to listening to me! Often at the end of one of my tales, I realized that I had said it many times; then they gently teased me, my credulous trust, my tender affection, and spoke to me yet of you! ... I thank them ... I owed them the greatest pleasure a mother can have.

A. de F ......
London, 1793.

that of *La Princesse de Clèves* (1678). It appeared in 1794 as her first novel. Mistress of Talleyrand, she opened a salon where he presided between 1783 and 1792. They had a son in 1785. The salon also saw Gouverneur Morris, Lavoisier, Condorcet, d'Holbach, Suard, and Marmontel. Talleyrand drew close to Staël at the onset of the Revolution, causing a rift. At the start of the Terror, Flahaut settled in London, leaving her husband in France. He was guillotined the same year. She traveled then to Switzerland where she met the Duc de Chartres, and on to Hamburg where she met her future husband, Dom José Maria de Sousa Botelho Mourão e Vasconcelos, Ambassador of Portugal in Denmark. Talleyrand helped her to return to France in 1797 and to be removed from the list of émigrés. She published *Émilie et Alphonse* in 1799, and *Charles et Marie* in 1802, the year she remarried. Souza worked at her son's career—even encouraging his liaison with Hortense de Beauharnais, which produced a grandson—but lost her influence at the Empire's fall. She then retired from public life, raising her grandson whose career followed that of his half-brother, Napoléon III. She is buried in Père Lachaise Cemetery.

Here is a later émigrée than Vigée Le Brun: Souza left Paris for exile in 1793. Souza's husband was executed in 1794, as *Adèle de Sénange* appeared, and she had separated from Talleyrand—a trimmer in politics with a gift for remaining close to power as it changed hands, from 1789 to 1815 and beyond. The Terror was a dark time for her as for countless others, and that is perhaps reflected in her text. It opens by stating its goal of having no "situations nouvelles," no characters who leave the common paths: ambrosia, surely, to all those who saw in the Terror the price paid by France for a focus both on novelty and on extraordinary characters. Souza goes on to state that her focus will be on "la suite de ces sentiments journaliers," which make up the ground of life, evoking both the fashionable contrast of revolution with evolution, the equally voguish focus on a gendered private sphere found in, say, David's 1784 *The Oath of the Horatii*, and finally, the contrast of everyday detail with the reign of abstraction that led to the guillotine—which was precisely Camus's argument in *L'Étranger* two centuries later. Souza does not name the Revolution in this preface, but one word—"encore", in paragraph two—depends on the Revolution for its weight of meaning.

The preface is rather oddly bisected by an edited quote from Spenser: the original reads,

> But a faint shadow of uncertain light;
> Such as a lamp whose light doth fade away;
> Or as the moon clothed with cloudy night
> Does shew to him that walks in fear and sad affright.

This is followed by an address to Souza's son (by Talleyrand) whose function is not entirely clear and where the word "vous" may surprise. Souza may have written this address as a *captatio benevolentiae*, an appeal to the reader's good will; or it may simply be her love and hope expressing themselves at a dark time for both, as we have seen. It is signed "A. de F ......" for Flahaut, her first married name.

Works

[Souza, Adélaïde de], *Œuvres complètes de Madame de Souza* (Paris: Garnier, 1865)

Adèle de Sénange (Genève: Slatkine Reprints, 1995)

Émilie et Alphonse, ou Danger de se livrer à ses premières impressions, 3 vols (Hambourg: P.F. Fauche; Paris: Charles Pougens, an VII/1799)

Charles et Marie (Paris: Maradan, an X/1802)

Eugène de Rothelin, 2 vols (Paris: H. Nicolle, 1808)

Eugénie et Mathilde, ou les Mémoires de la famille du Comte de Revel, 3 vols (Paris: F. Schoell, 1811)

La Comtesse de Fargy (Paris: Alexis Eymery, 1823)

La Duchesse de Guise, ou intérieur d'une famille illustre dans le temps de la Ligue; drame en trois actes (Paris: C. Gosselin, 1832)

Mademoiselle de Tournon (Paris: Firmin Didot, 1820)

Sources

Carpenter, Kirsty, *The Novels of Madame de Souza in Social and Political Perspective* (Bern: Peter Lang, 2007)

Chaumont, Jean-Philippe, *Archives du Général Charles de Flahaut et de sa famille* (Paris: Centre historique des Archives nationales, La documentation française, 2005)

Maricourt, André de, *Madame de Souza et sa famille. Les Marigny, les Flahaut, Auguste de Morny (1761–1836)* (Paris: Émile-Paul, 1907)

Mooij, Anne Louis Anton, *Caractères principaux et tendances des romans psychologiques chez quelques femmes-auteurs, de Mme Riccoboni à Mme de Souza, 1757–1826* (Groningen: de Waal, 1949)

12. Sophie de Grouchy or Sophie de Condorcet
8 April 1764–8 September 1822

Fig. 12. Sophie de Grouchy or Sophie de Condorcet, self portrait. Photo by Branor (2013). Wikimedia, https://upload.wikimedia.org/wikipedia/commons/f/f0/Sophiedecondorcet.jpg, CC BY 4.0.

Lettres sur la Sympathie

Lettre II

La sympathie dont nous sommes susceptibles pour les maux physiques, et qui est une partie de ce que nous comprenons sous le nom d'humanité, serait un sentiment trop peu durable pour être souvent utile, mon cher C***, si nous n'étions capables de réflexion autant que de sensibilité ; mais comme la réflexion prolonge les idées que nous ont apportées nos sens, elle étend et conserve en nous l'effet de la vue de la douleur, et l'on peut dire que c'est elle qui nous rend véritablement humains. En effet, c'est la réflexion qui fixe dans notre âme la présence d'un mal que nos yeux n'ont vu qu'un moment, et qui nous porte à le soulager pour en effacer l'idée importune et douloureuse ; c'est la réflexion qui, venant au secours de notre mobilité naturelle, force notre compassion à être active en lui offrant de nouveau les objets qui n'avaient fait sur elle qu'une impression momentanée ; c'est la réflexion qui, à la vue de la douleur, nous rappelant que nous sommes sujets de ce tyran destructeur de la vie, comme l'être que nous en voyons opprimé, nous rapproche de lui par un mouvement d'émotion et d'attendrissement sur nous-mêmes, et nous intéresse à ses maux, même lorsqu'ils pourraient plutôt repousser qu'attirer notre sensibilité ; c'est la réflexion enfin qui, par les habitudes qu'elle donne à notre sensibilité, en prolongeant ses mouvements, fait que l'humanité devient dans nos âmes, un sentiment actif et permanent qui, brûlant de s'exercer, va sans attendre qu'on l'excite, chercher le bonheur des hommes dans les travaux des sciences, dans les méditations de la nature, de l'expérience, et de la philosophie, ou qui, s'attachant à la douleur et à l'infortune, la suit partout, et en devient le consolateur, le dieu. Le sentiment de l'humanité est donc en quelque sorte, un germe déposé au fond du cœur de l'homme par la nature, et que la faculté de réfléchir va féconder et développer.

Mais quelques animaux, dira-t-on, sont susceptibles de pitié, et ne le sont pas de réflexion ?[1]

---

1 Bernier, Marc André, and Deidre Dawson, eds, *Les Lettres sur la sympathie de Sophie de Grouchy: philosophie morale et réforme sociale* (Oxford: Voltaire Foundation, 2010), pp. 38–39.

Translation: The sympathy of which we are capable for physical pains, and which is a part of what we comprehend under the name humanity, would be too short-lasting a feeling to be often useful, my dear C***, if we were incapable of reflection as much as of sensibility; but as reflection prolongs the ideas that our senses have brought us, it extends and conserves in us the effect of the sight of suffering, and one may say that it is this which makes us truly human. In fact, it is reflection which fixes in our soul the presence of a pain that our eyes have only seen a moment, and which leads us to remedy it to erase its importunate and painful idea; it is reflection which, coming to the help of our natural mobility, forces our compassion to be active in offering it again objects which had made only a momentary impression on it; it is reflection, which at the sight of pain, reminding us that we are subject to this life-destroying tyrant, like the being that we see oppressed by it, brings us toward them by a movement of emotion and tenderness directed toward ourselves, and interests us in their pains, even when they might rather repulse than attract our sensibility; it is reflection finally which, by the habits it gives to our sensibility, in prolonging its movements, makes humanity become an active and permanent sentiment in our souls which, burning to exercise itself, goes ahead without waiting to be excited, looking for the happiness of men in the works of the sciences, in the meditations of nature, of experience, and of philosophy, or which, attaching itself to pain and misfortune, follows it everywhere, and becomes its consoler, its god. The sentiment of humanity is thus in some sort a grain deposited at the bottom of man's heart by nature, and which the faculty of reflection will fertilize and develop.

But some animals, some will say, are capable of pity, and not of reflection?

12. Sophie de Grouchy or Sophie de Condorcet

Marie Louise Sophie de Grouchy was the daughter of François Jacques de Grouchy, Marquis de Grouchy, and Marie Gilberte Henriette Fréteau de Pény. Grouchy was born in Meulan in 1764 and died in Paris in 1822. In 1786, she married the mathematician and philosopher Marie Jean Antoine Nicolas de Caritat, Marquis de Condorcet. She was twenty-two, he was forty-two and a prominent Academician. After her marriage, Sophie de Condorcet started a salon attended by Turgot, Beaumarchais, Gouges, Staël, and many philosophers alongside foreign visitors such as Jefferson, Beccaria, and possibly Adam Smith. This salon later played an important role in Girondin politics. Condorcet allowed the Cercle Social, committed to equal rights for women, to meet at her house; her interest in women's rights may have helped to shape her husband's essay of 1790, "Sur l'admission des femmes au droit de cité." In 1793, after denouncing the Jacobin constitution, her husband went into hiding. Condorcet visited him secretly, encouraging him to write. The marquis composed his *Esquisse d'un tableau historique des progrès de l'esprit humain* (1795), which she later edited; Condorcet filed for divorce, with her husband's consent, since that would allow wife and daughter to keep the family assets. In 1794, he left hiding, was identified, and was handed over to the authorities. He was found dead in prison the next morning, likely by his own hand. Condorcet had her husband's last works published posthumously. Left penniless by his proscription and death, which preceded their planned divorce, Condorcet supported herself, her daughter, and her younger sister. She opened a shop to survive, putting aside her writing and translation work. Highly educated for her day, she became fluent in English and Italian and translated Adam Smith and Thomas Paine. Her most important publication is her eight *Lettres sur la sympathie,* added in 1798 to her translation of Smith's *Theory of Moral Sentiments* (1759). The translation was standard for the ensuing two centuries, while its eight letters on sympathy were largely ignored. In 1799, Condorcet resumed her salon, working between 1801 and 1804 to publish her husband's complete works. To the end, she adhered to her husband's political views, and under Consulate and Empire, her salon became a meeting place for opponents of the regime such as Fauriel. She witnessed the Bourbon reaction after 1815, dying in 1822 as she prepared a new edition of her husband's works.

The above passage opens Letter Two of the eight *Lettres sur la sympathie* Condorcet appended to her translation of Smith in 1798, though the text is some years older—her husband mentions the letters in his will, written in 1794. Letter Two opens with extended praise of reflection as a sort of mortar strengthening the brickwork of compassionate experience. Adam Smith belongs with Hutcheson and Hume to a Scottish tradition keen to find in sympathy a counterbalance to the self-interest promoted by Hobbes or La Rochefoucauld and central to the science of economics today. Condorcet is distinguished perhaps by a shift of emphasis: where Smith sees sympathy as a sort of spectacle retold in the viewing mind, Condorcet presents it in more material terms, as a chemistry of the heart, suggests a modern reviewer.[2] Condorcet seems untroubled by Smith's observation that we can have sympathy for the dead, though they do not contribute to it; the C*** her letters all address is her brother-in-law the *idéologue* Cabanis, whose *Rapports du physique et du moral de l'homme* (1802) cite her letters and codify a thoroughgoing materialist view of mind in the tradition of Condillac. Reducing mind to matter is a major undertaking, equivalent to Laplace's reduction of the heavens to Newtonian physics in his contemporary *Mécanique céleste* (1796), and it may have seemed more important than following Smith's theater metaphor. Condorcet does allege in Letter One that her English was poor as she began—"je n'entendais pas assez l'anglais pour lire l'original"—but that seems to have been corrected. Let us note that Rousseau also rejects Smith's theater metaphor, choosing instead to focus on pity; but much of this may be the detail that Condorcet feels can resolve into final unity, offering new tools to rehabilitate affectivity in moral thought.

Women enjoyed a longstanding premodern role as mediators of cutting-edge thought, and Condorcet, whose translation of Smith precedes her letters, follows in that tradition—it has been argued that her translator's lexicon is more physical than Smith's, which would be atypical for a rendering from English into French. Du Châtelet, who died in 1749, preceded her, translating Newton's *Principia mathematica* (1687) in the 1740s, but women translated a good deal throughout this period, it was a commonly exploited genre. Du Châtelet and Staël also

---

2   Marc André Bernier, "Les métamorphoses de la sympathie au siècle des Lumières", in *Les Lettres sur la sympathie (1798) de Sophie de Grouchy: philosophie morale et réforme sociale*, ed. Marc André Bernier and Deidre Dawson (Oxford: Voltaire Foundation, 2010), p. 14.

shared Condorcet's interest in moral philosophy. Condorcet meanwhile began her career as a translator through work on a text defending the early French Revolution by James Mackintosh, the Scottish Whig leader, in 1792.

Works

[Condorcet, Sophie de], Bernier, Marc André, and Deidre Dawson, eds, *Les Lettres sur la sympathie de Sophie de Grouchy: philosophie morale et réforme sociale* (Oxford: Voltaire Foundation, 2010)

Mackintosh, James, *Apologie de la Révolution française, et de ses admirateurs anglais* […], trans. Sophie de Grouchy (Paris: F. Buisson, 1792)

Smith, Adam, *Théorie des sentiments moraux* […], trans. Sophie de Grouchy (Paris: F. Buisson, 1798)

Sources

Arnold-Tétard, Madeleine, *Sophie de Grouchy, marquise de Condorcet: la dame de cœur* (Paris: Christian, 2003)

Bergès, Sandrine, and Eric Schliesser, *Sophie de Grouchy's Letters on Sympathy: A Critical Engagement with Adam Smith's The Theory of Moral Sentiments* (Oxford: Oxford University Press, 2019)

Bernier, Marc André, and Deidre Dawson, eds, *Les Lettres sur la sympathie de Sophie de Grouchy: philosophie morale et réforme sociale* (Oxford: Voltaire Foundation, 2010)

Boissel, Thierry, *Sophie de Condorcet, femme des Lumières, 1764–1822* (Paris: Presses de la Renaissance, 1988)

Brookes, Barbara, "The Feminism of Condorcet and Sophie de Grouchy," *Studies on Voltaire and the Eighteenth Century* 189 (1980), pp. 297–361

Brown, Karin, *Sophie Grouchy de Condorcet on Moral Sympathy and Social Progress* (Unpublished doctoral dissertation, City University of New York, 1997)

Brown, Karin, Sophie de Grouchy, *Letters on Sympathy (1798): A Critical Edition*, trans. James McClellan (Philadelphia: American Philosophical Society, 2008)

Kale, Steven, *French Salons: High Society and Political Sociability from the Old Regime to the Revolution of 1848* (Baltimore: The Johns Hopkins University Press, 2004)

Léger, Charles, *Captives de l'amour, d'après des documents inédits; lettres intimes de Sophie de Condorcet, d'Aimée de Coigny et de quelques autres cœurs sensibles* (Paris: C. Gaillandre, 1933)

Valentino, Henri, *Madame de Condorcet; ses amis et ses amours, 1764–1822* (Paris: Perrin, 1950)

13. Beate Barbara Juliane Freifrau von Krüdener
22 November 1764–25 December 1824

Fig. 13. Beate Barbara Juliane Freifrau von Krüdener, by S.-G. Counis. Photo by Xviona (2021). Wikimedia, https://upload.wikimedia.org/wikipedia/commons/3/3c/Barbara_von_Kr%C3%BCdener.jpg, CC BY 4.0.

Valérie ou Lettres de Gustave de Linar à Ernest de G...

Préface

Je me trouvais, il y a quelques années, dans une des plus belles provinces du Danemarck : la nature, tour à tour sauvage et riante, souvent sublime, avait jeté dans le magnifique paysage que j'aimais à contempler, là de hautes forêts, ici des lacs tranquilles, tandis que dans l'éloignement la mer du Nord et la mer Baltique roulaient leurs vastes ondes au pied des montagnes de la Suède, et que la rêveuse mélancolie invitait à s'asseoir sur les tombeaux des anciens Scandinaves, placés, d'après l'antique usage de ce peuple, sur des collines et des tertres répandus dans la plaine.

« Rien n'est plus poétique, a dit un éloquent écrivain, qu'un cœur de seize années. » Sans être aussi jeune, je l'étais cependant ; j'aimais à sentir et à méditer, et souvent je créais autour de moi des tableaux aussi variés que les sites qui m'environnaient. Tantôt je voyais les scènes terribles qui avaient offert à Shakespeare les effrayantes beautés de Hamlet ; tantôt les images plus douces de la vertu et de l'amour se présentaient à moi, et je voyais les ombres touchantes de Virginie et de Paul : j'aimais à faire revivre ces êtres aimables et infortunés ; j'aimais à leur offrir des ombrages aussi doux que ceux des cocotiers, une nature aussi grande que celle des tropiques, des rivages solitaires et magnifiques comme ceux de la mer des Indes.[1]

Beate Barbara Juliane Freifrau von Krüdener was born in Riga in 1764. Her father, Baron Otto Hermann von Vietinghoff, was a wealthy man and a leading freemason. Her mother, Countess Anna Ulrika von Münnich, was a strict Lutheran. Vietinghoff was educated in French, German, deportment, and sewing. In 1782, she married Baron Burkhardt Alexis Constantine Krüdener, sixteen years her senior. Well-traveled and cultured, the baron was reserved while the young Krüdener was more pleasure-loving and extravagant. In 1784, the couple had a son, named Paul after his godfather, the future tsar. Her husband became ambassador that year in Venice, then Munich in 1786, then Copenhagen in 1787. After the birth of a daughter, Krüdener traveled for her health. She was in Paris in 1789 when the Estates General met; there, she met Bernardin de

---

1 Beate Barbara Juliane Freifrau von Krüdener, *Valérie ou lettres de Gustave de Linar à Ernest de G ...*, ed. Michel Mercier (Paris: Klincksieck, 1974), p. 21.

Translation: Preface

I found myself, some years ago, in one of the most beautiful provinces of Denmark: nature, by turns wild and laughing, often sublime, had thrown into the magnificent landscape I loved to contemplate, here high forests, there tranquil lakes, while in the distance the North Sea and the Baltic rolled their vast waves at the foot of Sweden's mountains, and dreamy melancholy invited one to sit on the tombs of the old Scandinavians, placed, according to the ancient use of this people, on hills and mounds scattered in the plain.
    "Nothing is more poetic, said an eloquent writer, than a sixteen-year-old heart." Without being so young, I nevertheless was; I loved to feel and to meditate, and often I created around me paintings as varied as the sites which surrounded me. Sometimes I saw the terrible scenes which offered to Shakespeare the terrifying beauties of Hamlet; sometimes the softer images of virtue and love presented themselves to me, and I saw the touching shades of Virginia and Paul: I loved to make these lovable and unfortunate beings live again; I loved to offer them shade as sweet as that of the coconut trees, a nature as great as that of the tropics, shores solitary and magnificent like those of the Indian Ocean.

Saint-Pierre, Rivarol, and the cavalry captain Charles Louis de Frégeville, with whom she fell in love. The couple went to Copenhagen, where the baron refused a divorce; Krüdener set out for Riga, Saint Petersburg, Leipzig, and Switzerland. In 1800, her husband became ambassador in Berlin, where she joined him briefly before departing after Tsar Paul's death. The baron died in 1802. In December 1803, Krüdener published her novel *Valérie*, then returned to Riga, where she fell under the influence of the Moravian Brethren. She met a peasant to whom God had supposedly revealed that Napoleon was the Antichrist, and the latter days were at hand.[2] Krüdener visited the Moravians at Herrnhut, the mystic Jung-Stilling, and the pastor Fontaines, who all influenced her thought. In 1809, she founded a colony of the elect in Württemberg, which was dispersed by the government. Krüdener resumed her travels, to Riga where her mother lay dying, then Karlsruhe, Strasbourg, Geneva, and Baden in 1814, where Tsarina Elizabeth hoped she might bring Tsar Alexander peace of mind. The two met on 4 June 1815. She followed him to Paris, where a private door connected her lodgings to the tsar's and he prayed with her every evening. Chateaubriand attended these meetings, as did Duras, Constant, and Madame Récamier. On 26 September, the sovereigns of Russia, Austria, and Prussia proclaimed the Holy Alliance under this influence: it was to herald a new age of peace and goodwill on Earth. Krüdener later claimed she suggested the idea and the tsar submitted the draft for her approval.[3] In October, she left Paris, traveling in Switzerland before returning in 1818 to her estate in Livonia. Later, as the Greek War of Independence began, Krüdener announced the tsar's mission to take up arms for Greece; he wrote a polite letter telling her to leave Saint Petersburg. She died in the Crimea on 25 December 1824.

What might we say about this extract? Openings to fictions are revealing things. *Valérie* is an epistolary novel, and true to that tradition, Krüdener opens with a preface explaining how the letters we will read were obtained. Her framing narrator, we learn, met Gustave de Linar, and most of the letters are Gustave's. The two met in Denmark, site of Paul Henri Mallet's 1755 *Introduction à l'histoire du Dannemarc*, and Krüdener chooses to start by setting her scene. In the distance, the North Sea and

---

2   Francis Ley, *Madame de Krüdener et son temps 1764–1824* (Paris: Plon, 1961), pp. 268–270.
3   Ley, *Krüdener*, p. 513.

the Baltic meet: we are then near the Oresund Strait by Copenhagen—where Krüdener lived in 1787—with Sweden's Malmö and Scania across the strait. However, the 'Swedish mountains' Krüdener describes peak in Scania at 696 feet; her goal seems less accurate travelogue than mood-setting. Staël's *De l'Allemagne* (1810/1813) similarly says Germany's mountains are in the North, though they are in the South; but northern mountains had been a European trope ever since Ossian first appeared in 1760. Krüdener's six-paragraph preface is in fact packed with tropes, from the "sublime" of Burke's 1757 *A Philosophical Enquiry into the Origin of Our Ideas of the Sublime and Beautiful* to the "rêveuse mélancolie" of Rousseau's posthumous *Rêveries du promeneur solitaire* (1782). Even the tombs Krüdener mentions echo Volney's *Les Ruines* of 1792, and this is just the first paragraph; her second paragraph namechecks both Shakespeare's *Hamlet* (1603) and Bernardin de Saint-Pierre's 1788 *Paul et Virginie*, also quoting a line from Chateaubriand's 1801 *René* to announce that we are at the cutting edge of European fashion. The text itself goes on to cite the poet Klopstock and the *Frühromantiker* Tieck (in Gustave's diary and in Letter XXXV), who was then totally unknown in France and to whom an entire page is devoted. Krüdener is offering her readers a fresh Romantic universe, and her book sold out in Paris in 1803.

Works

[Krüdener, Julie de], *Autour de «Valérie»: œuvres de Mme de Krüdener / Julie de Krüdener*, ed. Michel Mercier, Francis Ley, and Elena Gretchanaia (Paris: H. Champion, 2007)

Écrits intimes et prophétiques de Madame de Krüdener (Paris: Éditions du Centre national de la recherche scientifique, 1975)

Le Camp de Vertus, ou la Grande revue de l'armée russe (Lyon: Guyot frères, 1815)

Valérie, ou, Lettres de Gustave de Linar à Ernest de G ... (Paris: Henrichs, 1803)

Sources

Ghervas, Stella, *Réinventer la tradition. Alexandre Stourdza et l'Europe de la Sainte-Alliance* (Paris: H. Champion, 2008)

Hilger, Stephanie M., *Women Write Back: Strategies of Response and the Dynamics of European Literary Culture, 1790–1805* (Amsterdam: Brill, 2009)

Knapton, Ernest John, *Lady of the Holy Alliance* (New York: Columbia University Press, 1939)

Ley, Francis, *Madame de Krüdener et son temps, 1764–1824* (Paris: Plon, 1961)

Ley, Francis, *Bernardin de Saint-Pierre, Madame de Staël, Chateaubriand, Benjamin Constant et Madame de Krüdener (d'après des documents inédits)* (Paris: Montaigne, 1967)

Mühlenbeck, Eugène, *Étude sur les origines de la Sainte-Alliance* (Paris: F. Vieweg, 1887)

Rossard, Janine, *Pudeur et romantisme: Mme Cottin, Chateaubriand, Mme de Krüdener, Mme de Staël, Baour-Lormian, Vigny, Balzac, Musset, George Sand* (Paris: A.G. Nizet, 1982)

Troyat, Henri, *Alexander of Russia: Napoleon's Conqueror* (New York: Dutton, 1982)

14. Anne Louise Germaine, Baronne de Staël-Holstein
22 April 1766–14 July 1817

Fig. 14. Anne Louise Germaine, baronne de Staël-Holstein, by F. Massot. Photo by Siren-Com (2011). Wikimedia, https://upload.wikimedia.org/wikipedia/commons/3/33/Madame_de_Sta%C3%ABl_en_Corinne_1807.jpg, CC BY 4.0.

Zulma

J'étais prisonnier chez les sauvages qui habitent le bord de l'Orénoque ; mais comme ma rançon était stipulée, je jouissais de quelque liberté parmi eux. Un long séjour dans leur contrée m'avait permis d'apprendre leur langue, et l'un de leurs vieillards me témoignait une amitié particulière ; son âge lui donnait des droits à l'exercice du gouvernement ; ces sauvages ne connaissant pas la première base de toute réunion sociale, la propriété, leurs peuplades errantes adoptaient pour chefs, ceux qui devaient à une longue expérience cet esprit conservateur, ange gardien des destinées humaines. Un matin je fus réveillé par le bruit des instruments militaires : je crus que la guerre allait recommencer ; le vieillard qui me protégeait vint à moi, et me dit : « Ce jour est le plus cruel de ma vie ; je vais donner à mes concitoyens une douloureuse preuve de mon dévouement ; je suis appelé par mon âge et le sort à juger un coupable ; sept d'entre nous sont condamnés à ce triste devoir. On dit que le crime qui va nous être exposé ne peut être pardonné ; mais quand ma voix prononcera la sentence de mort, mon cœur déchiré pourra-t-il savoir s'il n'abuse pas du droit de l'homme sur l'homme, et ne s'arroge pas la vengeance divine ? Après ce jugement, je serai huit jours sans vous voir ; c'est un usage établi parmi nous, que les juges, qui ont condamné à la peine de mort, restent enfermés seuls pendant une semaine, et soient rassemblés de nouveau après ce temps, pour confirmer, ou casser leur jugement. Dans votre pays, un second tribunal révise les décisions du premier ; ici nous en appelons de l'homme en société, à l'homme solitaire, de l'impression du moment, à la conscience éternelle : nous bénissons cette institution, puisque très souvent elle a fait révoquer des jugements sévères. Suivez-moi, mon ami, dans l'enceinte où l'on va plaider en présence du peuple ; vous y verrez la famille de l'accusé plus inquiète que lui-même, de l'arrêt qui sera prononcé ; car nos lois bannissent pour jamais les parents d'un enfant coupable, et souvent dans nos déserts ils périssent d'isolement et de misère. Cette responsabilité funeste est un préjugé qui nous est commun avec vous. Souvent les erreurs les plus composées s'admettent avant les vérités les plus naturelles, cependant nos mœurs errantes ne permettant pas au gouvernement une surveillance générale et constante, il nous était peut-être nécessaire de resserrer les liens des familles. Et cette punition rétroactive, de quelque manière que vous la jugiez, a produit cet heureux effet : venez donc, écoutez avec attention les motifs qui vont nous être présentés, et si vous excusez le crime que je serais prêt à condamner, hâtez-vous de m'en instruire, et sauvez à votre ami la douleur irréparable, le meurtre de l'innocent. » Alors je suivis ce bon vieillard vers la grande plaine, où le peuple était rassemblé. Je fus étonné d'en approcher sans être averti par aucun bruit, de la réunion d'un si grand nombre d'hommes. « Tous se recueillent, me dit le vieillard, dans la contemplation du malheur et de la mort, et ces guerriers si braves, versent des pleurs pour des dangers qu'ils ne partagent pas. »[1]

---

1   Germaine de Staël, *Zulma*, in Madame de Staël, *Œuvres de jeunesse*, ed. Simone Balayé and John Isbell (Paris: Desjonquères, 1997), pp. 107–108.

       Translation: I was a prisoner with the savages who live on the banks of the Orinoco; but as my ransom had been stipulated, I enjoyed a certain freedom among them. A long stay in their country had allowed me to learn their language, and one of their elders showed me a particular friendship; his age gave him rights to the exercise of government; these

Anne Louise Germaine, Baronne de Staël-Holstein was born and died in Paris, though she was Genevan through her father Jacques Necker, the wealthy minister of Finance for Louis XVI. Her mother was Suzanne Necker, in whose salon she met Buffon, Marmontel, Grimm, Gibbon, the *abbé* Raynal, and La Harpe among others. In 1786, after turning down Pitt, she married the older Erik Magnus, Baron Staël von Holstein, who was then made Ambassador of King Gustav III of Sweden at the court of France. The couple separated in 1800. Staël found fame early as a thinker and writer, with the *Lettres sur les ouvrages et le caractère de Jean-Jacques Rousseau* (1788), *De l'influence des passions sur le bonheur de l'individu et des nations* (1796), and *De la littérature considérée dans ses rapports avec les institutions sociales* (1800). Favoring the ideals of 1789—the Bastille fell three days after her father's first dismissal—Staël grew critical by 1791, as her lover Narbonne became Minister for War. She left France at the

> savages not knowing the first basis of all social gatherings, property, their wandering peoples adopted as leaders, those who owed to a long experience that conserving instinct which is a guardian angel of human destinies. One morning I was awakened by the sound of martial instruments: I thought that war would start back up; the elder who protected me came to me and said "This day is the most cruel of my life; I shall give to my fellow citizens a painful proof of my devotion; I am called by my age and fate to judge a guilty person; seven of us are condemned to this sad duty. They say that the crime which shall be shown to us cannot be pardoned; but when my voice pronounces the sentence of death, can my torn heart know if it does not abuse of the right of man over man, and take to itself divine vengeance? After this judgement, I shall go eight days without seeing you; it is a custom established among us, that the judges who have condemned someone to death stay shut up alone for a week, and be assembled again after this time, to confirm or nullify their verdict. In your country, a second tribunal revises the decisions of the first; here we call from man in society to solitary man, from the impression of the moment to eternal conscience: we bless this institution, because very often it has caused severe judgements to be revoked. Follow me, my friend, into the enclosure where speakers will plead in the presence of the people; you will see the family of the accused more worried than the accused about the verdict that will be pronounced; because our laws banish forever the parents of a guilty child, and often in our deserts they perish of isolation and destitution. This fatal responsibility is a prejudice we share with you. Often the most composite errors are admitted before the most natural truths, although with our wandering customs not allowing a general and constant surveillance by the government, it was perhaps necessary for us to strengthen the bonds of families. And this retroactive punishment, however you judge it, has produced this happy effect: come then, listen with attention to the motives that will be presented to us, and if you excuse the crime that I would be ready to condemn, hasten to inform me of it, and save your friend that irreparable grief, the murder of an innocent. "Then I followed this good elder toward the great plain where the people were assembled. I was astonished to approach it without being alerted by any noise to the presence of so great a number of men." "All are meditating, said the elder, in the contemplation of unhappiness and death, and these warriors who are so brave, shed tears for dangers they do not share."

September Massacres after saving several friends, staying in England before returning to Directoire Paris as a republican in 1795. Staël there reopened her salon, hosting a literary and political elite. Exiled by Bonaparte in 1803, she continued to publish with European success: the novels *Delphine* (1802) and *Corinne ou l'Italie* (1807), as well as the treatise *De l'Allemagne* (1810/1813), a book pulped by Napoleon's police. Her home in Coppet became a meeting-place for Europe's Romantics, from A.W. Schlegel, her children's tutor, to Sismondi and Byron, alongside her great love, the writer and politician Benjamin Constant: the *Groupe de Coppet*. Widowed in 1802, in 1811 she remarried a young Genevan officer, John Rocca, before fleeing Coppet for London via Moscow in an occupied Europe. Staël reopened her Parisian salon in 1814, receiving kings, ministers, and generals, campaigning also to end the slave trade but dying on Bastille Day, 1817. Her works, *De l'Allemagne* in particular, helped introduce Romanticism to Europe. She was praised by writers from Pushkin to Emerson or Leopardi. Major political works appeared posthumously: the *Considérations sur les principaux événements de la Révolution française* in 1818, and the *Dix années d'exil* in 1821.

Where to begin? Generally, for Staël scholarship, the answer is with *Corinne ou l'Italie*. Let us begin instead with her first published fiction, *Zulma*, which appeared in 1794, under the Terror; and certainly, the opening to this tale is striking. Our narrator, who seems to be European, is "prisonnier chez les sauvages," rather as Candide and Cacambo were prisoners of the *Oreillons* in Voltaire's *Candide*. But there the resemblance ends: for these South American "savages," in their customs, are as worthy of emulation as Voltaire's citizens of El Dorado in that same book, or as the Peruvians in Graffigny's *Lettres péruviennes*. Staël uses the death penalty to illustrate her thesis, somewhat fittingly, as the Terror unfolded over France: on the banks of the Orinoco, amid these apparent savages, the death penalty requires that seven judges isolate for a week after their verdict before confirming it. The relativity of laws is precisely Montesquieu's subject in *De l'esprit des lois* (1748); but this investigation into crime and punishment is more topical, reflecting notably Beccaria's *Dei delitti e delle pene* (1764)—*On Crimes and Punishments*—with its reasoned rejection both of the death penalty and of torture, a detail Staël remarks on in her *Considérations* of 1818. As Staël's judge here notes, "Cette responsabilité funeste est un préjugé qui nous est commun avec vous"—and indeed, the death penalty was not abolished in France for another 200 years. Who, one may ask, are the savages then, in 1794? For Staël invites that question. It is worth remembering that *Zulma* was originally conceived as an illustrative chapter in Staël's *De l'influence des passions* (1796), with its tight focus on the Revolution and the Terror that followed. Thus, the end of this first paragraph, in which the narrator is astonished at the crowd's silence, stands in direct contrast to the Parisian *sans-culotte* crowd at the guillotine, key player in the Terror, as Staël and her audience both knew.

A short note on Zulma herself, the defendant in this American trial. She has killed her unfaithful lover—one thinks of Staël's torrent of unanswered letters to her beloved Narbonne—and awaits her death unflinchingly, asking only to be allowed to address the crowd and the judges before judgement. She does this leaning on her offending bow. Zulma is not Staël's only non-European heroine; *Mirza*, published the following year, features an African heroine thirty years before Duras's *Ourika* (1823). All three heroines are given extensive voice, they are not voiceless. In Staël's case, each speaks to the assembled nation: theirs is a *public* voice, like that of Staël's Corinne in 1807, not a private one. Staël is closer to Gouges here than she might herself have suspected.

Works

Staël, Germaine de, *Œuvres complètes* [*OC*], ed. Auguste de Staël & Victor de Broglie, 3 vols (Genève: Slatkine Reprints, 1967)

Considérations sur les principaux événements de la Révolution française, ed. Lucia Omacini, 2 vols (Paris: Champion, 2017)

Corinne ou l'Italie, ed. Simone Balayé (Paris: Champion, 2000)

Correspondance générale, ed. B. Jasinski *et al.* (Paris: Pauvert, Hachette, Klincksieck-Champion, 1960–2017)

De la littérature considérée dans ses rapports avec les institutions sociales, ed. Axel Blaeschke (Paris: Garnier, 1997)

De l'Allemagne, ed. comtesse Jean de Pange with Simone Balayé, 5 vols (Paris: Hachette, 1958–1960)

Delphine, ed. Simone Balayé-Lucia Omacini, 2 vols (Genève: Droz, 1987–1990)

Des circonstances actuelles et autres essais politiques sous la Révolution, ed. Lucia Omacini (Paris: Champion, 2009)

Dix années d'exil, ed. Simone Balayé-Mariella Vianello Bonifacio (Paris: Fayard, 1996)

Lettres sur Rousseau, De l'influence des passions et autres essais moraux, ed. Florence Lotterie (Paris: Champion, 2008)

Du caractère de M. Necker, et de sa vie privée, OC II, 261–290

Œuvres, ed. Catriona Seth-Valérie Cossy (Paris: Gallimard, 2017)

Œuvres de jeunesse [*Lettres sur Rousseau, Zulma, Recueil de morceaux détachés*], ed. Simone Balayé and John Isbell (Paris: Desjonquères, 1997)

Œuvres dramatiques, ed. Aline Hodroge, Jean-Pierre Perchellet, Blandine Poirier, and Martine de Rougemont, 2 vols (Paris: Champion, 2021)

Sources

Cahiers staëliens (Paris, 1962–)

Balayé, Simone, *Les Carnets de voyage de Madame de Staël. Contribution à la genèse de ses œuvres* (Genève: Droz, 1971)

Balayé, Simone, *Madame de Staël. Lumières et Liberté* (Paris: Klincksieck, 1979)

Bredin, Jean-Denis, *Une singulière famille: Jacques Necker, Suzanne Necker et Germaine de Staël* (Paris: Fayard, 1999)

Burnand, Léonard and Poisson, Guillaume, eds, *Comment sortir de l'Empire?: le Groupe de Coppet face à la chute de Napoléon* (Genève: Slatkine, 2016)

Casillo, Robert, *The Empire of Stereotypes. Germaine de Stael and the Idea of Italy* (London: Palgrave MacMillan, 2006)

De Poortere, Machteld, *Les idées philosophiques et littéraires de Mme de Stael et de Mme de Genlis* (New York: Peter Lang, 2004)

Dubé, Pierre H., *Bibliographie de la critique sur Madame de Staël: 1789–1994* (Genève: Droz, 1998)

Fairweather, Maria, *Madame de Staël* (London: Constable, 2005)

Fontana, Biancamaria, *Germaine de Staël: A Political Portrait* (Princeton: Princeton University Press, 2016)

Garry-Boussel, Claire, *Statut et fonction du personnage masculin chez Madame de Staël* (Paris: Honoré Champion, 2002)

Genand, Stéphanie, *La Chambre noire: Germaine de Staël et la pensée du négatif* (Genève: Droz, 2016)

Goodden, Angelica, *Madame de Staël: The Dangerous Exile* (Oxford: Oxford University Press, 2008)

Herold, J. Christopher, *Germaine Necker de Staël* (Paris: Plon, 1962)

Hofmann, Étienne, ed., *Benjamin Constant, Madame de Staël et le Groupe de Coppet: Actes du Deuxième Congrès de Lausanne à l'occasion du 150e anniversaire de la mort de Benjamin Constant et du Troisième Colloque de Coppet, 15–19 juillet 1980* (Oxford: The Voltaire Foundation and Lausanne: Institut Benjamin Constant, 1982)

Isbell, John Claiborne, *The Birth of European Romanticism: Truth and Propaganda in Staël's De l'Allemagne* (Cambridge: Cambridge University Press, 1994)

Kohler, Pierre, *Madame de Staël et la Suisse* (Lausanne: Payot, 1916)

Lang, André, *Une vie d'orages, Germaine de Staël* (Paris: Calmann-Lévy, 1958)

Necker de Saussure, Albertine, *Notice sur le caractère et les écrits de Madame de Staël*, in OC III (*Œuvres posthumes*), pp. 1–24

Rosen, Julia von, *Kulturtransfer als Diskurstransformation: die Kantische Ästhetik in der Interpretation Mme de Staëls* (Heidelberg: C. Winter, 2004)

Wallenborn, Melitta, *Deutschland und die Deutschen in Mme de Staëls «De l'Allemagne»: Staaten, Landschaften und Menschen* (Frankfurt am Main: P. Lang, 1998)

Winegarten, Renee, *Germaine de Staël & Benjamin Constant: A Dual Biography* (New Haven: Yale University Press, 2008)

15. Constance Marie Pipelet or Constance, Princesse de Salm
7 September 1767–13 April 1845

Fig. 15. Constance Marie Pipelet or Constance, princesse de Salm, by J.-B. F. Desoria. Photo by Cecil (2007). Wikimedia, https://upload.wikimedia.org/wikipedia/commons/d/d6/Jean-Baptiste_Fran%C3%A7ois_Desoria_-_Portrait_de_Constance_Pipelet.jpg, CC BY 4.0.

« Sur la mort du jeune tambour Barra, âgé de quinze ans »

Jeune héros, espoir de ton pays,
Brave naissant dont la gloire s'honore,
C'en est donc fait, tes destins sont finis,
Et ton couchant a suivi ton aurore !

Quel furieux, altéré de trépas,
Leva sur toi son arme meurtrière ?
Cet assassin ne te voyait-il pas,
Couvert encor des baisers de ta mère ?

> Hélas ! ses yeux sont fermés pour toujours ;
> Grâces, Plaisirs, Amours, versez des larmes.
> Il tombe à peine au printemps de ses jours ;
> Il n'a connu que la gloire et les armes.
>
> Mais renfermons ces injustes regrets ;
> N'a-t-il pas dit : Je meurs pour ma patrie ?
> C'en est assez pour le cœur d'un Français,
> Et son trépas a compensé sa vie.[1]

Constance Marie Pipelet or Constance, Princesse de Salm was born in Nantes in 1767 and died in Paris in 1845. Her father Marie Alexandre de Théis was a poet and playwright. During her childhood, he retired and the family moved to Picardy, where she received a good education. In 1789, she married Jean-Baptiste Pipelet de Leury, a surgeon, and settled in Paris, publishing in the *Almanach des Muses* and other periodicals. In 1794, her *Sapho, tragédie mêlée de chants*, in three acts and in verse with music by Jean Paul Égide Martini, was performed in Paris, with over a hundred shows.[2] In 1795, Pipelet was the first woman admitted to the Lycée des arts. Her father died in 1796. She participated in the *Querelle des femmes auteurs* launched by Écouchard-Le Brun in 1797, writing her own *Épître aux femmes* (1797) in answer to his. Pipelet divorced in 1799. She wrote more epistles and cantatas, on the marriage of Napoleon for example, some read by her at the Athénée and afterwards published. She also published several ballads, for which she composed the melodies and the piano accompaniments. She ceased writing for the stage in 1800 after a poor reception for her drama *Camille, ou Amitié et imprudence*. In 1803, Pipelet married Joseph, Count zu Salm-Reifferscheidt-Dyck, who

---

1   Constance Marie Pipelet, *Œuvres de Madame la Princesse Constance de Salm*, 4 vols (Paris: Didot, 1842), II pp. 273–274.

> Translation: "On the Death of the Young Drummer Boy Barra, Aged Fifteen"
> Young hero, hope of your country, / Developing warrior of whom glory honors itself, / It is then over, your destinies are done, / And your setting has followed your dawn!
> What furious soul, drunk on death, / Raised over you his murderous weapon? / Did this assassin not see you, / Still covered by the kisses of your mother?
> Alas! his eyes are closed forever; / Graces, Pleasures, Loves, shed tears. / He falls barely in the springtime of his days; / He knew only glory and arms.
> But let us shut in these unjust regrets; / Did he not say: I die for my country? / It is enough for a Frenchman's heart, / And his death compensated for his life.

2   Jacqueline Letzter, Robert Adelson, *Women Writing Opera: Creativity and Controversy in the Age of the French Revolution* (Berkeley: University of California Press, 2001), p.35.

took the title of prince in 1816; she published thereafter as the Princesse de Salm. The couple lived alternately in Germany and in Paris, where Salm held a salon featuring Dumas, Stendhal, and other leading authors.

This brief text, "Sur la mort du jeune tambour Barra, âgé de quinze ans," consists of four decasyllabic quatrains, rhyming *abab*, with alternation of masculine and feminine rhymes as required by French tradition. Salm often writes longer pieces—epistles, for instance—but here, brevity is used to good effect. The story seems complete and there is little sense of pressure or constraint; on the contrary, Salm's sixteen lines feel roomy and comfortable. Silent e's are an important part of the music of French poetry and Salm uses them to advantage, tending to open lines with them for impact: "Jeune héros," "Brave naissant," "Grâces, Plaisirs." Striking or indeed poignant images are coined—"ton couchant a suivi ton aurore," "Couvert encore des baisers de ta mère"—and the latter may even have inspired Nerval's famous line in "El Desdichado," "Mon front est rouge encore du baiser de la Reine." A certain level of abstraction, not without precedent in French neoclassicism, shapes the narrative throughout, both lexically and syntactically, from "espoir de ton pays" in line one to "son trépas a compensé sa vie" in line sixteen. Abstraction provides order and balance in opposition to the early death that is the poem's topic, a feature of the elegiac tradition, though this elegy is unusually short. There is a sustained narrative: in stanza one, a young hero has died; in stanza two, we picture the killer; in stanza three, we call for tears from more abstractions that are as yet unknown to the young victim; in stanza four, we cease our tears in a wave of patriotism. The whole is highly skilled, indeed brilliant in its application of technique to the topic at hand, with just one awkward moment, that being the shift from second to third person in stanzas three and four, which the brief text does not seek to justify. Continuing with a revolutionary "tu" would pose almost no mechanical problems for the poet—just "Tu tombes à peine" with its extra syllable—which makes the decision even more curious.

Who is the Barra in the poem's title? A drummer in the republican army, Joseph Bara was killed at age fourteen by Vendéens in 1793. After his commander requested a government pension for his mother, the deceased Bara became a revolutionary icon. He is, for instance, the subject of an unfinished painting by David from 1794, *La Mort du jeune Bara*, painted in series with *La Mort de Marat*. This may seem an unexpected topic for a future princess, but it was in vogue under the Convention, with 1816 a long way off. Pipelet remained active in Paris throughout the Revolution, which may well reflect a certain bravery on her part, and republican patriotism is after all her subject.

Works

[Salm, Constance de], *Poésies de la princesse Constance de Salm* (Paris: Didot, 1811)

Mes Soixante ans, ou Mes Souvenirs politiques et litteraires (Paris: Didot, 1833)

Sources

Bied, Robert, "Le Rôle d'un salon littéraire au début du XIXe siècle: les amis de Constance de Salm," *Revue de l'Institut Napoléon* 133 (1977), pp. 121–160

Lauzon, Martine, *Une moraliste féministe: Constance de Salm* (Montréal, Université McGill, 1997)

Letzter, Jacqueline and Adelson, Robert G., *Women Writing Opera: Creativity and Controversy in the Age of the French Revolution* (Berkeley: University of California Press, 2001)

McNiven Hine, Ellen, *Constance de Salm. Her Influence and Her Circle in the Aftermath of the French Revolution: "A Mind of No Common Order"* (New York: Peter Lang, 2012)

Pascal, Jean-Noël, ed., "La Muse de la raison, Constance de Salm (1767–1845)," in *Cahiers Roucher-André Chénier No. 29* (2010), pp. 1–210

Pouget-Brunereau, Jeanne, *Presse féminine et critique littéraire: leurs rapports avec l'histoire des femmes de 1800 à 1830*, 2 vols (Paris: Bibliothèque Marguerite Durand, 1994)

Seth, Catriona, "Les Muses de l'Almanach. La poésie au féminin dans l'*Almanach des Muses*", in *Masculin/Féminin dans la poésie et les poétiques du 19th-century*, ed. Christine Planté (Lyon: Presses universitaires de Lyon, 2002), pp. 105–119

Seth, Catriona, "La femme auteur: stratégie et paradigmes. Le cas de Constance de Salm", in *La littérature en Bas-Bleus*, ed. Brigitte Louichon and Andrea Del Lungo (Paris: Garnier, 2010), pp.195–213

16. Henriette Lucie Dillon, Marquise de La Tour-du-Pin Gouvernet
25 February 1770–2 April 1853

Fig. 16. Auguste Danse, portrait of Henriette Lucy Dillon, Marquise de la Tour du Pin Gouvernet. Etching, 103 mm x 77 mm, ca. 1900–1925. © National Portrait Gallery, London (image ID: D15778), https://npgimages.com/search/?searchQuery=+marquise+de+La+Tour+du+Pin+Gouvernet.

Mémoires de la marquise de La Tour du Pin. Journal d'une femme de cinquante ans

Quelques jours après les événements que je viens de raconter, mon mari reçut un courrier lui annonçant la nomination de son père au ministère de la guerre. Nous repartîmes aussitôt pour Versailles. Alors commença ma vie publique. Mon beau-père m'installa au département de la Guerre et me mit à la tête de sa maison pour en faire les honneurs, de concert avec ma belle-sœur, également logée au ministère, mais qui, au bout de deux mois, devait nous quitter. J'occupai le bel appartement du premier avec mon mari. J'avais été si accoutumée, à Montpellier et à Paris, aux grands dîners, que ma nouvelle situation ne m'embarrassait aucunement. D'ailleurs, je ne me mêlais de rien que de faire les honneurs. Il y avait par semaine deux dîners de vingt-quatre couverts, auxquels l'on priait tous les membres de l'Assemblée constituante, à tour de rôle. Les femmes n'étaient jamais invitées. Mme de Lameth et moi étions assises vis-à-vis l'une de l'autre, et nous prenions à côté de nous les quatre personnages les plus considérables de la société, en observant de les choisir toujours dans tous les partis. Tant qu'on a été à Versailles, les hommes assistaient sans exception à ces dîners en habit habillé, et j'ai souvenir de M. de Robespierre en habit vert pomme et supérieurement coiffé avec une forêt de cheveux blancs. Mirabeau seul ne vint pas chez nous et ne fut jamais invité. J'allais souvent souper dehors, soit chez mes collègues, soit chez les personnes établies à Versailles pendant le temps de l'Assemblée nationale, comme on la nommait.[1]

Henriette Lucie Dillon, Marquise de La Tour-du-Pin Gouvernet was born in Paris in 1770 and died in Pisa in 1853. Her father was the Irish Jacobite colonel Arthur Dillon, her mother the lady-in-waiting Thérèse Lucy de Rothe. After her mother's death in 1782 and her father's posting abroad, Lucie lived in her maternal grandmother's house. She married Frédéric Séraphin, Comte de Gouvernet, later Marquis de La Tour-du-Pin, in 1787. He was the son of a French Minister of War. Gouvernet became lady-in-waiting to Marie-Antoinette and filled that role from 1787 to

---

1   Henriette Lucie Dillon, *Mémoires de la marquise de La Tour du Pin. Journal d'une femme de cinquante ans*, ed. le comte Christian de Liederkerke Beaufort (Paris: Mercure de France, 1989), pp. 124–125.

Translation: Some days after the events I have been describing, my husband received a letter announcing to him his father's appointment at the Ministry of War. We left at once for Versailles. Then began my public life. My father-in-law placed me in the Department of War and put me at the head of his household to receive visitors, in concert with my sister-in-law, also lodged in the ministry, but who would need to leave us two months later. I occupied the fine apartment on the first floor with my husband. I had been so accustomed, in Montpellier and in Paris, to grand dinners, that my new situation was no encumbrance to me. Besides, I took no part in anything but the social visits. Weekly there were two dinners of 24 places, to which were invited all the members of the Assemblée constituante, in turn. Wives were never invited. Mme de Lameth and I were seated facing each other, and we sat beside us the four most considerable members of the society, observing to choose them always from among all parties. As long as we were at Versailles, the men attended these dinners without exception in dress attire, and I recall M. de Robespierre in an apple green suit and superiorly coiffed with a forest of white hair. Mirabeau alone never came to call and was never invited. I often dined out, either with my colleagues, or with the persons established at Versailles during the time of the Assemblée nationale, as it was called.

1789. From Versailles, she witnessed the Estates General, the Women's March on Versailles, and the *Grande Peur*. From 1791–1792, her husband served as ambassador to the Dutch Republic in the Hague, where she joined him. During the Reign of Terror, she fled to the Gironde region. With the help of Madame Tallien, she secured a passport for herself and her husband, leaving for exile on a dairy farm near Albany, New York in 1794. She described this time as the happiest of her life. She was close to Talleyrand during his exile in the United States, returning to France with her husband in 1796 after the establishment of the Directoire. Bonaparte's Brumaire coup in November 1799 allowed her husband to resume his diplomatic career, and she continued to accompany him to his various appointments after the Bourbon Restoration. Their son was involved in the Duchesse de Berry's anti-Orléanist plot of 1831, and the couple again went into effective exile. Following her husband's death in 1837, Gouvernet moved to Italy, where she died. Her memoir was written to her only surviving child at the age of fifty and was not published until 1906.

Here is a lady-in-waiting to Marie-Antoinette discussing the onset of the Revolution: and in this extract, she idly recalls Robespierre in his apple-green costume and powdered wig as a guest in her salon. It is all rather unexpected. What then is going on?

Let us recall that the French aristocracy was by no means monolithic in their political opinions in 1789. This book's most extreme aristocrat, thus far, is Vigée Le Brun, whose parents were bourgeois. Not for nothing on 4 August 1789 did the nobles in the Assemblée surrender their feudal rights; the work of the *philosophes* over the preceding century had gone far to inculcate a vision of progress for France in which various institutions were seen as antiquated at best. And moreover, La Tour-du-Pin was daughter-in-law to the Minister for War. She had social obligations in support of his executive work. As she notes, these were dinners "auxquels l'on priait tous les membres de l'Assemblée constituante, à tour de rôle": Robespierre, member of the Assemblée for the Third Estate (he was a provincial lawyer), had every reason to expect an invitation. Besides, he had yet to order anyone's death. The only deputy not invited, La Tour-du-Pin notes acidly, was Mirabeau, on whom a lot of blame for the early Revolution had already fallen; he was also venal, the story went. There is in this extract a certain amount perhaps of world-weariness, a certain amount of executive knowledge that to get things done, there is no use whining, there is no use dreaming: decisions may be hard, but leaving them unmade is worse, as is surrendering to faction, resentment, and spite. La Tour-du-Pin had a job to do, and she did it. If that meant hosting the radical Robespierre, so be it, and she is not writing these memoirs at fifty to second-guess herself. Much of the beauty of her memoirs lies in that steady tone.

Let us note then the one detail this former lady-in-waiting permits herself, at the close of the paragraph in question. She talks of the Assemblée nationale with which the whole revolutionary circus started, and she adds four words: "comme on la nommait." That is very dry indeed.

Works

[La-Tour-du-Pin Gouvernet, Lucie de], *Mémoires de la marquise de La Tour du Pin. Journal d'une femme de cinquante ans*, ed. le comte Christian de Liederkerke Beaufort (Paris: Mercure de France, 1989)

Une dame et deux rois de cœur: correspondance inédite, 1833–1842, ed. Bertrand de Viviés (Nîmes: C. Lacour, 1996)

Sources

Lassère, Madeleine, *Lucie de La Tour du Pin, 1770–1853: marquise-courage* ([Bordeaux]: «SudOuest», 2014)

Moorehead, Caroline, *Dancing to the Precipice: The Life of Lucie de La Tour du Pin, Eyewitness to an Era* (London: HarperCollins, 2009)

Rohan Chabot, Alix de, *Madame de La Tour du Pin: le talent du bonheur* ([Paris]: Perrin, 1997)

Rossi, Henri, *Mémoires aristocratiques féminins 1789–1848* (Paris: Honoré Champion, 2000)

17. Marie Sophie Risteau Cottin
22 March 1770–25 August 1807

Fig. 17. Marie Sophie Risteau Cottin, by P.-F. Bertonnier. Photo by William C. Minor (2008). Wikimedia, https://upload.wikimedia.org/wikipedia/commons/0/0f/Sophie_Cottin.jpg, CC BY 4.0.

Claire d'Albe

Préface de l'auteur.

Le dégoût, le danger ou l'effroi du monde ayant fait naître en moi le besoin de me retirer dans un monde idéal, déjà j'embrassais un vaste plan qui devait m'y retenir longtemps, lorsqu'une circonstance imprévue, m'arrachant à ma solitude et à mes nouveaux amis, me transporta sur les bords de la Seine, aux environs de Rouen, dans une superbe campagne, au milieu d'une société nombreuse.

Ce n'est pas là où je pouvais travailler, je le savais ; aussi avais-je laissé derrière moi tous mes essais. Cependant la beauté de l'habitation, le charme puissant des bois et des eaux, éveillèrent mon imagination et remuèrent mon cœur ; il ne me fallait qu'un mot pour tracer un nouveau plan ; ce mot me fut dit par une personne de la société, et qui a joué elle-même un rôle assez important dans cette histoire. Je lui demandai la permission d'écrire son récit, elle me l'accorda ; j'obtins celle de l'imprimer, et je me hâte d'en profiter. Je me hâte est le mot, car ayant écrit tout d'un trait, et en moins de quinze jours, l'ouvrage qu'on va lire, je ne me suis donné ni le temps, ni la peine d'y retoucher. Je sais bien que, pour le public, le temps ne fait rien à l'affaire ; aussi il fera bien de dire du mal de mon ouvrage s'il l'ennuie ; mais s'il m'ennuyait encore plus de le corriger, j'ai bien fait de le laisser tel qu'il est.

Quant à moi, je sens si bien tout ce qui lui manque, que je ne m'attends pas que mon âge, ni mon sexe, me mettent à l'abri des critiques, et mon amour-propre serait assez mal à son aise, s'il n'avait une sorte de pressentiment que l'histoire que je médite le dédommagera peut-être de l'anecdote qui vient de m'échapper.[1]

Marie Sophie Risteau Cottin was born and died in Paris, daughter of Anne Suzanne Lecourt and Jacques François Risteau, a Bordeaux merchant and former director of the Compagnie des Indes, in a Calvinist family. She was raised by her uncle. Her mother was passionate about literature and art and Sophie shared that passion. In May 1789, she married Jean Paul Marie Cottin, a successful banker who had left Bordeaux to live in the capital. Cottin lived a retired life amid the revolutionary ferment. During the Terror, Jean Paul Marie Cottin was denounced as an aristocrat. On 13 September 1793, those who came for him found him lifeless in his bed. His wife was widowed at twenty-three

---

1   Marie Sophie Risteau Cottin, *Claire d'Albe* (Paris: Lebègue, 1820), pp. 5–8.

> Translation: Disgust, danger or the fear of the world having given rise in me to the need to retire into an ideal world, already I was embracing a vast plan which would keep me there for a long time, when an unexpected circumstance, tearing me from my solitude and my new friends, transported me to the banks of the Seine, in the neighborhood of Rouen, in a superb countryside, amid a numerous society.
>
> It is not here that I could work, I knew it; thus, I had left behind me all my essays. Yet the beauty of the habitation, the charm of the woods and the waters, awoke my imagination and moved my heart; I needed only a word to trace a new project; this word was said to me by a person of this society, and who herself played a fairly important role in this story. I asked for permission to write her story, she granted it to me; I received that of printing it; and I take haste to take advantage of that. I take haste is the word, for having written all in a rush, and in less than two weeks, the work one is about to read, I gave myself neither the time, nor the effort to retouch it. I know well that, for the public, time has no bearing on the matter; thus, it will do well to speak ill of my work if it finds it boring; but if it bored me still more to correct it, I did well to leave it as it is.
>
> As for me, I feel so well all that it is lacking, that I expect neither my age, nor my sex, to shelter me from criticisms, and my vanity would be fairly ill at ease, if it did not have a sort of presentiment that the story I am meditating will perhaps recompense it for the anecdote that has just escaped me.

and nearly ruined: she had paid a large part of their fortune to Fouquier-Tinville in a vain attempt to save two family members. She retired to Champlan, where she hid Vincent Marie de Vaublanc, condemned to death by the revolutionary tribunal. An accident of health—early menopause—prevented Cottin from having children. When in 1798 a friend was obliged to leave France, Cottin wrote *Claire d'Albe* (1799) in two weeks, published anonymously, and gave him the proceeds. She was removed from the list of émigrés that same year, visiting England and Italy. Her later works were headed "par l'auteur de *Claire d'Albe*," though the great success of *Malvina* (1800) and of *Amélie Mansfield* (1802) revealed her identity. She declined to publish her lyric pieces, which she considered less useful than her novels; she was no admirer of woman authors *per se*. Her poem *La Prise de Jéricho* with its Jewish heroine was first published posthumously by Suard in 1811. *Élisabeth ou les Exilés de Sibérie* (1806) meanwhile continued her success. *Mathilde ou Mémoires tirées de l'histoire des croisades* (1805) was more ambitious, but she died two years later at thirty-seven, of breast cancer, after months of suffering. She is buried in Père Lachaise Cemetery. Genlis found it necessary to attack her style and her character, but Lady Morgan visited Champlan in hope of meeting her.

Sophie Cottin had a short, hard life, dying at thirty-seven after early amenorrhea. Her husband died during the Terror; Cottin nearly ruined herself bribing the public prosecutor. She published her books anonymously. Let us look at the preface to her first published work.

"Le dégoût, le danger ou l'effroi du monde," she begins. This may seem after the fact—Robespierre had died in July 1794, four years earlier—but trauma takes its time, and four years is not so very long. Cottin was on French soil, but far from Paris, as she wrote in 1798; she was not caught up in the whirl of the days' events, the play of coup and countercoup that defined the Directoire. And so, she notes her retreat into an ideal world. This now—isolation and dream—is quite in keeping with a thousand Romantic novels across the West, it is already the theme of Rousseau's *Rêveries d'un promeneur solitaire* (1782). But this is not where Cottin's story begins; she instead describes her trip to Rouen, amid a "société nombreuse" and the superb natural scenery a Romantic reader might value. Here, a stranger says the word on which her novel rests, and after asking for permission from that person to write and then publish it, Cottin is ready to present her work to the world.

Cottin notes two more details: first, that she wrote the novel in under a fortnight; second, that she is unconcerned about critics of her age or of her sex (she was twenty-eight). The second point seems perhaps more relevant than the first: age and gender should indeed not determine reception, but work written in haste is often flawed. One might note Wordsworth's contemporaneous description of poetry as "a spontaneous outpouring of powerful emotion," but those words depend ultimately on what follows: "recollected in tranquility." There is a Romantic authenticity-topos which values work done quickly, improvised even, in distinction to the fruit of art; but in novel writing, readers may, like Wordsworth, want a certain amount of percolation to take place. A fortnight for a novel is a short time indeed. On the other hand, Cottin's clock ran out at the age of thirty-seven. Maybe she was right to work at speed.

Works

Cottin, Sophie, *Œuvres complètes*, 8 vols (Paris: Foucault, 1817)

Œuvres complètes de Mme Cottin, 12 vols (Paris: Bellavoine, 1825)

Correspondance complète. Tome I, Lettres de jeunesse, 1784–1794, ed. Huguette Krief and Mathilde Chollet (Paris: Classiques Garnier, 2021)

Claire d'Albe, 4 vols (Paris: Maradan, 1800)

Malvina, 4 vols (Paris: Maradan, 1800)

Amélie Mansfield, 4 vols (Paris: Maradan, 1802)

Mathilde ou Mémoires tirées de l'histoire des croisades, 6 vols (Paris: Giguet et Michaud, 1805)

Élisabeth ou les Exilés de Sibérie (Paris: Giguet et Michaud, 1808)

Sources

Call, Michael J., *Infertility and the Novels of Sophie Cottin* (Newark, NJ: University of Delaware Press, 2002)

Krief, Huguette, ed., *Vivre libre et écrire: anthologie des romancières de la période révolutionnaire (1789–1800)* (Oxford: Voltaire Foundation, 2005)

Lorusso, Silvia, *Le Charme sans la beauté, vie de Sophie Cottin* (Paris: Garnier, 2018)

18. Marie Françoise Sophie Gay
1 July 1776–2 March 1852

Fig. 18. Marie Françoise Sophie Gay, by J.-B. Isabey. Photo by M0tty (2021). Wikimedia, https://upload.wikimedia.org/wikipedia/commons/3/38/Marie_Fran%C3%A7oise_Sophie_Nichault_de_la_Valette-02.jpg, CC BY 4.0.

Anatole

— Eh bien, disait Richard, en brossant son habit de livrée, c'est donc après-demain que cette belle provinciale arrive ?

— Vraiment oui, répondit mademoiselle Julie, madame vient de m'ordonner d'aller visiter l'appartement qu'elle lui destine, pour savoir s'il n'y manque rien de ce qui peut être commode à sa belle-sœur ; je crois qu'on aurait bien pu se dispenser de faire meubler à neuf tout ce corps de logis ; madame de Saverny, accoutumée aux grands fauteuils de son vieux château, ne s'apercevra peut-être pas de tous les frais que madame a faits pour décorer son appartement à la dernière mode.

— C'est donc une vieille femme ?

— Point du tout, elle a tout au plus vingt-deux ans ; M. le comte est son aîné de plus de dix années, et madame la comtesse a bien au moins sept ou huit ans de plus que sa belle-sœur, puisqu'elle en avoue quatre.

— Et cette parente a-t-elle un mari, des enfants, une gouvernante ? Faudra-t-il servir tout ce monde-là ?

— Grâce au ciel, elle est veuve ; et je pense qu'elle est riche, car son mari était, je crois, aussi vieux que son château ; et l'on n'épouse guère un vieillard que pour sa fortune.

— Qui nous amène-t-elle ici ?

— Tout ce qu'il faut pour s'y établir, des gens, des chevaux ; enfin, jusqu'à sa nourrice.

— Ah ! C'est un peu trop fort. Je sais ce que c'est que ces grosses campagnardes, qui se croient le droit de commander à toute la maison, parce qu'elles ont nourri leur maîtresse ; ce sont de vieilles rapporteuses qui, sous prétexte de prendre les intérêts de leur cher nourrisson, vont leur raconter tout ce qui se fait ou se dit dans leurs antichambres ; Lapierre est bien libre de se mettre au service de celle-là ; quant à moi, je ne compte pas lui donner un verre d'eau.

— Ah ! tout cet embarras ne sera pas éternel, madame s'en lassera bientôt, surtout s'il est vrai que madame de Saverny soit aussi belle qu'on l'assure ; ne savez-vous pas, Richard, que deux jolies femmes n'ont jamais demeuré bien longtemps ensemble ?

Les remarques philosophiques de mademoiselle Julie furent interrompues par le retour du carrosse de madame de Nangis.[1]

---

1 Marie Françoise Sophie Gay, *Anatole* (Paris: Michel Lévy, 1863), pp. 3–4.

> Translation: -- Well then, said Richard, brushing his livery costume, it's tomorrow this beautiful provincial lady is arriving?
>
> Yes, indeed, replied Miss Julie, Madame has just ordered me to go visit the apartment she plans for her, to see if anything is missing that could be convenient for her sister-in-law; I believe that we could well have done without furnishing this whole main building like new; Madame de Saverny, accustomed to the big armchairs of her old chateau, will perhaps not notice all the expenses that Madame has made to decorate her apartment in the latest fashion.
>
> It's an old lady then?
>
> Not at all, she is at most twenty-two years old; the count is her senior by more than ten years, and the countess is at least seven or eight years younger than her sister-in-law, since she admits to four.
>
> And does this relative have a husband, children, a governess? Will we have to serve all that crowd?

Marie Françoise Sophie Gay, *née* Nichault de la Valette was born and died in Paris, daughter of the Italian Francesca Peretti and of Auguste Antoine Nichault de La Vallette, a financier. She was raised in a boarding establishment by Jeanne Marie Leprince de Beaumont, author of *la Belle et la Bête* (1756), alongside Claire de Duras, the future author of *Ourika* (1823), with a focus on music. Her father presented her aged two to Voltaire, who kissed her on the forehead; she also met the Vicomte de Ségur, Vergennes, the chevalier de Boufflers, and Alexandre de Lameth. In 1793, aged seventeen, she married the courtier Gaspard Liottier, divorcing in 1799 to marry Jean Sigismond Gay, Baron de Lupigny, soon after. In Aix-la Chapelle—a spa town—she met, among others, Pauline Bonaparte, who became a friend. Her salon drew many writers, artists, musicians, actors, and painters, among them Benjamin Constant, the Duc de Broglie, Chateaubriand, the Duc de Choiseul, Népomucène Lemercier, Jouy, Dupaty, and Talma, along with Juliette Récamier and the Marquise de Custine. In 1802, she published her first novel anonymously: *Laure d'Estell*. In 1803, she published a letter defending Staël's *Delphine*, after whom she named her daughter. She wrote songs and verse romances, both words and music—she had studied with Méhul. She also played the harp. Ten years after her first novel, in 1813, she published *Léonie de Montbreuse*, with the two initials of her name: Sainte-Beuve considered it her best work, but *Anatole* (1815), the story of a deaf-mute's loves, deserves attention.[2] Gay continued publishing

---

Heaven be thanked, she is a widow; and I think that she is rich, because her husband was, I believe, as old as his chateau; and one does not marry an old man except for his fortune.

Who is she bringing us here?

Everything she needs to establish herself, her people, her horses; frankly, down to her wet-nurse.

Ah! That's a bit rich. I know these fat country women who believe they have the right to order the whole house around because they nourished their mistress; they are old gossips who, under pretext of taking the interests of their dear nursling, go tell them everything done or said in their antechambers; Lapierre is quite free to put himself at the service of that one; as for me, I don't plan to fetch her a glass of water.

Ah! all this affair will not be eternal, Madame will soon grow tired of it, especially if it is true that Madame de Saverny is as beautiful as they say; don't you know, Richard, that two pretty women never lived long together?

Miss Julie's philosophical remarks were interrupted by the return of Madame de Nangis's carriage.

2 Charles-Augustin Sainte-Beuve, *Nouvelle galerie de femmes célèbres: tirée des Causeries du lundi, des Portraits littéraires, etc.* (Paris: Garnier, 1865), p. 551.

extensively after the Restoration, not only novels but also theatre, staging her one-act comedy the *Marquis de Pomenars* in 1819 at the Comédie-Française. Five-act comedies and dramas followed, staged at the Odéon and the Hôtel de Castellane. She also wrote several opera librettos, which met with some success. In 1826–1827, she traveled in Switzerland and Italy with her daughter. At her salon, one might see Hugo, Soumet, Lamartine, Vigny, Soulié, Sue, Balzac, Janin, or Dumas. Painters also came: Gérard, Girodet-Trioson, Isabey, Horace Vernet. After the July 1830 revolution, she brought out a series of historical novels which sold fairly well, enabling her to live off the proceeds: the *Duchesse de Châteauroux* (1834–1839), *Marie de Mancini* (1840), *Marie-Louise d'Orléans* (1842), *Ellénore* (1844–1846), the *Comte de Guiche* (1845). She also wrote the *Courrier de Versailles*, a sort of complement to the *Courrier de Paris* (1836–1848) by the Vicomte Charles de Launay (*i.e.*, her daughter).

In this passage from Gay, two servants are discussing the household doings: Richard and Julie. Richard is not a particularly common French name, making one wonder why Gay employs it. In Gay's youth, it was notorious in France because of the *Almanach du Bonhomme Richard* (1778), the French title for Ben Franklin's *Poor Richard's Almanac* (1732–1758), at just the time the name Julie was omnipresent as the heroine of Rousseau's *La Nouvelle Héloïse* (1761). Even allowing for Grétry's royalist anthem of 1785, "Ô Richard, ô mon roi," it seems hard to avoid the homespun bourgeois tone these two names carried, even as late as 1815. The maxims the servants offer have a similar patina of age to them: the countess is at most seven or eight years older than her sister-in-law, we read, since she admits to four; one only marries an old man for his fortune; two pretty women never lived together long. These well-worn channels of thought and wit have a slightly antiquated appeal, as does the fact that the lady being discussed is a widow, which was about the only way a woman of the Old Regime could escape tutelage. What then is new here? A couple of things. First, to open on the people, the *demos*, reviewing the doings of the great: this is routine in Shakespeare, from *Julius Caesar* (1599) to *Hamlet* (1603), and reminds us that Gay was a successful playwright after 1819. Second, for Richard to say "Faudra-t-il servir tout ce monde-là?" in a world after Mozart immediately recalls Leporello's opening refrain, *Non voglio più servir*, in Mozart's 1787 *Don Giovanni*. These two novelties are perhaps common enough by 1815. But third, *Anatole* is the story of the loves of someone who is deaf and mute. That now is a very Romantic storyline: the Romantic era turns again and again to protagonists facing adversity and stigma, from Hugo's Quasimodo to Duras's impotent Olivier, finding in these unknown souls our common humanity after all. One is reminded of André Chénier's *boutade*, which again had become omnipresent by the 1820s: "Sur des pensers nouveaux faisons des vers antiques." 1815 was a transitional year if ever there was one—it opened on Louis XVIII, transitioned back to Napoleon for the Hundred Days, then back to Louis XVIII again after Waterloo—and it is only fitting to find such a mix of old and new in Gay's new novel. Her daughter, as noted, was the writer Delphine Gay de Girardin, her niece was the writer Hortense Allart; Voltaire kissed her on the forehead; Hugo visited her salon. She is, in a sense, a liminal figure, or a pivotal figure if one prefers. She is obviously competent. One might expect to find more written about her than seems to be the case.

Works

[Gay, Sophie], *Œuvres complètes de Sophie Gay* (Paris: M. Lévy, 1864–1885)

Laure d'Estell, 3 vols (Paris: C. Pougens, an X/1802)

Anatole, 2 vols (Paris: Firmin-Didot, 1815)

Le Marquis de Pomenars, comédie en un acte et en prose (Paris: Ladvocat, 1820)

Une Aventure du chevalier de Grammont, comédie en trois actes et en vers (Paris: Tardieu, 1822)

Marie, ou la pauvre fille, drame en trois actes et en prose (Paris: Ponthieu & Barba, 1824)

Théobald, épisode de la guerre de Russie, 4 vols (Paris: Ponthieu, Dupont, 1828)

Le Moqueur amoureux, 2 vols (Paris: Levavasseur, 1830)

Un Mariage sous l'empire, 2 vols (Paris: Vimont, 1832)

Scènes du jeune âge, 2 vols (Paris: Dumont, 1834)

Souvenirs d'une vieille femme (Paris: Ledoux, 1834)

La Duchesse de Châteauroux, 2 vols (Paris: Dumont, 1834)

Le Chevalier de Canolle, opéra-comique en trois actes (Paris: Lemoine, 1836)

La Comtesse d'Egmont, 2 vols (Paris: Dumont, 1836)

Les Salons célèbres, 2 vols (Paris: Dumont, 1837)

Marie de Mancini, 2 vols (Paris: Dumont, 1839)

Marie-Louise d'Orléans, 2 vols (Paris: Dumont, 1842)

Ellénore, 4 vols (Paris: Dumont & Pétion, 1844–1846)

Le Comte de Guiche, 3 vols (Paris: L. de Potter, 1845)

Le Mari confident, 2 vols (Paris: A. Cadot, 1849)

Sources

Johnston, Joyce, *Women Dramatists, Humor, and the French Stage: 1802–1855* (New York: Palgrave Macmillan, 2014)

Malo, Henri, *Une muse et sa mère: Delphine Gay de Girardin* (Paris: Émile-Paul Frères, 1924)

Manecy, Jules, *Une famille de Savoie: celle de Delphine Gay* (Aix-les-Bains: E. Gérente, 1904)

19. Claire Louisa Rose Bonne, Duchesse de Duras
27 February 1777–16 January 1828

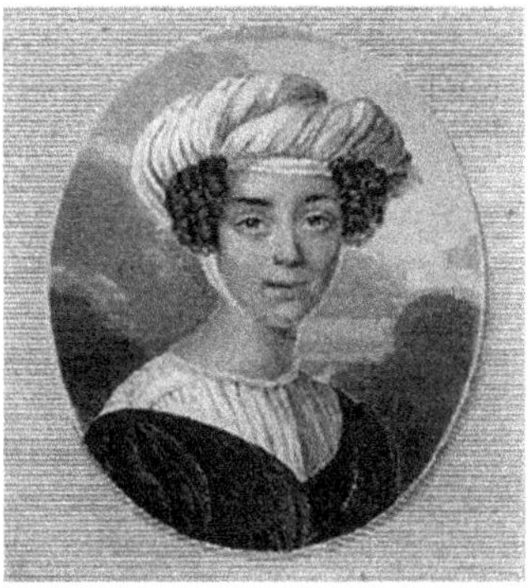

Fig. 19. Claire Louisa Rose Bonne, duchesse de Duras. Photo by Paola Severi Michelangeli (2011). Wikimedia, https://upload.wikimedia.org/wikipedia/commons/f/fb/Claire_de_Duras.jpg, CC BY 4.0.

Ourika

Je fus rapportée du Sénégal, à l'âge de deux ans, par M. le chevalier de B., qui en était gouverneur. Il eut pitié de moi, un jour qu'il vit embarquer des esclaves sur un bâtiment négrier qui allait bientôt quitter le port : ma mère était morte, et on m'emportait dans le vaisseau, malgré mes cris. M. de B. m'acheta, et, à son arrivée en France, il me donna à Mme la maréchale de B., sa tante, la personne la plus aimable de son temps, et celle qui sut réunir aux qualités les plus élevées la bonté la plus touchante.

Me sauver de l'esclavage, me choisir pour bienfaitrice Mme de B., c'était me donner deux fois la vie : je fus ingrate envers la Providence en n'étant point heureuse ; et cependant le bonheur résulte-t-il toujours de ces dons de l'intelligence ? Je croirais plutôt le contraire : il faut payer le bienfait de savoir par le désir d'ignorer, et la fable ne nous dit pas si Galatée trouva le bonheur après avoir reçu la vie.

Je ne sus que longtemps après l'histoire des premiers jours de mon enfance. Mes plus anciens souvenirs ne me retracent que le salon de Mme de B. ; j'y passais ma vie, aimée d'elle, caressée, gâtée par tous ses amis, accablée de présents, vantée, exaltée comme l'enfant le plus spirituel et le plus aimable.

Le ton de cette société était l'engouement, mais un engouement dont le bon goût savait exclure ce qui ressemblait à l'exagération ; on louait tout ce qui prêtait à la louange, on excusait tout ce qui prêtait au blâme, et souvent, par une adresse encore plus aimable, on transformait en qualités les défauts mêmes. Le succès donne du courage ; on valait près de Mme de B. tout ce qu'on pouvait valoir, et peut-être un peu plus, car elle prêtait quelque chose d'elle à ses amis sans s'en douter elle-même ; et, en la voyant, en l'écoutant, on croyait lui ressembler.[1]

Claire Louisa Rose Bonne, Duchesse de Duras, *née* de Coëtnempren de Kersaint was born in Brest in 1777, daughter of an admiral, and died in Nice in 1828. Present in her youth at her parents' salon, she left France for her mother's properties in Martinique after her father's guillotining with the Girondins on 4 December 1793, traveling on four years later to

---

1   Claire Louisa Rose Bonne, *Ourika*, ed. Roger Little (Exeter: University of Exeter Press, 1998), pp. 6–7. Spelling modernized by John Claiborne Isbell.

    Translation: I was brought back from Senegal, at the age of two, by M. le chevalier de B., who was governor there. He took pity on me, one day when he saw slaves being loaded on a slave ship which was soon to leave port; my mother was dead, and they were carrying me off in the vessel, despite my cries. M. de B. bought me, and, at his arrival in France, he gave me to Mme la maréchale de B., his aunt, the most amiable person of her time, and she who knew how to combine the most elevated qualities with the most touching kindness.

    Saving me from slavery, choosing for my benefactress Mme de B., this was to give me life twice over; I was ungrateful to Providence in not being happy; and yet does happiness always result from these gifts of the intelligence? I would rather think the opposite: one must pay for the benefit of knowing by the desire not to know, and the fable does not tell us whether Galatea found happiness after having received life.

    I only knew long afterward the story of the first days of my childhood. My oldest memories only retrace for me the salon of Mme de B.; I spent my life there, loved by her, caressed, spoiled by all her friends, flooded with presents, praised, exalted like the wittiest and most lovable child.

    The tone of this society was enthusiasm, but an enthusiasm from which good taste knew how to exclude all that resembled exaggeration; one praised all that lent itself to praise, one excused all that lent itself to blame, and often, by a still more amiable address, one transformed defects themselves into qualities. Success gives courage; one was worth, near Mme de B., all that one could be worth, and perhaps a little more, since she lent something of herself to her friends without suspecting this herself; and in seeing her, in hearing her, one thought to resemble her.

the United States, Switzerland, and finally London where she married Amédée Bretagne Malo de Durfort, Duc de Duras in 1797. Returning to Paris in 1800, she obtained her husband's removal from the list of émigrés in 1807. At the Restoration, Chateaubriand's friendship opened doors, though it was she who later furthered his political career. She was also the friend of Staël and of Rosalie de Constant, Benjamin's cousin. Her husband was admitted to court, and their salon became a major center for Parisian literary and social life. Duras had no interest in a career herself, and it was at Chateaubriand's insistence that she published *Ourika* anonymously in 1823, one of the three brief novels she produced, along with *Édouard* (1825) and *Olivier ou le Secret*, written in 1822. When Duras chose not to publish *Olivier*, Latouche brought out a version he attributed to her. *Les Mémoires de Sophie* and *Amélie et Pauline* appeared in 2011, while *Le Moine du Saint-Bernard* remains unpublished. As Sainte-Beuve notes, Duras often presents oppressed and marginalized protagonists, whose race or social origin makes happiness impossible for them. Tragedy recurs. Discounted for some time after her death as an author of brief sentimental romances, Duras has been reassessed by modern theory as a postmodern theorist on the question of identity. One might surmise that she had been systematically misread.

Ourika is narrated by a young woman saved from enslavement in Senegal, brought to Paris and presented to a friend as a gift. At fifteen, she discovers prejudice, which her society education had not previously revealed to her. Her beloved, who is born French, marries a Frenchwoman and Ourika retires to a convent to die young. *Édouard* meanwhile is the story of a love made impossible by social difference, and in *Olivier ou le Secret*, first published in 1971, the protagonist is impotent. Duras in short is interested in star-crossed lovers and the obstacles that separate them. Let us look then at this passage, in which the protagonist is not only a Black woman, but also the narrator. This is quite radical in 1823 and is apparent from her opening words. "Je fus rapportée du Sénégal," the novel begins after a brief framing preface; it appeared in a society where the slave trade continued, premised upon the treatment of human beings as objects. Staël similarly gives Mirza a voice in her eponymous tale of 1795; but Mirza's voice remains mediated throughout by a European narrator. Duras has gone one step further on the path of empathy, that same Romantic path of empathy that led

Hugo to give voice to Quasimodo, or Blake to give voice to his chimney sweep. Finally, we might note that Boufflers brought two slaves back from Senegal in 1786, not one, and Staël's 1795 tale uses the name of the second, Ziméo, for her heroine Mirza's beloved.

Slavery was abolished by the first French republic in 1794. It was reinstated by Napoleon in 1802—Joséphine was from Martinique—which cost France Haiti as Toussaint Louverture led the island to freedom. He was captured by the French in their ill-fated expedition to reconquer the island—they failed—and died in a Pyrenean prison. In Fort-de-France, Martinique, a public statue of Joséphine, decapitated when I visited in 1997, has since been torn down. Staël worked with Wilberforce to end the French slave trade at the Congress of Vienna in 1814, and it was banned north of the Niger; but the trade continued, like the institution of slavery itself, until the Second Republic banned both in 1848. That is Duras's context. It is worth noting the particularity that Chateaubriand, who encouraged Duras to publish, lived in a château (Combourg) paid for in part by slave trade money.

This extract spends some time flattering the woman and family who received Ourika as a gift in 1786. That is all well and good, and the Beauvau family, like Ourika, were real people and still present in Paris in 1823, when this tale was published. But the tale is not all sweetness and light; it is star-crossed, and Ourika's love for Charles cannot be fulfilled. The novel *Édouard*, where the obstacle is class, attracts less attention these days—it seems less radical—but the unpublished *Olivier ou le secret*, where the obstacle is impotence, does attract attention, not least because of its curious place in a French tradition Margaret Waller retraces in *The Male Malady* (1992). It is unclear what made so many French heroes in this period so paralyzed; they do resemble René, as Chateaubriand noted, but the tradition starts earlier, and it continued beyond Austerlitz and the burning of Moscow.

Works

[Duras, Claire de], *L'amante et l'amie: lettres inédites 1804–1828. François de Chateaubriand, Delphine de Custine, Claire de Duras*, ed. Marie-Bénédicte Diethelm and Bernard Degout (Paris: Gallimard, 2017)

Ourika, ed. Roger Little (Exeter: University of Exeter Press, 1998)

Édouard (Paris: Mercure de France, 1983)

Olivier ou le Secret (Paris: Éditions José Corti, 1971)

Mémoires de Sophie, suivi de Amélie et Pauline: Romans d'émigration, ed. Marie-Bénédicte Diethelm (Paris: éditions Manucius, 2011)

Sources

Allan, Stacie, *Writing the Self, Writing the Nation: Romantic Selfhood in the Works of Germaine de Staël and Claire de Duras* (Berlin: Peter Lang, 2019)

Crichfield, Grant, *Three Novels of Madame de Duras: Ourika, Edouard, and Olivier* (Paris: Mouton, 1975)

Kadish, Doris Y., Massardier-Kenney, Françoise, et al., *Translating Slavery: Gender and Race in French Women's Writing, 1783–1823* (Kent, OH: Kent State University Press, 1994)

Kadish, Doris Y., *Fathers, Daughters, and Slaves: Women Writers and French Colonial Slavery* (Liverpool: Liverpool University Press, 2012)

Pailhès, Gabriel, *La Duchesse de Duras et Chateaubriand* (Paris: Perrin, 1910)

Métais-Thoreau, Odile, *Une femme rare: Dans les pas de la duchesse de Duras* (Brissac: Petit Pavé, 2010)

20. Claire Élisabeth Jeanne, Comtesse de Rémusat
5 January 1780–16 December 1821

Fig. 20. Claire Élisabeth Jeanne, comtesse de Rémusat, by G. Descamps. Photo by Benj73 (2020). Wikimedia, https://upload.wikimedia.org/wikipedia/commons/c/c0/Comtesse_de_R%C3%A9musat_-.jpg, CC BY 4.0.

Mémoires de Madame de Rémusat [...]

Le mardi matin, Mme Bonaparte me dit : « Tout est inutile ; le duc d'Enghien arrive ce soir. Il sera conduit à Vincennes, et jugé cette nuit. Murat se charge de tout. Il est odieux dans cette affaire. C'est lui qui pousse Bonaparte ; il répète qu'on prendrait sa clémence pour de la faiblesse, et que les jacobins seraient furieux. Il y a un parti qui trouve mauvais qu'on n'ait pas eu égard à l'ancienne gloire de Moreau, et qui demanderait pourquoi on ménagerait davantage un Bourbon ; enfin Bonaparte m'a défendu de lui en parler davantage. Il m'a parlé de vous, ajouta-t-elle ensuite ; je lui ai avoué que je vous avais tout dit ; il avait été frappé de votre tristesse. Tâchez de vous contraindre. »

Ma tête était montée alors : « Ah ! qu'il pense de moi ce qu'il voudra ! Il m'importe peu, madame, je vous assure, et, s'il me demande pourquoi je pleure, je lui répondrai que je pleure sur lui. »

Enfin, à l'heure du dîner, il fallut descendre et composer son visage. Le mien était bouleversé. Bonaparte jouait encore aux échecs, il avait pris fantaisie à ce jeu. Dès qu'il me vit, il m'appela près de lui, me disant de le conseiller ; je n'étais pas en état de prononcer quatre mots. Il me parla avec un ton de douceur et d'intérêt qui acheva de me troubler. Lorsque le dîner fut servi, il me fit mettre près de lui, et me questionna sur une foule de choses toutes personnelles à ma famille. Il semblait qu'il prît à tâche de m'étourdir, et de m'empêcher de penser.

On annonça le général Hullin; le Premier consul repoussa la table fortement, se leva, et, entrant dans la galerie voisine du salon, il demeura tout le reste de la soirée avec Murat, Hullin et Savary. Il ne reparut plus, et cependant moi, je rentrai chez moi plus tranquille. Je ne pouvais me persuader que Bonaparte ne fût pas ému de la pensée d'avoir dans les mains une telle victime. Je souhaitais que le prince demandât à le voir ; et c'est ce qu'il fit en effet, en répétant ces paroles : « Si le Premier consul consentait à me voir, il me rendrait justice, et comprendrait que j'ai fait mon devoir. » Peut-être, me disais-je, il ira lui-même à Vincennes, il accordera un éclatant pardon.[1]

Claire Élisabeth Jeanne, Comtesse de Rémusat was the daughter of Charles Gravier de Vergennes, councillor at the Parlement of Burgundy

---

1 [Claire Élisabeth Jeanne de Rémusat], *Mémoires de Madame de Rémusat* [...] (Paris: Les Amis de l'Histoire, 1968), pp. 97–98.

> Translation: Tuesday morning, Mrs. Bonaparte said to me: "All is useless; the Duke d'Enghien arrives this evening. He will be taken to Vincennes and judged tonight. Murat takes charge of everything. He is odious in this affair. It is he who pushes Bonaparte; he repeats that one would take his clemency for weakness, and that the Jacobins would be furious. There is a party that finds it bad that Moreau's former glory was not respected, and which would ask why one should sooner make allowances for a Bourbon; frankly, Bonaparte forbade me from speaking more with him about it. He spoke to me of you, she then added; I avowed to him that I had told you everything; he was struck by your sadness. Try to constrain yourself."
>
> My blood was up then: "Ah! Let him think of me what he likes! Madam, I assure you, I am little concerned, and if he asks me why I weep, I shall say I weep for him."
>
> Finally, at the hour of dinner, one had to go down and compose one's face. Mine was overwhelmed. Bonaparte was still playing chess, he had taken a fancy to this game. As soon as he saw me, he called me to him, telling me to counsel him; I was not in a state to pronounce four words. He spoke to me with a tone of sweetness and interest which completed my trouble. When dinner was served, he put me next to him, and questioned me on a host of topics all personal to my family. It seemed that he took it upon himself to confuse me and to stop me thinking.
>
> General Hullin was announced; the First Consul pushed back the table vehemently, got up and entering the gallery next to the salon, he spent the rest of the evening with Murat, Hullin and Savary. He did not reappear, and yet I, I returned to my chambers more tranquil. I could not persuade myself that Bonaparte would not be moved at the thought of having such a victim in his hands. I wished that the prince would ask to see him; and that is what he did in fact, in repeating these words: "If the First Consul consented to see me, he would do me justice, and would understand that I have done my duty." Perhaps, I said to myself, he will go to Vincennes himself, he will grant a splendid pardon.

and Paris director of taxes, 1784–1789—guillotined with her grandfather on 24 July 1794—and of Adélaïde de Bastard, daughter of a councillor at the Parlement of Toulouse. Rémusat left an important correspondence, notably with her husband and her son Charles. Sainte-Beuve called her "à peu près la seule femme avec qui [Napoléon] causât."[2] At her father's death in 1794, Madame de Vergennes took refuge with her two daughters in Saint-Gratien near Montmorency. In 1796, the sixteen-year-old Claire married Auguste Laurent de Rémusat, aged thirty-four, a family friend and widower. They had two sons. In 1802, aged twenty-two, she was chosen by Madame Bonaparte, wife of the First Consul, as lady of honor at the Tuileries. Her husband was named a prefect of the palace. Both rose at court over the years, and the couple hosted a successful salon. Talleyrand penned her portrait in 1811, as did her son Charles in 1857.[3] She died aged forty-one and is buried in Père-Lachaise Cemetery.

Besides her unpublished novels, Rémusat kept memoirs which she burned in 1815 during Napoleon's Hundred Days. Then, reading Staël's *Considérations sur la révolution française* in 1818, as an exchange of letters with her son reveals, she was struck with the urge to relate what she knew, notably of "ce malheureux homme," her name for Bonaparte. Her early death ended the memoirs with just three of five planned sections complete. Here, then, is her memory of the year 1804 and the seizure of the Duc d'Enghien, a *prince du sang* and only heir of the Condé line, at his home across the Rhine in the Holy Roman Empire. Bonaparte had received news that Enghien was involved with Cadoudal's royalist conspiracy earlier that year: this was false, though Enghien had earlier borne arms against Robespierre's republic in the émigré *armée de Condé*. Enghien was taken to Vincennes, where Savary prevented any interview between him and the First Consul. Hulin executed him in the castle moat at dawn: a pillar marks the spot. There is no evidence of Murat's involvement in the affair, despite Joséphine's long speech. Savary was a man of blood; Murat was an ardent republican, but also a soldier, future marshal of the Empire and King of Naples. The claim looks like slander. The execution shocked Europe, though Napoleon continued to defend his action even in his will on Saint Helena. Fouché, a chief of police

---

2   *Mémoires de Madame de Rémusat, 1802–1808*, ed. Paul de Rémusat, 3 volumes (Paris: Calmann-Lévy, 1880), I, p.32.
3   *Mémoires de Madame de Rémusat* (1880), I, pp. 23–24.

less pliable than Savary, said of it: *C'est pire qu'un crime, c'est une faute.* Bonaparte made himself emperor that December.

What is Rémusat's reaction? Disbelief, to begin with. The passage ends with her still believing Bonaparte would pardon Enghien if only they met; in reality, the arrest seems either Savary's or Napoleon's idea, and Napoleon later devoted some effort to saying he would do it again. On the other hand, after reporting Joséphine's long speech about Murat, Rémusat does nothing to confirm or contradict it. Both women seem open to the age-old trope that separates a benevolent but misled ruler from their nasty counsellors—one might wish for clearer eyes, but perhaps they are there in Rémusat's name for the man: "ce malheureux homme." She was lady-in-waiting to Napoleon's wife and rose like her husband in his service, but as her memoirs reveal, a good mind maintains its independence. In all, this is an interesting, even revealing passage, and the writer's son played a significant, though still-occluded role in the Paris of the 1820s. It is a little startling, then, to find not one monograph devoted to Rémusat in the catalogue of the Bibliothèque nationale de France, nor anywhere else for that matter.

Works

[Rémusat, Claire de], *Essai sur l'éducation des femmes*, published by her son Charles de Rémusat (Paris: Ladvocat, 1825)

«*Je vous dirai, cher ami*»: *lettres de madame de Rémusat à son mari, 1804–1813*, ed. Hannelore Demmer ([Paris]: Mercure de France, 2016)

Lettres de Madame de Rémusat, 1804–1814, published by her grandson Paul de Rémusat, 2 vols (Paris: C. Lévy, 1881)

Mémoires de Madame de Rémusat [...], ed. Pierre-André Weber (Paris: Les Amis de l'Histoire, 1968).

Sources

The Bibliothèque nationale de France lists no study of Rémusat in their holdings, and I have identified none elsewhere. There is however a more general survey:

Rossi, Henri, *Mémoires aristocratiques féminins 1789–1848* (Paris: Honoré Champion, 2000)

21. Adélaïde Charlotte Louise Éléonore, Comtesse de Boigne
19 February 1781–10 May 1866

Fig. 21. Adélaïde Charlotte Louise Éléonore, comtesse de Boigne, by J.-B. Isabey. Photo by PBrieux (2020). Wikimedia, https://upload.wikimedia.org/wikipedia/commons/7/7c/Ad%C3%A9la%C3%AFde_d%27Osmond%2Ccomtesse_de_Boigne_par_Jean-Baptiste_Isabey.jpg, CC BY 4.0.

Mémoires de la comtesse de Boigne née d'Osmond. Récits d'une tante

Il serait assurément fort peu intéressant pour un autre de connaître mes opinions personnelles en 1814. Mais c'est une recherche qui m'amuse de me rendre ainsi compte de moi-même aux différentes époques de ma vie et d'observer les variations qui les ont marquées.

J'avais perdu en grande partie mon anglomanie ; j'étais redevenue française, si ce n'est politiquement, du moins socialement ; et, comme je l'ai dit déjà, le cri des sentinelles ennemies m'avait plus affecté que le bruit de leur canon. J'avais éprouvé un mouvement très patriotique, mais fugitif. J'étais de position, de tradition, de souvenir, d'entourage et de conviction royaliste et légitimiste. Mais j'étais bien plus antibonapartiste que je n'étais bourbonienne ; je détestais la tyrannie de l'Empereur que je voyais s'exercer.

Je considérais peu ceux de nos princes que j'avais vus de près. On m'assurait que Louis XVIII était dans d'autres principes. L'extrême animosité qui existait entre sa petite Cour et celle de Monsieur le comte d'Artois pouvait le faire espérer. J'avais quitté l'Angleterre avant que les vicissitudes de l'exil l'y eussent amené, et je me prêtais volontiers à écouter les éloges que ma mère faisait du Roi, malgré le tort qu'il avait, à ses yeux, d'être un constitutionnel de 1789.

C'était sur ce tort même que se fondaient mes espérances ; car, en me recherchant bien, je me retrouve toujours aussi libérale que le permettent les préjugés aristocratiques qui m'accompagneront, je crains, jusqu'au tombeau.[1]

Adélaïde Charlotte Louise Éléonore, Comtesse de Boigne was born in Versailles in 1781 and died in Paris in 1866. Daughter of René Eustache, Marquis d'Osmond and of Éléonore Dillon, she was the playmate of the first dauphin, Louis Joseph Xavier François de France (1781–1789) at Versailles, her mother being the lady of honor of Madame Adélaïde. Her father included politics and economics in her education, with a

---

1   Adélaïde Charlotte Louise Éléonore de Boigne, *Mémoires de la comtesse de Boigne née d'Osmond. Récits d'une tante*, ed. Jean-Claude Berchet, 2 vols (Paris: Mercure de France, 1979), p. 219.

> Translation: It would surely be of little interest for another to know my personal opinions in 1814. But it is a study that amuses me thus to make acquaintance with myself at the different epochs of my life and to observe the variations that marked them.
>
> I had in great measure lost my Anglomania; I had become French again, if not politically, then at least socially; and as I have already said, the cry of enemy sentries had affected me more than the noise of their cannon. I had experienced a very patriotic movement, but a fugitive one. I was by position, by tradition, by memory, by entourage and by conviction royalist and legitimist. But I was far more Antibonapartist than I was Bourbonian; I detested the emperor's tyranny that I saw being exercised.
>
> I had little consideration for those of our princes whom I had seen at close range. People assured me that Louis XVIII had other principles. The extreme animosity which existed between his little Court and that of Monsieur the Comte d'Artois made it possible to hope. I had left England before the vicissitudes of exile had brought him there, and I willingly lent an ear to the praises my mother made of the King, despite the error he had, in her eyes, of being a Constitutional of 1789.
>
> It was on this very error that my hopes were founded; because, in examining myself well, I find myself still as liberal as is allowed by the aristocratic prejudices that will accompany me, I fear, to the tomb.

penchant for English liberalism. She emigrated in 1792 with the king's aunts, befriending the future Queen of the French in Naples. During emigration in England in 1798, she married the soldier and adventurer Benoît, Comte de Boigne (1751–1830). They were childless. A mutually agreed separation in 1802 left the countess both freedom and a pension. Boigne then returned to France in 1804 and found herself until the fall of the Empire in the royalist circles Napoléon tolerated, with ties to Staël and Madame Récamier. At the return of the Bourbons in 1814, she acquired a leading position in society, first following her father, ambassador to Turin and London, then settling permanently in Paris. Her salon united the old nobility with the worlds of politics, diplomacy, and literature. From the start of the 1820s, the countess was a leading proponent of the medievalizing Troubadour style the Romantics brought into vogue, used in two rooms of the hôtel d'Osmond, where the Opéra Garnier now stands. The July Monarchy was the zenith of her fame. The d'Osmond family were closely tied to the Orléans, and Boigne was a good friend of Marie Amélie de Bourbon, Queen of the French. Her salon grew more explicitly political: Charles de Rémusat, visiting in 1832, noted the guests Broglie, Guizot, and Thiers, for instance, alongside Mérimée, remarking that Boigne's constant goodness did not prevent her spotting a flaw or a ridicule. Proust read her memoirs with enthusiasm and based Madame de Beausergent on her.[2] It had taken ten years in court for the memoirs to come out unexpurgated, with several aristocratic families attempting to censor them. The countess was also the author of two novels, *La Maréchale d'Aubemer, nouvelle du XVIIIe siècle* (1866) and *Une passion dans le grand monde* (1867), which both appeared posthumously.

1814 was a very different year than 1815. In 1814, Louis XVIII, younger brother of Louis XVI, returned with a concession to twenty-five years of Revolution and empire, the Charte which he had *octroyée* or granted and which made of him a constitutional monarch, not an absolute one. He returned, of course, on the back of the Prussians, the Russians, and the English, who had ended by defeating Napoleon after his ill-fated march on Moscow. The emperor seemed safely lodged on Elba. In 1815, he was to land in Cannes, and after a triumphal march on

---

2 François Wagener, *La Comtesse de Boigne (1781–1866)* (Paris: Flammarion, 1997), pp. 427–428.

Paris, to rule once more for the Hundred Days and make of Waterloo, in the words of the Duke of Wellington, "a damned close-run thing." Louis XVIII then returned once again, with perhaps somewhat less legitimacy than one year previously.

What does the Comtesse de Boigne, former playmate at Versailles of the first dauphin—Louis XVIII's nephew—make of a king's return to Paris after twenty-five years of blood and dreams? Well, she begins rather adroitly by saying that her opinions on the topic would be of little interest to others. To herself, however, she sees interest in the question. These memoirs, after all, later spent ten years waiting to be published. So then, she had lost her anglomania, she tells us: her parents had taught her English liberalism, and by 1814, she was disenchanted either with it or with its country of origin, fierce enemy of France for the past quarter-century and now an occupying power. Boigne explains her royalist and legitimist background, adding that she was far more antibonapartist than she was Bourbonian: she had spent the previous decade in Imperial France, and was happy to see the emperor fall, but still felt pain to hear foreign sentries calling out in the Paris streets. She was a patriot. Staël, somewhat similarly, had hoped in 1814 to see Napoleon victorious but killed in battle.

Boigne then turns to the returning Bourbons, noting her low esteem for the Bourbon princes she had seen close up. Louis XVIII, she had been assured, had different principles to the others—evidently more readiness for constitutional rule—as the author's contrast with Artois, his absolutist younger brother and the future Charles X, last of his line, suggests. As Boigne notes, it was on Louis's constitutionalism that her hopes were grounded. Like her friend Staël, she was unready to see twenty-five years of French suffering and effort swept under the carpet as if they had not occurred. In that, Boigne separated from her mother, who called Louis's openesss to the ideals of 1789 a fault. This was the position of the Ultras around the Comte d'Artois, of whom it was said, "Ils n'ont rien oublié ni rien appris."

So, the kings came back in 1814; Louis XVIII even numbered himself non-consecutively, to indicate the unhappy reign of Louis XVII, son of Louis XVI, from the Parisian prison in which the boy died aged ten. This was the world of Balzac's *Le Colonel Chabert* (1832), where Chabert returns from the Napoleonic wars to find himself wiped from history.

It was the world of Chateaubriand's 1814 pamphlet *De Buonaparte, des Bourbons, et de la nécessité de se rallier à nos souverains légitimes*, with its telltale 'u' in the name Bonaparte; it was also the world where Benjamin Constant wrote Napoleon's Hundred-Day constitution. It was a France bitterly divided.

Works

[Boigne, Adélaïde de], *Mémoires de la comtesse de Boigne née d'Osmond. Récits d'une tante*, ed. Jean-Claude Berchet, 2 vols (Paris: Mercure de France, 1979)

Sources

Vanderboegh, David S., *The Life and Works of Adèle d'Osmond, Comtesse de Boigne: 1781–1866* (Lewiston, NY: Edwin Mellen Press, 2002)

Wagener, Françoise, *La comtesse de Boigne: 1781–1866* (Paris: Flammarion, 1997)

22. Marceline Félicité Josèphe Desbordes-Valmore
20 June 1786–23 July 1859

Fig. 22. Marceline Félicité Josèphe Desbordes-Valmore, by Nadar. Photo by Paola Severi Michelangeli (2011). Wikimedia, https://upload.wikimedia.org/wikipedia/commons/1/1b/Marceline_Desbordes-Valmore_1.jpg, CC BY 4.0.

Poésies inédites

« Les Roses de Saadi »

J'ai voulu ce matin te rapporter des roses ;
Mais j'en avais tant pris dans mes ceintures closes
Que les nœuds trop serrés n'ont pu les contenir.

Les nœuds ont éclaté. Les roses envolées
Dans le vent, à la mer s'en sont toutes allées.
Elles ont suivi l'eau pour ne plus revenir ;

> La vague en a paru rouge et comme enflammée.
> Ce soir, ma robe encore en est tout embaumée ...
> Respires-en sur moi l'odorant souvenir.[1]

Marceline Félicité Josèphe Desbordes-Valmore was born in Douai in 1786 and died in Paris in 1859. Daughter of Catherine Lucas and Félix Desbordes, a painter and cabaret owner ruined by the Revolution, Desbordes left France at fifteen with her mother in 1801, seeking financial support from a wealthy cousin in Guadeloupe. Yellow fever took her mother in 1803; revolt agitated the island, and the cousin's finances were ruined in their turn. Desbordes returned to her father in Douai, becoming an actress at the age of sixteen, first touring in the provinces, then performing in Paris at the Odéon and the Opéra-Comique, thanks to Grétry, then in Brussels in 1815, where she played Rosine in Beaumarchais's *Le Barbier de Séville* (1775). She often played *ingénues*, meeting Talma, Marie Dorval, and Mademoiselle Mars who remained her lifelong friend. From 1808–1812, Desbordes stopped acting while engaged to Eugène Debonne, a member of Rouen society, by whom she had a son; but the family refused any marriage to a former actress. Desbordes therefore left her fiancé and resumed acting. Their son died in 1816. In 1817, she married an actor, Prosper Lanchantin, known as Valmore, whom she met in Brussels. She had four more children, of whom one, Hippolyte, survived his mother; one may have been the child of the playwright Henri de Latouche, the great love of her life. In 1819 Desbordes-Valmore published her first volume of poetry, *Élégies et Romances*, which opened the pages of *La Muse française* to her. *Poésies de Mme Desbordes-Valmore* followed in 1820. After 1823, she definitively abandoned theater for poetry, publishing *Élégies et poésies nouvelles* (1824), *Pleurs* (1833), *Pauvres fleurs* (1839), and *Bouquets et Prières*

---

[1] Marceline Félicité Josèphe Desbordes-Valmore, *Poésies inédites* in *Les Œuvres poétiques de Marceline Desbordes-Valmore*, ed. M. Bertrand, 2 vols (Grenoble: Presses universitaires de Grenoble, 1973), II p. 509, pp. 735–736.

> Translation: "Saadi's Roses"
> I wanted this morning to bring you back some roses; / But I had taken so many in my closed belts / That the knots, over-tight, could not hold them.
> The knots burst. The roses flown / in the wind, all went to the sea. / They followed the water not to return;
> The wave seemed from it red and as if aflame. / This evening, my dress is still completely embalmed from it ... / Breathe its scented memory on me.

(1843). Her works earned her a royal pension under Louis Philippe and several academic distinctions. She also wrote prose, including tales for children in prose and verse. In 1833, she published an autobiographical novel, *L'Atelier d'un peintre*. She died in 1859, having survived almost all of her children. Desbordes-Valmore was known as "Notre-Dame-des-Pleurs" in reference to the dramas which marked her life. In 1859, the Académie française gave her a posthumous prix Lambert; her admirers include Sainte-Beuve, who writes at length about her, Balzac, Baudelaire, Verlaine, and Aragon. Clearly among the most gifted French poetesses since Louise Labé, she brought the eleven-syllable line to French and contributed to the idea of *Romances sans paroles*. She also published in Picard.

And so, we come to "Les Roses de Saadi." First, one may ask, is what it describes possible? There have been critics who doubted it. At this point, it is worth recalling that Desbordes-Valmore is imitating a passage in the thirteenth-century Persian poet Saadi's *Gulistan*: she is the maker of the music of her poem, not its content. But it is also quite possible to overstuff a garment with roses and have the knots come undone. Why ever not? The objection gives some insight into why the Romantics were unfond of critics. The story, then, goes thus: the speaker gathered roses for her addressee this morning. The knots came undone, and the roses flew off in the wind into the sea. The water was red and as if on fire. The speaker's dress still smells of it; she invites the addressee to smell that memory. This conceit is fresh and resonant. Roses have a long history in poetry: Desbordes-Valmore, echoing her source Saadi, says she has not one rose to offer, but instead a memory of roses. She also has a tale to tell, of roses gathered and then lost to the ocean, with the ocean's strange sea-change into red flame beneath that weight. There is a magical quality to the whole thing, and Desbordes-Valmore works to make her poem as like a spell as possible. First, it is nine lines long. Short poems are hard: Desbordes-Valmore has told every necessary detail of this somewhat complex story, and not a syllable more. There is no filler. She has done so with an elegant play between end-stopped and enjambed lines: the excess roses enjamb to their dispersal, then the flying roses enjamb into the wind. The other seven lines are all end-stopped and a complete thought—a level of simplicity that is not so easy to achieve, as any practicing poet will know. Finally, her rhyme scheme is new: *aab ccb ddb*, three tercets which alternate masculine and feminine alexandrines as French tradition required, with a refrain on *-ir* to hold the whole together. It is, in short, a cameo fully the equal of, say, those of Théophile Gautier's 1852 *Émaux et camées*. It is chiseled. But it doesn't look chiseled, it looks effortless. And that is hard indeed. Just as Alphonse de Lamartine's rather longer "Le Lac" (1820) has more structure than is sometimes thought, so Desbordes-Valmore, another canonical Romantic, has built her music into something new and strange, despite its seeming simplicity and flow. She has cast a spell on us. Saadi, that Persian Sufi poet from the tradition which produced Rumi, Hafiz, and Omar Khayyam, might have been content to see his work thus rendered into French.

Works

[Desbordes-Valmore, Marceline], *Les Œuvres poétiques de Marceline Desbordes-Valmore*, ed. M. Bertrand, 2 vols (Grenoble: Presses universitaires de Grenoble, 1973)

Vingt-deux lettres (Paris: L'Arbre, 1986)

Les Petits Flamands (Genève: Droz, 1991)

Domenica (Genève: Droz, 1992)

L'Atelier d'un peintre (Paris: Miroirs Éditions, 1992)

Contes (Lyon: Presses Universitaires de Lyon, 1996)

Huit femmes (Genève: Droz, 1999)

Les Veillées des Antilles (Paris: L'Harmattan, 2006)

Sources

Ambrière, Francis, *Le siècle des Valmore, Marceline Desbordes-Valmore et les siens*, 2 vols (Paris: Seuil, 1987)

Bertrand, Marc, *Une femme à l'écoute de son temps*, (Paris: Jacques André, 2009)

Bertrand, Marc, *La liberté sans effroi: (re)lire Marceline Desbordes-Valmore* (Lyon: Jacques André éditeur, 2017)

Boulenger, Jacques, *Marceline Desbordes-Valmore, sa vie et son secret* (Paris: Plon, 1927)

Boutin, Aimée, *Maternal Echoes: The Poetry of Marceline Desbordes-Valmore and Alphonse de Lamartine* (Newark: University of Delaware Press, 2001)

Cavallucci, Giacomo, *Bibliographie critique de Marceline Desbordes-Valmore, d'après des documents inédits. II, Prose et correspondance* (Naples: R. Pironti, [ca 1930])

Clancier, Georges-Emmanuel, *Marceline Desbordes-Valmore ou le génie inconnu* (Paris: Seghers, 1983)

Desbordes, Lucie, *Le Carnet de Marceline Desbordes-Valmore* (Paris: Bartillat, 2016)

Descaves, Lucien, *La Vie douloureuse de Marceline Desbordes-Valmore* (Paris, 1898)

Duflot, Marianne, *L'Éros du souvenir d'enfance dans les contes de Marceline Desbordes-Valmore* (Rennes: Université Rennes 2, 2008)

Duhamel, Yvonne, *Marceline Desbordes-Valmore: bibliothèque municipale de Douai: exposition organisée pour le centième anniversaire de sa mort... [28 juin-30 septembre 1959]* (Douai: Bibliothèque municipale de Douai, 1959)

Effertz, Julia, *Songbirds on the Literary Stage: The Woman Singer and Her Song in French and German Prose Fiction, from Goethe to Berlioz* (New York: Peter Lang, 2015)

Jasenas, Éliane, *Marceline Desbordes-Valmore devant la critique* (Paris: Minard, 1962)

Mariéton, Paul and Vial, Eugène, eds, *Marceline Desbordes-Valmore et ses amis lyonnais, d'après une série de lettres inédites* (Paris: la Connaissance, 1923)

Moulin, Jeanine, *Marceline Desbordes-Valmore* (Paris: Seghers, 1955)

Paliyenko, Adrianna M., *Genius Envy: Women Shaping French Poetic History, 1801– 1900* (University Park (Penn.): Pennsylvania State University Press, 2016)

Planté, Christine, ed., *J'écris pourtant: bulletin de la Société des études Marceline Desbordes-Valmore*: N° 1 (Douai: Société des études Marceline Desbordes-Valmore, 2017-)

Sesma, Manuel Garcia, *Le Secret de Marceline Desbordes-Valmore* (Lyon: La Guillotière, 1945)

Zweig, Stefan, *Marceline Desbordes-Valmore* (Paris, 1924)

23. Hortense Thérèse Sigismonde Sophie Alexandrine Allart de Méritens
7 September 1801–28 February 1879

Fig. 23. Hortense Thérèse Sigismonde Sophie Alexandrine Allart de Méritens, by S. Allart. Photo by BeatrixBelibaste (2022). Wikimedia, https://upload.wikimedia.org/wikipedia/commons/3/35/Hortense_Allart_by_Sophie_Allart.jpg, CC BY 4.0.

Lettres sur les ouvrages de Madame de Staël

Lettre I.
Des lettres sur Rousseau.

Le premier ouvrage connu de madame de Staël a été l'expression de son enthousiasme pour celui de nos grands écrivains avec lequel elle devait avoir le plus de rapport.

C'est un beau début pour le talent que l'examen d'un sublime génie. Madame de Staël, élevant un monument à la gloire de J.-J. Rousseau, put déjà faire prévoir quel serait son talent, si l'on peut jamais prévoir ce qui doit étonner.

Nous n'examinerons pas ces cinq lettres en détail. Nous ne dirons pas les endroits où il nous semble qu'elle a trop ou pas assez loué ; nous ne ferons point remarquer la justesse de certains aperçus, et la profondeur et la force naissantes de ses pensées. Nous jetterons sur ces lettres un coup d'œil général.

Madame de Staël s'élève en parlant de l'auteur qui a le mieux su toucher son cœur, ébranler son âme, de celui avec lequel elle s'est trouvée le plus de sympathie.

On ne l'accusera pas d'exagération. Elle se contient dans son admiration ; elle veut être sage dans son enchantement. Quoiqu'elle avoue que plusieurs des idées de Rousseau sont fausses, elle le reconnaît, à tout prendre, l'homme de la nature et de la vérité. Elle a dit beaucoup sur lui ; il ne nous semble pas cependant qu'elle ait tout dit. En examinant ses plus forts écrits, elle n'a point parlé d'un des grands effets qu'ils produisent. Elle a loué l'Emile, mais elle n'a pas fait l'observation que cet ouvrage révèle, pour ainsi dire, les droits de l'homme. On se sent fier et libre après l'avoir lu ; il donne le sentiment de la grandeur et de la dignité humaines ; c'est une école de liberté autant que de morale.

Remontant toujours aux sources des idées de l'homme, pour trouver la vérité dans sa pureté première, Rousseau a ramené l'humanité à la liberté naturelle comme aux sentiments primitifs. Donnant toujours les théories abstraites, travaillant d'une manière spéculative, il a fait le Discours sur l'inégalité des conditions, il a fait le Contrat social ; génie universel et profond, il a jeté les bases immuables, il a révélé les principes éternels, laissant à d'autres le soin de construire sur ces bases et de faire l'application de ces principes. Il vous fait l'homme de l'indépendance en vous faisant l'homme de la nature. Et en effet l'espèce humaine, dans son innocence, est à la fois libre et sensible. La perfection de la société, c'est d'avoir consacré ces vertus de fierté et de sentiment que la nature indique. Dans ses progrès elle s'écarte quelquefois de la vraie route. Les hommes qui, comme Rousseau, viennent, lorsqu'elle est déjà avancée dans sa course, lui rappeler ses devoirs et la raffermir dans la vérité, sont certainement les plus utiles. On a attribué la révolution française à une foule de causes. Sans doute la masse des années et des événements amena cette grande secousse ; mais, parmi les progrès de la raison humaine qui l'ont produite, Rousseau a fait faire les plus forts, les plus hardis et les plus rapides.[1]

---

1   Hortense Allart, *Lettres sur les ouvrages de Madame de Staël* (Paris: Bossange, 1824), pp. i–ii, 1–4.

23. Hortense Thérèse Sigismonde Sophie Alexandrine Allart de Méritens

Hortense Thérèse Sigismonde Sophie Alexandrine Allart de Méritens [Prudence de Saman L'Esbatx] was born in Milan and died in Montlhéry, losing her father, Nicolas Jean Gabriel Allart, at the age of sixteen and her mother, Marie Françoise Gay, translator of Ann Radcliffe, four years later. She was also the niece of Sophie Gay and cousin of Delphine de Girardin, both featured here . Her father died penniless in 1817. The young Allart wrote to Henri Galien Bertrand in 1819, volunteering to travel to Saint Helena to nurse the ex-emperor, Napoleon. Bertrand later offered her a job as a governess; she worked for him for two years and was there impregnated and abandoned by the Portuguese Comte de Sampayo. In 1824, amid this liaison, she published her letters on Staël.

Translation: The first known work of Mme de Staël was the expression of her enthusiasm for the one of our great writers with whom she must have had the greatest connection.

It is a fine start to talent to examine a sublime genius. Mme de Staël, elevating a monument to the glory of J.-J. Rousseau, could already reveal what was to be her talent, if one can ever reveal early that which is to astonish.

We will not examine these five letters in detail. We will not name the places where it seems to us she has too much or too little praised; we will not point out the justice of certain insights, and the growing depth and force of her thoughts. We will offer a general overview of these letters.

Mme de Staël lifts herself in speaking of the author who best knew how to touch her heart, overthrow her soul, him with whom she felt the most sympathy.

One will not accuse her of exaggeration. She is contained in her admiration; she wishes to be wise in her enchantment. Although she acknowledges that several ideas of Rousseau's are false, she recognizes him, all things considered, as the man of nature and truth. She spoke about him at length; it does not however seem to us that she said everything. In examining his strongest writings, she did not speak of one of the great effects they produce. She praised Émile but did not make the observation that this work reveals, so to speak, the rights of man. One feels proud and free after having read it; it gives the sentiment of human grandeur and dignity; it is a school of freedom as much as of ethics.

Going back always to the sources of man's ideas, to find the truth in its first purity, Rousseau brought humanity to natural liberty as to first or primitive feelings. Always giving abstract theories, working in a speculative fashion, he wrote the Discourse on the Inequality of Conditions, he wrote the Social Contract; a universal and profound genius, he laid down immovable bases, he revealed eternal principles, leaving to others the care to construct on these bases and to make the application of these principles. He gives you independent man in giving you natural man. And in fact the human species, in its innocence, is both free and sensitive. The perfection of society is to have consecrated these virtues of pride and sentiment which nature indicates. In its progress, it sometimes loses sight of the true road. Men who, like Rousseau, come, when it is already advanced in its course, to remind it of its duties and strengthen it in its truths, are certainly the most useful. The French Revolution has been attributed to a host of causes. Doubtless the mass of years and of events brought on this great convulsion; but, among the advances in human reason which produced it, Rousseau made the strongest, the boldest and the most rapid.

Gertrude followed in 1828, under the name Hortense Allart de Thérase, then books on history and politics. In 1832, she began a longstanding liaison with George Sand. Her autobiography on the topic was a *succès de scandale* in 1873. A believer in free love, Allart demanded an improvement in women's condition, participating in the *Gazette des femmes*. She also wrote on philosophy, in her *Novum organum ou sainteté philosophique* (1857), and had liaisons with Chateaubriand, Bulwer-Lytton, Cavour, and Sainte-Beuve.[2] Between 1838 and 1879, she corresponded with Marie d'Agoult, also featured in this volume. In 1843, she married Napoléon Louis Frédéric Corneille de Méritens de Malvézie, an architect she left the following year. She is buried with her two sons in Bourg-la-Reine.

One work which seems to have escaped Staël scholars is Allart's 1824 *Lettres sur les ouvrages de Madame de Staël*. It was Allart's first major publication, at the age of twenty-three; almost exactly Staël's age when she published her own first major work, the *Lettres sur Jean-Jacques Rousseau* (1788). As Allart writes, "C'est un beau début pour le talent que l'examen d'un sublime génie." The book is relatively long—144 pages—and contains a series of letters on Staël's major works, precisely Staël's own 1788 format. What are we to make of this? First, Staël had died in 1817, and her last major work, the *Dix années d'exil*, appeared with her complete works in 1821. The young Allart is not only topical; hers may be the first monograph devoted to Staël's complete works ever written. Second, Allart has embraced her youthful model's method: one of enthusiasm, which is not the same as blindness. Thus, she notes absences in the works she admires so readily: in the *Lettres sur Rousseau*, for instance, she writes, "il ne nous semble pas cependant qu'elle ait tout dit"—notably, the way that Rousseau's *Emile* (1762) reveals the rights of man. One feels, writes Allart in the masculine, "fier et libre après l'avoir lu."

This passage of Allart's is describing the same work of Rousseau's to which Genlis was responding in 1782, but it feels like we are in a different universe. Allart swims gladly in the sea of enthusiasm into which Genlis dips her toe. Allart's is undeniably a critical approach, though perhaps an uncommon one today; in 1824, year of the *Chambre retrouvée* with its crushing Ultra majority, this gushing Romantic praise for Staël

---

2   There is a book on the topic: André Billy, *Hortense et ses amants, Chateaubriand, Sainte-Beuve, etc.* (Paris: Flammarion, 1961).

and Rousseau together was cutting edge. Thus, Allart writes of the Revolution: "parmi les progrès de la raison humaine qui l'ont produite, Rousseau a fait faire les plus forts, les plus hardis et les plus rapides." The work deserves some attention for that Romantic liberalism as well, in the allegedly 'preromantic' decade before 1830's *bataille d'Hernani*.

Works

Allart, Hortense, *Lettres sur les ouvrages de Madame de Staël* (Paris: Bossange, 1824)

Gertrude (Paris: Dupont, 1828)

L'Indienne, suivi du Convict (Paris: Vimont, 1833)

Settimia (Bruxelles: Wahlen, 1836)

La Femme et la démocratie de nos temps (Paris: Delaunay et Pinard, 1836)

Histoire de la république de Florence (Paris: Delloye, 1843)

Novum organum ou sainteté philosophique (Paris: Garnier frères, 1857)

Essai sur la religion intérieure (Paris: chez tous les libraires, 1864)

Les enchantements de Prudence, Avec George Sand (Paris: Michel Lévy, 1873)

Les nouveaux enchantements (Paris: C. Lévy, 1873)

Derniers enchantements (Paris: M. Lévy, 1874)

Lettres inédites à Sainte-Beuve (1841–1848) avec une introduction et des notes, ed. Léon Séché (Paris: Société du Mercure de France, 1908)

Lettere inedite a Gino Capponi (Genova: Tolozzi, 1961)

Nouvelles lettres à Sainte-Beuve, 1832–1864 ; les lettres de la collection Lovenjoul (Genève: Droz, 1965)

Sources

Bertelà, Maddalena, *Hortense Allart entre Madame de Staël et George Sand, ou, Les femmes et la démocratie* (Pisa: Edizioni ETS, 1999)

Billy, André, *Hortense et ses amants, Chateaubriand, Sainte-Beuve, etc.* (Paris: Flammarion, 1961)

Charton, Ariane, *Le Roman d'Hortense* (Paris: Albin Michel, 2009)

Ciureanu, Petre, *Hortense Allart e Anna Woodcock; con lettere inedite* (Genoa: Tolozzi, 1961)

Decreus, Juliette, *Henry Bulwer-Lytton et Hortense Allart, d'après des documents inédits* (Paris: Minard, 1961)

Dupêchez, Charles, *Hortense et Marie. Une si belle amitié (1838–1876)* (Paris: Flammarion, 2018)

Hollstein Hansen, Helynne, *Hortense Allart: The Woman and the Novelist* (Lanham, MD: University Press of America, 1998)

Séché, Léon, *Hortense Allart de Méritens dans ses rapports avec Chateaubriand, Béranger, Lamennais, Sainte-Beuve, G. Sand, Mme d'Agoult* (Paris: Mercure de France, 1908)

Vier, Jacques, *La comtesse d'Agoult et Hortense Allart de Meritens sous le Second Empire d'après une correspondance inédite* (Paris: Lettres modernes, 1960)

Walton, Whitney, *Eve's Proud Descendants: Four Women Writers and Republican Politics in Nineteenth-century France* (Stanford, CA: Stanford University Press, 2000)

24. Flore Célestine Thérèse Henriette Tristán y Moscoso [Flora Tristan]
7 April 1803–14 November 1844

Fig. 24. Flore Célestine Thérèse Henriette Tristán y Moscoso [Flora Tristan], by J. Laure. Photo by FreCha (2018). Wikimedia, https://upload.wikimedia.org/wikipedia/commons/8/80/Flora_Tristan_par_Jules_Laure.jpg, CC BY 4.0.

Pérégrinations d'une paria

Péruviens,

J'ai cru qu'il pourrait résulter quelque bien pour vous de ma relation : c'est pourquoi je vous en fais hommage. Vous serez surpris sans doute, qu'une personne qui fait si rarement usage d'épithètes laudatives en parlant de vous ait songé à vous dédier son ouvrage. Il en est des peuples comme des individus : moins ils sont avancés et plus susceptible est leur amour-propre. Ceux d'entre vous qui liront ma relation en prendront d'abord de l'animosité contre moi, et ce ne sera que par un effort de philosophie que quelques-uns me rendront justice. Le blâme qui porte à faux est chose vaine ; fondé, il irrite ; et, conséquemment, est une des plus grandes preuves de l'amitié. J'ai vécu parmi vous un accueil tellement bienveillant, qu'il faudrait que je fusse un monstre d'ingratitude pour nourrir contre le Pérou des sentiments hostiles. Il n'est personne qui désire plus sincèrement que je le fais votre prospérité actuelle, vos progrès à venir. Ce vœu de mon cœur domine ma pensée, et, voyant que vous faisiez fausse route, que vous ne songiez pas, avant tout, à harmoniser vos mœurs avec l'organisation politique que vous avez adoptée, j'ai eu le courage de le dire, au risque de froisser votre orgueil national.

J'ai dit, après l'avoir reconnu, qu'au Pérou, la haute classe est profondément corrompue, que son égoïsme la porte, pour satisfaire sa cupidité, son amour du pouvoir et ses autres passions, aux tentatives les plus anti-sociales ; j'ai dit aussi que l'abrutissement du peuple est extrême dans toutes les races dont il se compose. Ces deux situations ont toujours, chez toutes les nations, réagi l'une sur l'autre. L'abrutissement du peuple fait naître l'immoralité dans les hautes classes, et cette immoralité se propage et arrive, avec toute la puissance acquise dans sa course, aux derniers échelons de la hiérarchie sociale [...]

Le Pérou était, de toute l'Amérique, le pays le plus avancé en civilisation, lors de sa découverte par les Espagnols ; cette circonstance doit faire présumer favorablement des dispositions natives de ses habitants et des ressources qu'il offre. Puisse un gouvernement progressif, appelant à son aide les arts de l'Asie et de l'Europe, faire reprendre aux Péruviens ce rang parmi les nations du Nouveau-Monde ! C'est le souhait bien sincère que je forme.

Votre compatriote et amie,
Flora Tristan
Paris, Août 1836.[1]

---

1   Flora Tristan, *Pérégrinations d'une paria*, 2 vols (Paris: Indigo, 1999), I, pp. 7–8.

   Translation: Peruvians,
   I thought some good could come for you from my narrative: that is why I make you an offering of it. You will doubtless be surprised, that a person who so rarely makes use of laudative epithets in speaking of you might think to dedicate her work to you. It is with peoples as with individuals: the less they are advanced, the more susceptible is their vanity. Those of you who will read my relation will at first feel animosity against me, and it will only be by an effort of philosophy that some of you will do me justice. Blame which goes awry is a vain thing; founded, it irritates; and consequently, it is one of the greatest proofs of friendship. I received among you so benevolent a welcome, that I would have to be a monster of ingratitude to nourish hostile sentiments against Peru. No person desires

24. Flore Célestine Thérèse Henriette Tristán y Moscoso

Flore Célestine Thérèse Henriette Tristán y Moscoso [Flora Tristan] was born in Paris and died in Bordeaux, daughter of Mariano de Tristán y Moscoso, a Peruvian aristocrat, and Anne Pierre Laisnay, a Parisian bourgeoise who had emigrated to Spain during the Revolution. The couple were married by a refractory priest, but Mariano never took the time to regularize his marriage. He died soon after their return to Paris in 1807, a blow which affected Flora's existence. She notes in the *Pérégrinations* (1838): "Mon enfance heureuse s'acheva, à quatre ans et demi, à la mort de mon Père." Absent a civil marriage, Flora's mother was unable to prove her right to the family's home in Vaugirard; they were expelled from it and the property was seized by the state. Flora imagined herself a descendant of Moctezuma II or a daughter of Simón Bolívar, a frequent houseguest. Bolívar however left Bilbao over nine months before Flora's birth, making his paternity unlikely. Mother's and daughter's financial hardship helped precipitate her marriage at seventeen to André Chazal, for whose brother she worked as a colorist. The idyll ended quickly: he was jealous, mediocre, and violent. Flora read Rousseau, Lamartine, and above all Staël, managing to escape in 1825 while pregnant with their third child Aline, future mother of Paul Gauguin. She obtained a separation of goods in 1828, living thereafter under assumed names to escape her husband. For ten years, she

---

more sincerely than myself your current prosperity, your progress to come. This wish of my heart dominates my thought, and seeing that you were on a false path, that you were not thinking, above all, to harmonize your customs with the political organization you have adopted, I had the courage to say it, at the risk of offending your national pride.

I said, after having recognized it, that in Peru, the upper class is profoundly corrupted, that its egoism leads it, in order to satisfy its cupidity, its love of power and other passions, to the most antisocial attempts; I also said that the stupidity of the people is extreme in all the races of which it is composed. These two situations have always, among every nation, reacted the one to the other. The stupidity of the people gives birth to the immorality of the upper classes, and this immorality propagates itself and arrives, with all the power collected in its course, at the last steps of the social hierarchy [...]

Peru was, of all America, the land most advanced in civilization, at its discovery by the Spanish; this circumstance must make for favorable presumptions as to the native dispositions of its inhabitants and the resources it offers. May a progressive government, calling to its aid the arts of Asia and Europe, allow Peruvians to resume this rank among the nations of the New World! This is the quite sincere wish I form.

Your compatriot and friend,
Flora Tristan
Paris, August 1836.

traveled, working as a lady's companion while completing the education she had missed as a child. The period features in her 1840 *Promenades dans Londres*. Her maternal family however sided with Chazal, so Flora placed Aline at an institution and left for Peru hoping to be recognized by her paternal family. She there presented herself as single. Her uncle in Arequipa, who lodged her, denied her her father's full inheritance, granting her just one fifth of the estate as a natural child and agreeing to pay her a pension for some years.[2] Flora then returned to France after a short stay in Lima, with her first book in the making, *Pérégrinations d'une paria*. It was to appear in 1838; her uncle suppressed her pension, but the funds she had already received let her live free from financial worry. Meanwhile, reaching Paris in 1835, Flora was located by Chazal, who abducted Aline. Years of custody battles ensued, with Aline fleeing her father after a second abduction to rejoin her mother amid allegations of violence and incest. Chazal was released after some months in prison: Flora obtained a French 'separation of body' in 1838. That year, Chazal punctured her lung with a pistol shot. He returned to prison for twenty years, and Flora was at last able to use her name Tristan. She committed herself to organizing the working classes, in a religious framework alien to Marx or Engels. She published *L'Union ouvrière* in 1843. Proudhon knew her, Marx cites her. Today, Tristan increasingly appears to be a major and tireless fighter in the history of socialism and of women's rights. Paid subscribers to her work included Béranger, Victor Considérant, George Sand, Eugène Sue, Agricol Perdiguier, Paul de Kock, Desbordes-Valmore, Louis Blanc and others. She died of typhoid fever in Bordeaux, perhaps aggravated by the bullet wound. André Breton wrote of her, "Il n'est peut-être pas de destinée féminine qui, au firmament de l'esprit, laisse un sillage aussi long et aussi lumineux."[3]

"L'affranchissement des travailleurs," writes Tristan, "sera l'œuvre des travailleurs eux-mêmes." This is a ringing, revolutionary formulation, as is the following formulation, also her work: "L'homme le plus opprimé peut opprimer un être, qui est sa femme. Elle est le prolétaire du prolétaire même." Tristan's life was ruined by her marriage

---

2   Flora Tristan, *Pérégrinations d'une paria* (Biarritz: Transhumance, 2014), pp. 234–239.
3   *Flora Tristan. La Paria et son rêve*, ed. Stéphane Michaud (Paris: Sorbonne Nouvelle, 2003), p. 8.

at seventeen to a man who eventually shot her in the chest; in France from 1816 to 1884, divorce was illegal, and the best Tristan could do was see him imprisoned for twenty years, after his early release the first time. She fled the country more than once, hence her 1840 *Promenades dans Londres* and her 1838 *Pérégrinations d'une paria*, dedicated to the people of Peru. The word *paria* was given to French by Bernardin de Saint-Pierre in *La Chaumière indienne* (1791); few words are, one might argue, more quintessentially Romantic. In Jean Valjean, in Heathcliff and Jane Eyre, in Faust and Don Giovanni, Europe's Romantic writers celebrated the outcast, the Promethean rebel, the pariah. Tristan's arresting title was thus well-chosen for a Romantic age. Her writings, however, are generally shelved with politics, not with literature, and it is as an uncompromising socialist that she is remembered today. Not a Marxist—her framework is mystical, and she died four years before the *Communist Manifesto* (1848)—but a precursor, she is part of the current of mystical socialism in France that included Saint-Simon, Fourier, and Lamennais, not to mention the later Victor Hugo, chronicled in Frank-Paul Bowman's *Le Christ des barricades* (1987). Tristan, in short, made something of her life.

In this opening dedication, Tristan appeals to the people of Peru, once the most advanced civilization in all America, she writes, now groaning under the dead hand of civil and religious corruption. Tristan, like the excommunicated Lamennais, is no friend of the established church. The book caused a scandal in newly independent Peru—Tristan had known the Liberator Bolívar as a child in Vaugirard—and it ended her pension from her uncle. Tristan might have guessed as much, but that likely would not have stopped her: she saw her role as Messianic, speaking and fighting on behalf both of the working classes everywhere and of the proletarian's proletarians: the women of the world. Tristan's accident of ancestry—her father was a Peruvian aristocrat—turned her gaze to the developing world as it did few others in that age: Garibaldi, prior to Rome and Italy, fought for Uruguayan independence. This gives Tristan's writing a specific modern energy, a sort of authenticity rarely matched by the writers of the period, of either gender. One might find something analogous in the works of Gouges, who went to the guillotine for what she wrote. It is no surprise that Marx chose to cite Tristan in his writings.

Works

Tristan, Flora, *Pérégrinations d'une paria*, 2 vols (Paris: Indigo, 1999)

Nécessité de faire un bon accueil aux femmes étrangères (Paris: Delaunay, 1835)

Méphis (Paris: Ladvocat, 1838)

Promenades dans Londres (Paris: Delloye, 1840)

L'Union ouvrière, suivie de lettres de Flora Tristan, ed. Daniel Armogathe and Jacques Grandjonc (Paris: Éditions des Femmes, 1986)

Le Tour de France. Journal 1843–44, 2 vols (Paris: La Découverte, 1980)

L'Émancipation de la Femme ou Le Testament de la Paria (Paris: La Vérité, 1846)

Sources

Baelen, Jean, *La vie de Flora Tristan: socialisme et féminisme au XIXe siècle* (Paris: Éditions du Seuil, 1972)

Bloch-Dano, Évelyne, *Flora Tristan La Femme-messie* (Paris: Grasset, 2001)

Bloch-Dano, Évelyne, *Flora Tristan: « J'irai jusqu'à ce que je tombe »* (Paris: Éd. Payot & Rivages, 2006)

Bloch-Dano, Évelyne, *Flora Tristan: une femme libre* (Paris: Librairie générale française, 2018)

Cross, Máire and Gray, Tim, *The Feminism of Flora Tristan* (Oxford: Berg, 1992)

Cross, Máire Fedelma, *In the Footsteps of Flora Tristan: A Political Biography* (Liverpool: Liverpool University Press, 2020)

Debré, Jean-Louis and Bochenek, Valérie, *Ces femmes qui ont réveillé la France* (Paris: Fayard, 2013)

Desanti, Dominique, *Flora Tristan: la femme révoltée* (Paris: Hachette, 1972)

Gaudefroy, Olivier, *Flora Tristan: une insoumise sous le règne de Louis-Philippe* (Paris: Syllepse, 2022)

Gerhard, Leo, *Flora Tristan: la révolte d'une paria* (Paris: Les éditions de l'Atelier, 1994)

Hart, Kathleen, *Revolution and Women's Autobiography in Nineteenth-century France* (Amsterdam: Rodopi, 2004)

Iribarne González, María de la Macarena, *Flora Tristán y la tradición del feminismo socialista* (Madrid: Congreso de los Diputados, 2012)

Krulic, Brigitte, *Flora Tristan* (Paris: Gallimard, 2022)

Leprohon, Pierre, *Flora Tristan* (Antony: Éditions Corymbe, 1979)

Michaud, Stéphane, ed., *Un fabuleux destin: Flora Tristan* (Dijon: éditions universitaires de Dijon, 1985)

Michaud, Stéphane, *Flora Tristan: La paria et son rêve* (Paris: Sorbonne nouvelle, 2003)

Perrot, Michelle, *Des femmes rebelles—Olympe de Gouges, Flora Tristan, George Sand* (Paris: Elyzad poche, 2014)

Puech, Jules-L., *La vie et l'œuvre de Flora Tristan: thèse principale pour le doctorat ès-lettres* (Paris: M. Rivière, 1925)

Sanchez, Luis Alberto, *Flora Tristán: una mujer sola contra el mundo* (Caracas: Biblioteca Ayacucho, 1992)

Sommella, Vincenzo, *Flora Tristan: vivere nell'avvenire* (Roma: Prospettiva, 2010)

25. Delphine Gay de Girardin [Vicomte de Launay]
24 January 1804–29 June 1855

Fig. 25. Delphine Gay de Girardin [Vicomte de Launay], by L. Hersent. Photo by PancoPinco (2015). Wikimedia, https://upload.wikimedia.org/wikipedia/commons/f/fa/Louis_Hersent_-_Delphine_de_Girardin.jpg, CC BY 4.0.

Lettres parisiennes du vicomte de Launay par Madame de Girardin

Lettre première

28 septembre 1836.
 Événement du jour. — Paris provincial. — L'Ennuyeux et l'Ennuyé. — Esméralda. — Thémistocle et Scipion l'Africain dénoncés au commandant de la garde nationale.
 Il n'est rien arrivé de bien extraordinaire cette semaine : une révolution en Portugal, une apparition de république en Espagne, une

nomination de ministres à Paris, une baisse considérable à la Bourse, un ballet nouveau à l'Opéra, et deux capotes de satin blanc aux Tuileries.

 La révolution de Portugal était prévue, la quasi-république était depuis longtemps prédite, le ministère d'avance était jugé, la baisse était exploitée, le ballet nouveau était affiché depuis trois semaines : il n'y a donc de vraiment remarquable que les capotes de satin blanc, parce qu'elles sont prématurées : le temps ne méritait pas cette injure. Qu'on fasse du feu au mois de septembre quand il fait froid, bien, cela est raisonnable : mais que l'on commence à porter du satin avant l'hiver, cela n'est pas dans la nature.

 Le spectacle et les promenades, voilà ce qui occupe la capitale en ce moment. Dieu merci, les courses sont terminées ; la dernière n'était point brillante : toujours les mêmes femmes, toujours les mêmes chevaux ; et puis toujours ce même et ennuyeux incident, ce cheval forcé de courir tout seul ; et l'on vous condamne à regarder niaisement ce lutteur sans adversaire, ce triomphateur sans rival. Depuis longtemps le *solo équestre* nous a paru la plus ingénieuse des mystifications. Bref, tout cela était médiocre et faisait dire aux mauvais plaisants que cette pauvre *Société d'encouragement* était toute découragée.[1]

Delphine Gay de Girardin [Vicomte de Launay] was born in Aix-la-Chapelle (Aachen) and died in Paris, daughter of Sophie Nichault de la Vallette, writer and *salonnière*, here featured, and of Jean Sigismond

---

1 Delphine Gay de Girardin, *Lettres parisiennes du vicomte de Launay par Madame de Girardin*, ed. Anne Martin-Figuier, 2 vols (Paris: Mercure de France, 1986), I pp. 9–10.

 Translation: 28 September 1836.
  Event of the day. — Provincial Paris. — The Boring and the Bored. — Esméralda. — Themistocles and Scipio Africanus denounced to the commander of the National Guard.
  Nothing very extraordinary happened this week: a revolution in Portugal, the appearance of a republic in Spain, a nomination of ministers in Paris, a considerable drop in the stock exchange, a new ballet at the opera, and two white satin hoods at the Tuileries.
  The revolution in Portugal was expected, the quasi-republic had for some time been predicted, the ministry was judged in advance, the drop was exploited, the new ballet posted for the past three weeks: the only remarkable thing, then, is the white satin hoods, because they are premature: the weather did not merit this insult. Let one make fires in the month of September when it is cold, good, that is reasonable: but let one begin to wear satin before winter, that is not in nature.
  The spectacle and the promenades, that is what occupies the capital at this moment. Thank the Lord, the races are over; the last was not brilliant: always the same women, always the same horses; and then always that same dull incident, that horse forced to run alone; and you are condemned to watch like a fool this fighter with no adversary, this victor with no rival. For ages now the *equestrian solo* has seemed to us the most ingenious of mystifications. In brief, all that was mediocre and made the ill-willed say that this poor *Encouragement Society* was quite discouraged.

Gay, receiver-general of the revolutionary department of the Roer. Delphine was raised in Aix-la-Chapelle and Paris in her mother's salon, named Delphine in honor of Staël's heroine and belonging like her mother to Nodier's romantic circle. By sixteen, she had met Vigny, Latouche, Soumet, and Émile Deschamps, publishing her first poems in *La Muse française*, followed by *Essais poétiques* (1824) and *Nouveaux Essais poétiques* (1825). Her marriage to Émile Delamothe, known as Émile de Girardin, in 1831, opened new literary horizons to her—notably her dazzling chronicles in the newspaper *La Presse*, published from 1836–1848 under the name of Charles de Launay, which had great success. Her best-known works of fiction include the novel *Le Marquis de Pontanges* (1835); a group of tales, *Contes d'une vieille fille à ses neveux* (1832); *La Canne de Monsieur de Balzac* (1836), and *Il ne faut pas jouer avec la douleur* (1853). Her prose and verse dramas include *L'École des journalistes* (1840); *Judith* (1843); *Cléopâtre* (1847); *Lady Tartuffe* (1853); and the one-act comedies *C'est la faute du mari* (1851), *La joie fait peur* (1854), *Le Chapeau d'un horloger* (1854), and *Une femme qui déteste son mari* (1856), which appeared posthumously. Girardin wielded a considerable influence on contemporary literary society, not least in her salon frequented by Gautier, Balzac, Musset, Hugo, Laure Junot d'Abrantès, Desbordes-Valmore, Lamartine, Janin, Sandeau, Liszt, Dumas *père*, and George Sand among others. She wrote under several pseudonyms.

Girardin, crowned like Staël's Corinne at the Capitol in Rome in 1827,[2] had by 1830 given up poetry for prose and the theatre, and this was likely a good thing. She was, as it happens, an unusually witty person, as seen both in her novels—*La Canne de Monsieur de Balzac* (1836)—and in her chronicles for *La Presse*. The loss of that wit would have diminished and impoverished the July Monarchy.

Our extract is her opening entry in *La Presse*, 28 September 1836. Girardin's method here is litotes or ironic understatement: nothing extraordinary has happened, she writes, just the usual revolution in Portugal, republic in Spain, new ministers in Paris, drop in the Stock Exchange, new ballet at the Opera, and two white satin hoods at the Tuileries (the royal palace). Girardin promptly explains how all but the satin hoods are routine, if not banal occurrences; the hoods, on the contrary, deserve attention. The very syntax puts major political

---

[2] *Encyclopedia Britannica*, 11th edition, "Girardin, Delphine de."

events on a par with fashion, then undercutting them by Girardin's insistence that the fashion *faux pas* is more significant. Here is a world, like Balzac's, in which economic and political realities are not invisible; they are simply thrown in the pot with fashion and reduced. This, one might say, is a voice which has seen a revolution or two and decided they are not worth the effort, the time and expense. Instead, in an almost Parnassian retreat, the voice will speak passionately and knowledgeably about white satin hoods in September. To which one might rejoin: is this mere frivolity, mere whipped cream? And the answer might be: on the contrary. Because the fashion *faux pas* is not on the streets of Paris, it is at the Tuileries: the speaker maintains a diplomatic discretion, but the conceit is that the entire July Monarchy belongs not to the earth-shaking world of revolutions and republics, but to the world of the fashion *faux pas*, of white satin hoods in September. It is a small place, and what it engages in are small things. It is no coincidence that the chronicles also feature fulsome praise of Louis Napoléon Bonaparte, the future Napoléon III; Louis Philippe, in a perhaps mistaken bid to outflank the legitimists, promoted the first Napoleon somewhat unrelentingly—the Arc de Triomphe, the Invalides in Paris—and the public was more than happy to find in the unremarkable nephew, who had never won a battle, a fitting heir to his uncle, that remarkable man. This is, in short, a world immediately familiar to readers of Balzac; but it also prepares the Second Empire, in all its puffery and disappointment. That, after all, is true of the July Monarchy itself.

Works

[Girardin, Delphine de], *Œuvres complètes de madame Émile de Girardin, née Delphine Gay*, 6 vols (Paris: Henri Plon, 1860–1861)

Lettres parisiennes du vicomte de Launay par Madame de Girardin, ed. Anne Martin-Figuier, 2 vols (Paris: Mercure de France, 1986)

Essais poétiques (Paris: Imprimerie de Gaultier-Laguionie, 1824)

Nouveaux essais poétiques (Paris: Urbain Canel, 1825)

Le Dernier Jour de Pompéi (Paris: P. Dupont, 1828)

Contes d'une vieille fille à ses neveux (Paris: Librairie de Charles Gosselin, 1832)

Le Lorgnon (Paris: Librairie Charles Gosselin, 1832)

La Canne de M. de Balzac (Paris: Librairie de Dumont, 1836)

L'école des Journalistes, comédie (Paris: Marchant, 1839)

Judith, tragédie (Paris: Tresse, 1843)

Cléopâtre, tragédie (Paris: M. Lévy, 1847)

C'est la faute du mari, comédie (Paris: M. Lévy, 1851)

Lady Tartufe, comédie (Brussels: Lelong, 1853)

La joie fait peur, comédie (Paris: M. Lévy, 1854)

Sources

Bondy, François, *Une femme d'esprit en 1830, Madame de Girardin* (Paris: Hachette, 1928)

Court-Perez, Françoise, ed., *Delphine de Girardin et son temps, actes de la journée d'étude organisée à l'Université de Rouen en juin 2015* (Rouen: CÉRÉdI, 2016)

Finch, Alison, *Women's Writing in Nineteenth-century France* (Cambridge: Cambridge University Press, 2000)

Gautier, Théophile, *Portraits et souvenirs littéraires* (Paris: Michel Lévy, 1875)

Giacchetti, Claudine, *Delphine de Girardin, la muse de Juillet* (Paris: L'Harmattan, 2004)

Johnston, Joyce Ann Carlton, *Laughing Fit to Kill: Aspects of Wit in the Works of Delphine Gay de Girardin* (Unpublished doctoral dissertation, Indiana University, 2001)

Lassère, Madeleine, *Delphine de Girardin: journaliste et femme de lettres au temps du romantisme* (Paris: Perrin, 2003)

Malo, Henri, *Une muse et sa mère: Delphine Gay de Girardin* (Paris: Émile-Paul Frères, 1924)

Malo, Henri, *La Gloire du vicomte de Launay, Delphine Gay de Girardin* (Paris: Émile-Paul, 1925)

Manecy, Jules, *Une famille de Savoie: celle de Delphine Gay* (Aix-les-Bains: E. Gérente, 1904)

Séché, Léon, *Muses romantiques: Delphine Gay, Mme de Girardin, dans ses rapports avec Lamartine, Victor Hugo, Balzac, Rachel, Jules Sandeau, Dumas, Eugène Sue et George Sand* (Paris: Mercure de France, 1910)

Thérenty, Marie-Ève, *Femmes de presse, femmes de lettres: de Delphine de Girardin à Florence Aubenas* (Paris: CNRS éditions, 2019)

26. Amantine Lucile Aurore Dupin, Baronne Dudevant [George Sand]
1 July 1804–8 June 1876

Fig. 26. Amantine Lucile Aurore Dupin, baronne Dudevant [George Sand], by A. Charpentier. Photo by Mathiasrex (2010). Wikimedia, https://upload.wikimedia.org/wikipedia/commons/e/ee/George_Sand.PNG, CC BY 4.0.

Les Maîtres Sonneurs

Première veillée

Je ne suis point né d'hier, disait, en 1828, le père Étienne. Je suis venu en ce monde, autant que je peux croire, l'année 54 ou 55 du siècle passé. Mais, n'ayant pas grande souvenance de mes premiers ans, je ne vous parlerai de moi qu'à partir du temps de ma première communion, qui eut lieu en 70, à la paroisse de Saint-Chartier, pour lors desservie par M. l'abbé Montpérou, lequel est aujourd'hui bien sourd et bien cassé.

Ce n'est pas que notre paroisse de Nohant fût supprimée dans ce temps-là ; mais notre curé étant mort, il y eut, pour un bout de temps, réunion des deux églises sous la conduite du prêtre de Saint-Chartier, et nous allions tous les jours à son catéchisme, moi, ma petite cousine, un gars appelé Joseph, qui demeurait en la même maison que mon oncle, et une douzaine d'autres enfants de chez nous.

Je dis mon oncle pour abréger, car il était mon grand-oncle, frère de ma grand'mère, et avait nom Brulet, d'où sa petite-fille, étant seule héritière de son lignage, était appelée Brulette, sans qu'on fît jamais mention de son nom de baptême, qui était Catherine.

Et, pour vous dire tout de suite les choses comme elles étaient, je me sentais déjà d'aimer Brulette plus que je n'y étais obligé comme cousin, et j'étais jaloux que Joseph demeurait avec elle dans un petit logis distant d'une portée de fusil des dernières maisons du bourg, et du mien d'un quart de lieue de pays : de manière qu'il la voyait à toute heure, et qu'avant le temps qui nous rassembla au catéchisme, je ne la voyais pas tous les jours.[1]

Amantine Lucile Aurore Dupin, Baronne Dudevant [George Sand] was born in Paris in 1804 and died in the château of Nohant-Vic in 1876. Daughter of Maurice Dupin de Francueil, who died in 1808, and of Sophie Victoire Delaborde, she wrote over seventy novels and fifty volumes of diverse works including tales, plays, and political tracts, a lady of infinite variety. Sand caused scandals in her love life and also in fashions she started: masculine dress, a male pseudonym. At Nohant,

---

1   George Sand, *Les Maîtres Sonneurs*, ed. P. Salomon and J. Mallion (Paris: Garnier, 1980), pp. 7–9.

   Translation: First Watch
   I was not born yesterday, said, in 1828, Old Étienne. I came into this world, as much as I can believe it, in the year 54 or 55 of the last century. But, not having great recollection of my first years, I will speak to you of me only from the time of my first communion, which happened in 70, in the parish of Saint-Chartier, then served by M. the abbé Montpérou, who today is quite deaf and quite broken.
   It is not that our parish of Nohant was suppressed in that time; but our curate being dead, there was, for a patch of time, a union of the two churches under the conduct of the Saint-Chartier priest, and we went every day to his catechism, me, my little cousin, a lad named Joseph, who lived in the same house as my uncle, and a dozen other children from our village.
   I say my uncle to be brief, because he was my great-uncle, my grandmother's brother, and his name was Brulet, which is why his granddaughter, being the only heir to his line, was named Brulette, without our ever using her baptismal name, which was Catherine.
   And to tell you at once things as they were, I already felt myself loving Brulette more than I was obliged to as a cousin, and I was jealous that Joseph stayed with her in a little lodging a rifle shot away from the last houses of the town, and a quarter of a league of countryside from mine: so that he saw her at all hours, and before the time that brought us together for catechism, I did not see her every day.

she welcomed Liszt, Chopin, d'Agoult, Balzac, Flaubert, Delacroix, and others. She corresponded with Hugo, though the two never met, and sought his pardon from Napoléon III.[2] She inspired Ledru-Rollin and helped found three newspapers. Her works often feature the Berry countryside, from her first feminist novels of revolt—*Indiana* (1832), *Lélia* (1833)—to her novels describing proletarians—*Le Compagnon du Tour de France, Mauprat* (1837)—or peasants—*La Mare au diable* (1846), *François le Champi* (1848), *La Petite Fadette* (1849), *Les Maîtres sonneurs* (1853). She also wrote autobiography—*Histoire de ma vie* (1855). Her plays were largely unpublished in her lifetime. Aurore was raised in Nohant by her mother and grandmother, with two years in a convent from 1818 to 1820. In 1822, her mother broke with the paternal family to bring Aurore to Paris. The two soon quarreled; Aurore met François Casimir Dudevant, a lawyer at the royal court, and married him that same year. A prenuptial agreement preserved for Aurore her 500,000-franc fortune. The couple returned to Nohant. In 1824, Casimir slapped her in public; he also began drinking and having affairs. Aurore's first liaison, between 1827 and 1828, raises some questions about the paternity of her daughter Solange. She met Jules Sandeau during July 1830, moving to Paris in 1831 for a sort of *vie de Bohême*. She and Sandeau wrote the novel *Rose et Blanche* (1831) for the *Figaro* run by Henri de Latouche and signed it J. Sand. *Indiana* followed in 1832, then *Valentine* three months later, making George Sand famous. She broke with Sandeau and had a brief, unhappy liaison with Mérimée. In 1833, *Lélia* followed, to great success. That year, Sand formed an intimate friendship with Marie Dorval which caused some scandal; she also met Alfred de Musset, who moved in with her. In December, they left for Italy, where both fell gravely ill and each was unfaithful, ending their liaison but not their correspondence. Sand wrote *Mattea* (1835), *Leone Leoni* (1835), *André* (1834), and *Jacques* (1833), then returned to France. Attempted reconciliations followed, and later, memoirs on every side. A liaison with Michel de Bourges helped to make of Sand a republican, under police surveillance. Musset also introduced Sand to Liszt, who became a close friend; come 1836, Sand was visiting d'Agoult's salon alongside Liszt, Lamennais—excommunicated after his *Paroles d'un croyant* (1834)—Heine, Mickiewicz, and Chopin.

---

2 *George Sand. Victor Hugo. Correspondance croisée*, ed. Danielle Bahiaoui (Nîmes: HB Éditions, 2004), pp. 19–26.

Lamennais and, by Sainte-Beuve's intermediary, Pierre Leroux had a great impact on Sand's move toward socialism and mark her novels, as did her later friendship with Louis Blanc. Her liaison with Chopin began in 1838; it lasted ten years, ending when Solange married the sculptor Clésinger and broke with her mother. The failure of the 1848 Revolution left Sand wondering whether peoples can be happy; in 1852, she wrote several letters to the new emperor asking for clemency for his political opponents. In 1857, she met Flaubert at a dinner with Gautier, the Goncourt brothers, Renan, Taine, Dumas *fils*, and Sainte-Beuve. Sand is among the first Frenchwomen to live by her pen, a life made possible by the spread in literacy during the nineteenth century. She faced misogyny, indeed scandal, and overcame it, though neglected for decades after her death, and even Virginia Woolf questions her use of a pseudonym.[3] She reinvented herself more than once, becoming in the end the *bonne dame de Nohant* whose works now appear in the Pléiade. No woman writer in this book better engineered her posterity.

This is our only text published under the Second Empire. In brief, the July Monarchy fell in February 1848 to a revolution that brought in the Second Republic. On 10 December 1848, Louis Napoléon Bonaparte won a surprise 74% of the popular vote for president. He then proclaimed himself president for life, and emperor in January 1852. "History repeats itself," wrote Marx about these exact events, "first as tragedy, then as farce." *Les Maîtres Sonneurs* appeared the following year.

In 1853, Sand was the best-known woman writer in France, famous since *Indiana* in 1832. From early scandal she had moved to socialism and republicanism around 1836, and then later retired to Nohant to write novels about peasant life. Since Sand began her career as a *révoltée*, one may ask whether this was the settling of age or rather a new revolt, a reinvention of herself as *la bonne dame de Nohant*, a demonstration of mastery and independence. Perhaps it was both. In any case, above is the opening of *Les Maîtres Sonneurs*.

On 10 December 1848, the French intelligentsia discovered to its surprise that 74% of France wanted no part of their republic; they wanted an emperor back. Sand remarked in 1849, "mon cœur est un

---

3 Virginia Woolf, *A Room of One's Own*, ed. David Bradshaw and Stuart N. Clarke (Oxford: Wiley & Sons, 2015), p. 37.

cimetière,"[4] and one imagines that the crushing of her republican hopes had their share in her disappointment. It seems reasonable to argue that Sand's series of peasant novels (1846–1853) reflect in part this nagging truth. If Sand is to speak for France, how can she ignore three quarters of the nation? This is perhaps one reason our extract not only focuses on peasant life; it is narrated by *le père Étienne*, in a Berry dialect that rings true to me at least—*souvenance, mes premiers ans*. That is part of the enduring appeal of this text, and it distinguishes Sand's voice here from, say, Duras's Ourika, who speaks with the elegance of the Beauvau family, or Daniel Stern's *Nélida* (1846), which opens on a peasant scene described by an urbane narrator. There is of course more to this great novel—it leaves us wondering, for instance, whether Joset sells his soul to the devil for his art—but it is perhaps fitting to resituate the play of the fantastic, as in those two other novels in Sand's peasant series, *La Petite Fadette* (1849) and *La Mare au diable* (1846), in the rural landscape from which they all spring. Just as Sand hears the true voice of her peasant narrator, so she works hard to indicate his mindset, the milieu he inhabits in which magic is perhaps less startling than to a Parisian reader. Perhaps this work of discovery and reclamation would let Sand and her readers better understand how the nation chose Napoléon le Petit to end the republic of which she had dreamed, preferring to have that little man sit on a throne above it.

Selected Works

Sand wrote over a hundred novels and short stories, from 1829 as Aurore Dudevant (some with Jules Sandeau), then from *Indiana* in 1832 as George Sand. A critical edition of her complete works is in progress.

Sand, George, *Les Maîtres Sonneurs*, ed. P. Salomon and J. Mallion (Paris: Garnier, 1980) [1853]

Indiana, 2 vols (Paris: H. Dupuy, 1832)

Lélia, 2 vols (Paris: Dupuy & Tenré, 1833)

Lettres d'un voyageur, 2 vols (Paris: Bonnaire, 1837)

---

[4] Évelyne Bloch-Dano, *Le Dernier Amour de George Sand* (Paris: Éditions Grasset, 2010), p. 11.

Mauprat, 2 vols (Paris: Bonnaire, 1837)

Le Compagnon du tour de France, 2 vols (Paris: Perrotin, 1840)

Consuelo, 8 vols (Paris: L. de Potter, 1843)

La Comtesse de Rudolstadt, 5 vols (Paris: L. de Potter, 1844)

Le Péché de Monsieur Antoine (Lunel: Ararauna, 2021) [1845]

La Mare au diable (Paris: Gallimard, 1999) [1846]

François le Champi (Paris: Gallimard, 2005) [1848]

La Petite Fadette (Paris: Gallimard, 2004) [1849]

Histoire de ma vie, 1855 in *Œuvres autobiographiques*, 2 vols (Paris: Gallimard, 1978)

Elle et Lui (Paris: Hachette, 1859)

Monsieur Sylvestre (Paris: M. Lévy, 1866)

Contes d'une grand'mère (Paris: Maxi-Livres, 2005) [1873/1876]

Journal intime, 1834 in *Œuvres autobiographiques*, 2 vols (Paris: Gallimard, 1978)

Théâtre, 17 vols (Paris: Indigo & côté femmes, 1997–2009)

Lubin, Georges, *Correspondance: 1812–1876*, 25 vols (Paris: Classiques Garnier, 1964–1991)

Lubin, Georges, *Correspondance: suppléments 1821–1876*, vol. 26 (Tusson: Éditions du Lérot, 1995)

Sources

There are over a hundred monographs and conference proceedings devoted to George Sand. A selection follows.

Bernard-Griffiths, Simone and Auraix-Jonchière, Pascale, eds, *Dictionnaire George Sand*, 2 vols (Paris: Champion, 2015)

Bouchardeau, Huguette, *George Sand: la lune et les sabots* (Paris: Editions Robert Laffont, 1990)

Brem, Anne-Marie de, *Le Monde de George Sand* (Paris: Editions du Patrimoine, 2004)

Canavaggio, Pierre, *George Sand et Alfred de Musset: les amants impossibles* (Paris: Alphée-Jean-Paul Bertrand, 2009)

Caors, Marielle, *George Sand: de voyages en romans* (Paris: Royer, 1993)

Caors, Marielle, *George Sand et les arts: Actes du colloque international organisé du 5 au 9 septembre 2004 au Château d'Ars* (Clermont-Ferrand: Presses universitaires Blaise-Pascal, 2006)

Chauvel, Geneviève, *Le roman d'amour de George Sand* (Clermont-Ferrand: De Borée, 2018)

Dauphin, Noëlle, ed., *George Sand: Terroir et histoire* (Rennes, Presses universitaires de Rennes, 2006)

Diaz, Brigitte and Hoog-Naginski, Isabelle, eds, *George Sand: pratiques et imaginaires de l'écriture* (Caen: Presses universitaires de Caen, 2006)

Didier, Béatrice, *George Sand écrivain: un grand fleuve d'Amérique* (Paris: Presses universitaires de France, 1998)

Dufour, Hortense, *George Sand: la somnambule* (Monaco: du Rocher, 2004)

Greilsamer, Claire and Laurent, *Dictionnaire George Sand* (Paris: Perrin, 2014)

Harvey, Cynthia, ed., *Les règles du jeu au féminin: Indiana ou la conquête d'un espace de liberté* (University of Quebec at Rimouski: Tangence, 2010)

Jack, Belinda Elizabeth, ed., *George Sand: A Woman's Life Writ Large* (New York: Alfred A. Knopf, 2000)

James, Henry (trans. Jean Pavans), *George Sand* (Paris: Mercure de France, 2004)

Karénine, Wladimir, *George Sand: sa vie et ses œuvres*, 4 vols (Paris: Plon, 1899–1926)

Laporte, Dominique, Powell, David, and Daunais, Isabelle, eds, *Née romancier je fais des romans ...: George Sand et ses personnages 1804–2004* (Laval: Département des littératures de l'Université Laval, 2003)

Lubin, Georges, *George Sand en Berry* (Paris: Hachette, 1967)

Lubin, Georges, *Album Sand* (Paris, Gallimard, 1973)

Margerie, Diane de, *Aurore et George* (Paris: Albin Michel, 2004)

Martin-Dehaye, Sophie, *George Sand et la peinture* (Paris: Royer, 2006)

Maurois, André, *Lélia: ou la vie de George Sand* (Paris: Hachette, 1952)

Powell, David, *Le Siècle de George Sand* (Amsterdam: Rodopi, 1998)

Rastoueix-Guinot, Brigitte, *George Sand — Marie Dorval — Jules Sandeau: histoire intime* (Paris: L'Harmattan, 2015)

Reid, Martine, *George Sand: Biographie* (Paris: Folio, 2013)

27. Louise Angélique Bertin
15 January 1805–26 April 1877

Fig. 27. Louise Angélique Bertin, by V. Mottez. Photo by Adam Cuerden (2019). Wikimedia, https://upload.wikimedia.org/wikipedia/commons/9/98/Louise_Bertin_by_Victor_Mottez.jpg, CC BY 4.0.

Glanes

L'aube n'a point encor repris sa robe blanche
    Et sera longue à s'en vêtir ;
Mais l'épi mûr là-haut depuis hier se penche ;
    « Allons ! enfants, il faut partir !

– Non, ce n'est pas le jour, non mère, c'est la lune
    Qui, dans la chambre, vient danser ;
C'est son rayon tremblant sur notre armoire brune
    Que devant toi tu vois passer. »

La mère, pétrissant une blonde farine,
    Prépare le repas du jour ;
Et près du four brûlant une vieille voisine
    Viendra veiller jusqu'au retour.

> Puis elle appelle encor ; et si l'enfant ne cède,
>   Sa rude main l'a secoué,
> Car le jour qui paraît doit, au jour qui précède,
>   Par le travail être noué.
>
> Les enfants paresseux, à cette voix sévère,
>   Enfin se lèvent en pleurant,
> Et tous, d'un pas boudeur, de la pauvre chaumière
>   Ils s'éloignent en murmurant.
>
> La mère vigilante, à travers la montagne,
>   A chacun montre le chemin,
> Gourmande le plus grand qui court dans la campagne,
>   Soutient le petit par la main.
>
> Si, comme en un sentier, dans le ruisseau limpide,
>   Les enfants, pieds nus, vont courir,
> Et s'arrêtent craintifs au courant trop rapide,
>   Elle est là pour les secourir.
>
> Ils implorent son aide, et de leurs mains vermeilles
>   S'attachent à son tablier,
> Comme on voit se suspendre une grappe d'abeilles
>   A la fleur qu'elle fait plier.[1]

Louise Angélique Bertin was born in Roches near Bièvres in 1805 and died in Paris in 1877. Daughter of Louis François Bertin, owner of the *Journal des Débats*, and of Geneviève Aimée Victoire Boutard,

---

1   Louise Angélique Bertin, *Glanes* (Paris: René, 1842), pp. 3–4.

    Translation: Dawn has not yet taken back up its white robe / And will be long to dress itself in it; / But the ripe ear up there has been leaning since yesterday; / "Come! children, we must leave!

    No, it is not day, no mother, it's the Moon / Which, in the bedroom, comes dancing; / It is its trembling ray on our brown wardrobe / That you see passing before you."

    The mother, kneading a blond flour, / Prepares the day's meal; / And near the burning stove an old neighbor / Will come watch till their return.

    Then she calls again; and if the child does not yield, / Her rough hand will have shaken him, / For the day which appears must, to the day which precedes, / Be linked by work.

    The lazy children, at this severe voice, / Get up at last while crying, / And all, with a sulky step, from the poor cottage / They depart grumbling.

    The watchful mother, across the mountain, / Shows to each the path, / Scolds the biggest who runs in the fields, / Holds the little one by the hand.

    If, as in a path, in the limpid brook, / The children, barefoot, go running, / And stop fearful at the too-rapid current, / She is there to help them.

    They ask her aid, and with their red hands / Cling to her apron, / As one sees a cluster of bees hang itself / from the flower it makes bend.

Louise Angélique was taught by her father after 1811, when France's independent press ended for a time, while her mother, a pianist, likely taught her that instrument. She studied voice with François Joseph Fétis, along with Italian-style composition. For counterpoint, she turned to Reicha, also the teacher of Berlioz and Liszt. Her major works were operas: *Fausto* (1831) and an opéra-comique, *Le Loup-garou* (1827), with libretto by Scribe, which garnered some success. In 1836, the Opéra staged a grander work, *La Esmeralda*, performed for only six nights due to rowdy audiences reflecting her father's exposed political position.[2] Victor Hugo wrote the libretto but faced censorship in his turn; his *Le Roi s'amuse* similarly closed after one performance in 1832. Critics were condescending to this disabled woman—after contracting polio, she walked with crutches—seeing in her work consolations for her physical infirmity, where Berlioz, who is something of an authority, thought her harmony "virile, forte et neuve," adding "Mlle Bertin est l'une des têtes de femmes les plus fortes de notre temps."[3] This failure may have discouraged the composer from trying again. Bertin also left twelve cantatas, some instrumental work including six ballades for the piano, five chamber symphonies (all manuscript), and two volumes of poetry, the first awarded a prize by the Académie française. Berlioz dedicated to her the first version of his *Les Nuits d'été*, op. 7, in 1841.

Bertin awaits rediscovery as a composer, and there is argument she merits it. Our focus however is on her two volumes of lyric poetry; let us begin by suggesting that this piece is not the equal of Desbordes-Valmore's "Les Roses de Saadi" (written 1848, published 1860). That however is a high bar. On publication in 1842, *Glanes* won a prize from the Académie française, so the Académie found value in this collection. First, in this poem's plot, there is some blurring of boundaries between the human protagonists and the botany that opens and closes the piece. We have, then, a mother readying her children for the day. They are off, but Bertin won't say where they are headed. Are they gleaning, as the collection's title might suggest? The poems are all untitled and this one gives no reason to think that; indeed, the mother has "une blonde farine" to hand already. What we have instead is a somewhat traditional

---

2   Michèle Friang and Pierrette Germain, *Louise Bertin, compositrice, amie de Victor Hugo* (Sampzon: Éditions Delatour France, 2019), pp. 55–70.

3   Friang and Germain, *Louise Bertin*, p. 68.

vision of mother and children—a mother hen of sorts—with touches to reduce the risk of cliché here: she has a "rude main" and a "voix sévère", yet she is "là pour les secourir" as needed. Bertin might have done better with another subject—I've found no evidence that she had children—but the range of topics on offer to women poets in 1842 was more limited than today, and she did please the Académie. Let's turn then to the music and the metaphors. Structurally, this is eight quatrains of alternating masculine and feminine rhymes as well as of alexandrines and octosyllables. The form is demanding and Bertin seems at ease within it, though there is a moment—"Non, ce n'est pas le jour, non mère..."—where the repeated "non" is somewhat clunky. As for metaphors, perhaps the opening "épi mûr" is indeed a presage of gleaning, though harvesters go unmentioned; in counterargument, the family are in "la montagne", which is not really gleaning country. Let us leave the opening "épi mûr" as unexplained as Bertin makes it. The closing metaphor, for its part, is lovely: the children hang at their mother's apron as a "grappe"—perfect word, meaning a cluster or bunch of grapes—of bees hangs at a flower. The rather Lamartinian poem perhaps began with that very observation. In all, this is a flawed poem, but one sees why it might appeal to the Académie in 1842. Bertin's music seems her strong suit, if Berlioz's testimony counts for something, as one imagines it should. Perhaps this is why she waited thirty years before publishing another poetry collection.

Works

Bertin, Louise, *Glanes* (Paris: René, 1842)

Nouvelles glanes (Paris: Charpentier, 1876)

Sources

Boneau, Denise Lynn, *Louise Bertin and Opera in Paris in the 1820s and 1830s* (Unpublished doctoral dissertation, University of Chicago, 1989)

Friang, Michèle and Germain, Pierrette, *Louise Bertin, compositrice, amie de Victor Hugo* (Sampzon: Éditions Delatour France, 2019)

28. Marie Catherine Sophie de Flavigny, Comtesse d'Agoult [Daniel Stern]
31 December 1805–5 March 1876

Fig. 28. Marie Catherine Sophie de Flavigny, comtesse d'Agoult [Daniel Stern], by H. Lehmann. Photo by B2Belgium (2019). Wikimedia, https://upload.wikimedia.org/wikipedia/commons/6/69/%22Marie_de_Flavigny%22_de_Henri_Lehmann_%28Petit_Palais%2C_Paris%29_%2848740090161%29.jpg, CC BY 4.0.

Nélida

> Alle Erscheinungen dieser Zeit zeigen
> dass die Befriedigung im alten Leben
> sich nicht mehr findet.
> Hegel.

C'était au mois de juin ; le soleil, à son midi, inondait l'horizon de clartés ; pas un nuage ne voilait la splendeur du ciel. Une chaude brise glissait sur l'étang et se jouait dans les roseaux sonores. Près de la rive, à l'ombre d'un rideau de peupliers, sommeillait un couple de cygnes. Le nénuphar ouvrait ses ailes blanches sur le miroir des eaux. Dans une barque, amarrée au tronc d'un saule dont les rameaux flexibles formaient au-dessus de leurs têtes une voûte mobile et fraîche, deux beaux enfants étaient assis, qui se tenaient par la main. Le plus âgé pouvait avoir une douzaine d'années; c'était un garçon robuste, hardiment découplé, aux yeux noirs, au teint brun : un enfant des campagnes, épanoui au soleil, accoutumé à se jouer librement au sein de la mère nature. L'autre était une jeune fille qui paraissait avoir un ou deux ans de moins. Rien n'égalait la pureté de ses traits ; mais son corps frêle avait déjà cette grâce inquiétante des organisations trop délicates ou trop hâtivement développées ; son cou, d'une blancheur mate, fléchissait sous le poids de sa chevelure d'or ; une pâleur maladive couvrait ses joues ; un léger cercle entourait ses yeux d'azur ; tout trahissait dans cette créature charmante l'alanguissement des forces vitales.[1]

Marie Catherine Sophie de Flavigny, Comtesse d'Agoult [Daniel Stern] was born in Frankfurt-am-Main and died in Paris, daughter of Alexandre Victor François de Flavigny, a French nobleman who had emigrated during the Revolution, and Maria Elisabeth Bethmann, from an old family of German Jewish bankers converted to Protestantism. The family returned to France after Marie's birth, her father encouraging her love of French literature, her mother promoting her interest in German: Marie spoke both languages fluently. Visiting Frankfurt, she met Goethe who gave her a blessing. Educated from 1819–1821 in a

---

1   Daniel Stern, *Nélida*, ed. Charles F. Dupêchez (Paris: Calmann-Lévy, 1987), pp. 1–2.

    Translation: All appearances of this time show that the satisfaction in the old life is no longer to be found. Hegel.
    It was the month of June; the sun, at its noon, inundated the horizon with light; not a cloud veiled the splendor of the sky. A hot breeze slid over the pond and played in the sonorous rushes. Near the shore, in the shadow of a curtain of poplars, slept a couple of swans. The waterlily opened its white wings on the mirror of the waters. In a boat, tied to the trunk of a willow whose flexible branches made a fresh and mobile vault over their heads, two lovely children were seated, holding each other by the hand. The elder could be about twelve years old; it was a stout boy, boldly decoupled, with black eyes, with sun-browned skin; a country child, flourishing in the sun, accustomed to play freely in the heart of mother nature. The other was a young girl who seemed one or two years younger. Nothing equaled the purity of her features; but her frail body already had that disquieting grace of organizations either too delicate or too hastily developed; her neck, of a matte whiteness, bent beneath the weight of her golden tresses; an unhealthy paleness covered her cheeks; a light circle surrounded her azure eyes; all betrayed in this charming creature the languishing of vital forces.

convent, she pursued her education reading Chateaubriand, Rousseau, and Lamartine. In 1827, she married Charles Louis Constant, Comte d'Agoult, a cavalry colonel and steward of Madame the Dauphine, and they had two daughters, the first of whom died in childhood. Her salon drew writers and musicians from Vigny to Chopin to Heine. In 1833 she began her liaison with Liszt, the composer and virtuoso, and she left her husband for him in 1835, the two traveling through Italy together. She later divided her time between Rome, London, Paris, and the Rhineland. D'Agoult and Liszt had three children, notably Cosima who later married Richard Wagner. And d'Agoult began to publish. *Nélida* (1846) is an anagram of their last child's name, Daniel—he died aged twenty of tuberculosis—as well as of her own male pseudonym; readers found in it echoes of her liaison with Liszt. Her *Histoire de la Révolution de 1848*, published in 1850, remains a reference point for historians and marks her shift to non-fiction. D'Agoult, by now an ardent republican, hosted a leading republican salon under the Second Empire and is buried in Père Lachaise Cemetery. Her relations with Sand were complex; Balzac put her in his early novel *Béatrix* (1839) as the title character, for which she hated him thereafter. She maintained a long correspondence with Allart. Hugo, at her death, remarked in his private notebooks: "Peu de talent, petite âme."[2]

Opening one's first novel with an epigraph from Hegel, in German no less, is a bold move. The quotation reads, in essence: "All appearances of this time show that satisfaction in the old life is no longer to be found." The Comtesse d'Agoult, one might speculate, is concerned to be taken seriously—an entirely understandable position for an intelligent, serious woman in that place and time. Hugo, let us observe, was reluctant to accord her that honor. D'Agoult's grasp of German was rare in France in 1846, and she is right to make use of it; one thinks of her early meeting with Goethe, as of her years with Liszt, whose native tongue was German.

After the epigraph, we find elegant prose. This is all well and good, but Sand, no stranger to elegant prose, had already begun to show what could be done with an "enfant des campagnes" when the author allows them to narrate the novel instead of just starring in it. There is, briefly put,

---

2   Victor Hugo, *Choses vues*, ed. Hubert Juin (Paris: Gallimard, 2002), p. 1332.

a disconnect or disjunction between d'Agoult's Hegel, her sophisticated style, and the heroes she presents to us. This disconnect was not unknown in the mid-nineteenth century, but d'Agoult knew Sand, and one has the feeling she was gifted and imaginative enough to do otherwise. Finding the poetry in the everyday is perhaps more interesting than bringing it in on a platter. In short: this is interesting, elegant writing, and the epigraph from Hegel is possibly the most resonant part of that interest, in this very short extract. Certainly, d'Agoult deserves to be read today with some attention, and Hugo's remark at her death says as much about Hugo as about his intended target.

Works

d'Agoult, Marie, *Correspondance générale*, ed. Charles Dupêchez (Paris: H. Champion, 2003-)

Valentia, Hervé, Julien (Paris: Calmann-Lévy, 1883)

Nélida (Paris: Amyot, 1846)

La Boîte aux lettres (Paris: Calmann-Lévy, 1883)

Ninon au couvent, ou Il ne faut jamais manquer à ses amis (Paris: Calmann-Lévy, 1883)

Lettres républicaines (Paris: Amyot, 1848)

Esquisses morales et politiques (Paris: Pagnerre, 1849)

Florence et Turin: études d'art et de politique (Paris: Michel Lévy, 1862)

Histoire de la Révolution de 1848 (Paris: Charpentier, 1862)

Essai sur la liberté considérée comme principe et fin de l'activité humaine (Paris: Michel Lévy, 1863)

Dante et Goethe (Paris: Didier, 1866)

Histoire des commencements de la république aux Pays-Bas (Paris: M. Lévy, 1872)

Esquisses morales (Paris: Calmann Lévy, 1880)

Mes souvenirs, 1806–1833 (Paris: Calmann Lévy, 1880)

Mémoires (1833–1854) (Paris: Calmann-Lévy, 1927)

Gut, Serge and Bellas, Jacqueline, eds, *Franz Liszt — Marie d'Agoult, Correspondance* (Paris: Fayard, 2001)

Sources

D'Alessandro, Maurizio, *Franz Liszt negli anni romani e nell'Albano dell'800* (Bari: Florestano edizioni, 2019)

Bolster, Richard, *Marie d'Agoult: The Rebel Countess* (New Haven: Yale University Press, 2000)

Bory, Robert, *Une retraite romantique en Suisse: Liszt et la comtesse d'Agoult* (Lausanne: SPES, 1930)

Charton, Ariane, *Marie d'Agoult, une sublime amoureuse* (Aix-en-Provence: Kirographaires, 2011)

Colombo, Laura, *Marie d'Agoult: autoritratto di un intellettuale romantica* (Reggio Emilia: Diabasis, 1997)

Colombo, Laura and Piva, Franco, eds, *Marie d'Agoult-Daniel Stern: eroina romantica e intellettuale Europea* (Verona: Edizioni Fiorini, 2006)

Desanti, Dominique, *Daniel ou Le visage secret d'une comtesse romantique, Marie d'Agoult* (Paris: Stock, 1980)

Destouches, Camille, *La passion de Marie d'Agoult* (Paris: Fayard, 1959)

Dupêchez, Charles, *Marie d'Agoult, 1805–1876* (Paris: Plon, 1994)

Dupêchez, Charles, *Hortense et Marie: une si belle amitié* (Paris: Flammarion, 2018)

Guggenheim, Suzanne, *Madame d'Agoult, et la pensée européenne de son époque* (Firenze: L. S. Olschki, 1937)

Menou, Jean-Claude, *Le voyage-exil de Franz Liszt et Marie d'Agoult en Italie: 1837–1839* (Arles: Actes Sud, 2015)

Monod, Marie Octave, *Daniel Stern, comtesse d'Agoult, de la Restauration à la IIIe république* (Paris: Plon, 1937)

Ollivier, Daniel, *Autour de Mme d'Agoult et de Liszt* (Paris: Bernard Grasset, 1941)

Rain, Henriette, *Les enfants du génie—Blandine, Cosima et Daniel Liszt* (Paris: Presses de la Renaissance, 1986)

Saint Bris, Gonzague, *Marie, l'ange rebelle* (Paris: Belfond, 2007)

Stock-Morton, Phyllis, *The Life of Marie d'Agoult, alias Daniel Stern* (Baltimore: The Johns Hopkins University Press, 2000)

Vier, Jacques Albert, *La Comtesse d'Agoult et son temps* (Paris: A. Colin, 1959–1963)

Zavatti, Giovanna, *Perché e nonostante: l'amicizia tra Giuseppe Mazzini e la contessa Marie D'Agoult* (Milano: Ares, 2000)

29. Julienne Joséphine Gauvin [Juliette Drouet]
10 April 1806–11 May 1883

Fig. 29. Julienne Joséphine Gauvin [Juliette Drouet], by C.-É.-C. de Champmartin. Photo by Vassil (2013). Wikimedia, https://upload.wikimedia.org/wikipedia/commons/9/96/Maison_de_Victor_Hugo_Juliette_Drouet_Champmartin_27122012.jpg, CC BY 4.0.

Lettres à Victor Hugo. Correspondance 1833–1882

Dimanche.
4 h. du soir [1833].

Je rentre bien triste et bien découragée de tout. Je souffre, je pleure, je me plains tout haut, tout bas, à Dieu, à toi, et je voudrais mourir une bonne fois pour en finir avec toutes les misères, toutes les déceptions, toutes les douleurs. On dirait vraiment que mon bonheur s'est envolé avec les beaux jours, et compter les voir revenir lui et eux serait presque de la folie car en regardant autour de moi et au-dedans de moi je trouve la saison bien avancée pour les beaux jours, et pour les jours heureux. Pauvre fou qui t'étonnes de me voir regretter si amèrement une journée de bonheur, on voit bien que tu n'as pas attendu le bonheur d'aimer et d'être aimé jusqu'à vingt-six ans. Pauvre poète qui avez fait *Les Feuilles d'automne* avec de l'amour, des rires d'enfants, des yeux noirs, et bleus, des cheveux bruns, et blonds, du bonheur en quantité vous n'avez pas observé combien une journée triste et pluvieuse comme celle d'aujourd'hui fait jaunir et tomber les feuilles les plus vertes et les mieux attachées. Donc vous ne savez pas ce qu'une journée sans bonheur comme celle-ci, peut ôter de confiance et de force pour l'avenir. Vous ne le savez pas, car vous vous étonnez quand je pleure, vous vous fâchez presque contre ma douleur. Tu vois donc bien que tu ne sais pas ce que c'est que mon amour, tu vois bien que j'ai raison de regretter de t'aimer autant puisque cet amour t'est inutile et importun. Oh ! je t'aime c'est bien vrai ! Je t'aime malgré toi, malgré moi malgré tout le monde entier, malgré Dieu, malgré le Diable qui s'en mêle aussi. Je t'aime, je t'aime, je t'aime. Heureuse ou malheureuse gaie ou triste je t'aime. Fais de moi ce que tu voudras, je t'aime.[1]

Julienne Joséphine Gauvain [Juliette Drouet] was born in Fougères and died in Paris, Victor Hugo's companion for over fifty years. Her mother, Marie Marchandet, was a seamstress; her father, Julien Gauvain, was a

---

1   Juliette Drouet, *Lettres à Victor Hugo. Correspondance 1833–1882*, ed. Evelyn Blewer (Paris: Fayard, 2001), p. 20.

   Translation: Sunday. 4 p.m. [1833]
   I return quite sad and quite discouraged with everything. I suffer, I weep, I complain aloud, quietly, to God, to you, and I would wish to die once and for all to have an end of all the miseries, all the disappointments, all the pains. One would say truly that my happiness flew off with the fine days, and to count on seeing them return, it and they, would be almost madness because in looking around me I find the season well advanced for fine days and for happy ones. Poor madman who is astonished to see me regret so bitterly a day of happiness, one sees well that you did not wait for the happiness of loving and being loved until twenty-six. Poor poet who wrote the *Feuilles d'automne* with love, with children's laughter, with black eyes, and blue ones, with brown hair, and blonde, with happiness in quantity you have not observed how much a day sad and rainy like today will make the greenest and best attached leaves grow yellow and fall. And so you do not know what a day without happiness like this one can remove in the way of confidence and force for the future. You do not know it, because you grow astonished when I weep, you almost grow angry at my pain. You see well then that you do not know what my love is, you see well that I am right to regret loving you so much because this love is useless to you and importunate. Oh! I love you, that is very true! I love you despite yourself, despite me, despite the whole world, despite God, despite the Devil who has his part in this. I love you, I love you, I love you, I love you. Happy or unhappy gay or sad I love you. Do with me what you wish, I love you.

tailor. Julienne lost her mother some months after her birth, her father the following year, and was placed like her siblings with a wet-nurse, then later in a convent, before being raised by an uncle, Drouet, who moved to Paris and whose name she took. Around 1825, she became the mistress of the sculptor James Pradier, who may have modeled the Strasbourg statue after her on the Place de la Concorde.[2] The couple had a child, Claire, whom he recognized two years later. Pradier encouraged her to act, and she began in 1828, taking her uncle's name. Not a natural actress, Drouet was booed in *Marie Tudor* (1833). She was however extremely beautiful, and Victor Hugo, seeing her that year, began to fall in love. Auditioning for the queen in *Ruy Blas* (1838), she was passed over perhaps in part due to a frank letter from Madame Hugo, contrasting her place in Hugo's affections with her talent as an actress. She abandoned acting and instead devoted herself to Hugo—he required of her a cloistered life, going out only in his company. Their liaison was public knowledge, Hugo even leading her daughter Claire's funeral cortège with Pradier. In 1852, having organized Hugo's flight from the Second Empire, Drouet accompanied her lover to exile in Jersey, then Guernsey, but without sharing his roof. He rented a little house for her within eyesight, but was not faithful, cheating on her for instance in 1873 with Blanche, her chambermaid. She wrote him over 22,000 letters during the fifty years of their liaison.

Looking for Drouet's letters, you will find them at the Bibliothèque nationale de France not under D for Drouet, but under H for Hugo. Our title is *Destins de femmes*, and Drouet's destiny was to be subsumed by the man she loved to the point of disappearance. In the fifty years of their affair—for it was an affair, he remained for a half-century with his wife and children—she was not to leave her home except in his company. In Guernsey, a smallish island, Drouet even had her little house within eyesight of the Hugo property, where Madame Hugo could see it. Reading the thirty biographies here given, one is struck more than once by how badly men at least were prepared to behave when they thought they could get away with it. Flaubert, in our closing chapter, trashed Louise Colet as an artist after their breakup and her reputation has not recovered almost two centuries later. "All power corrupts," wrote Lord

---

2   Jean-Pierre Barbier, *Juliette Drouet. Sa vie—son œuvre* (Paris: Grasset, 1913), p. 21.

Acton, "and absolute power corrupts absolutely." How did Drouet feel about this? Let us look at her letter, almost the first she wrote to the great man. It is 1833.

The first thing that strikes the eye is her prose. It is very good. In its openness to passion, it is not without analogy to the extract from Lespinasse near the start of this book. Drouet is evidently overwhelmed with passion in this text, and yet she exerts mastery over the prose she uses to express it. "A spontaneous outpouring of powerful emotion [...] recollected in tranquility," wrote Wordsworth, seeking to define poetry in 1798, but there is no evidence here of multiple drafts: Drouet is not Flaubert. Instead, one has the impression that this is simply how she writes, almost without lifting the pen from the paper. "Je souffre, je pleure, je me plains tout haut, tout bas, à Dieu, à toi, et je voudrais mourir une bonne fois pour en finir avec toutes les misères, toutes les déceptions, toutes les douleurs," she writes; "Je t'aime, je t'aime, je t'aime," she adds, switching between *tu* and *vous* at the drop of a hat. Victor Hugo was clearly a vain man, but he was also a gifted writer, and one imagines that the relationship would not have lasted for the 20,000 letters it generated from Drouet had she had no gift for prose. One might take a moment to suggest that Drouet suffered from depression—again, quite understandably—but it seems fitting to end here by stating that prose combining this amount of passion with this musicality of expression is not a given. One finds it in Juliette Drouet, the lady who spent fifty years sitting at home waiting for Hugo to come and visit.

Works

[Drouet, Juliette], *Juliette Drouet, Victor Hugo: « mon âme à ton cœur s'est donnée »: [exposition, Paris, Maison de Victor Hugo, 1er décembre 2006–4 mars 2007]* (Paris: Maison de Victor Hugo, 2006)

Lettres à Victor Hugo. Correspondance 1833–1882, ed. Evelyn Blewer (Paris: Fayard, 2001)

Drouet, Juliette, *Souvenirs 1843–1854*, ed. Gérard Pouchain (Paris: Des Femmes, 2006)

Sources

Barbier, Jean-Pierre, *Juliette Drouet: sa vie, son œuvre par des documents inédits* (Paris: B. Grasset, 1913)

Huas, Jeanine, *Juliette Drouet ou la Passion romantique* (Paris: Hachette, 1970)

Huas, Jeanine, *Juliette Drouet: le bel amour de Victor Hugo* (Paris: G. Lachurié, 1985)

Lafargue, Pascale, *Juliette Drouet, une destinée* (Paris: Lanore, 2004)

Naugrette, Florence and Simonet-Tenant, Françoise, eds, *Juliette Drouet épistolière: actes du colloque de Paris, 16–17 septembre 2017* (Paris: Eurédit, 2019)

Novarino, Albine, *Victor Hugo-Juliette Drouet: dans l'ombre du génie* ([Paris]: Acropole, 2000)

Pouchain, Gérard and Sabourin, Robert, *Juliette Drouet, ou La dépaysée* (Paris: Fayard, 1992)

Souchon, Paul, *Juliette Drouet, inspiratrice de Victor Hugo* (Paris: J. Tallandier, 1942)

Troyat, Henri, *Juliette Drouet: la prisonnière sur parole* (Paris: Flammarion, 1997)

30. Louise Colet
15 August 1810–9 March 1876

Fig. 30. Louise Colet, by F.X. Winterhalter. Photo by Guise (2021). Wikimedia, https://upload.wikimedia.org/wikipedia/commons/d/d1/Louise_Colet.jpg, CC BY 4.0.

Mementos

Journal
Paris samedi 14 juin 1845

Pourquoi commencer ce journal aujourd'hui plutôt qu'il y a dix ans quand je suis arrivée à Paris, quand, pleine d'enthousiasme, curieuse de tout voir, de tout connaître, j'avais encore des illusions sur les grands hommes, sur les sentiments, sur la gloire ! Oh ! c'est qu'alors ma vie était trop pleine, mes espérances trop vives, je voyais ma carrière (littéraire trop belle), je n'aurais pas perdu un instant à réfléchir, à quoi bon ? il fallait marcher au bonheur, aux succès qui m'attendaient. Aujourd'hui, tout m'a fait défaut. Je vais écrire chaque soir mes impressions et mes actes, non pour me distraire, c'est impossible, mais pour que ce journal (document informe) me serve dans ma vieillesse (si je vieillis) à rédiger la confession de ma vie. Ce sera le seul roman que je pourrai bien faire et qui vaudra la peine d'être lu. Dans tous les ouvrages de ce genre que j'ai essayé d'écrire, je sais que le souffle de vérité a manqué. Ce n'est pas le courage et la franchise qui me manquaient pour décrire les sentiments et les événements, tels que je les avais éprouvés ou observés dans la vie, c'était le courage du cœur exigeant qui se refusait de descendre de l'idéal à la réalité. J'en cite un exemple, le dernier roman (ou plutôt nouvelle) que j'ai écrit ou que j'écrirai jamais, il est encore inachevé en ce moment, c'est *Eudoxie Mallet*. J'écrivais ces pages sur l'empire du sentiment que je voulais y peindre, sentiment en réalité si incomplet, si inférieur à l'amour de Frédéric et de Diane que mon cœur souffrait mille tortures tandis que je forçais mon récit à exprimer non ce que j'exprimais à XXX mais ce que j'aurais voulu qu'il fût pour moi. Ecrire la vérité de ma faiblesse et de mes déceptions pour les livrer au public sous une forme littéraire était au-dessus de mes forces, c'était bien amer de le subir.[1]

Louise Colet, *née* Révoil was born in Aix-en-Provence in 1810 and died in Paris in 1876. In 1834, she met and married Mouriès Hippolyte Raymond Colet, a professor of composition at the Conservatoire de musique in Paris, following him there. A year after her arrival in

---

1 Louise Colet, *Mementos*, ed. Joëlle Gardes (Paris: Kimé, 2018), pp. 15–16.

   Translation: Diary Paris Saturday 14 June 1845
     Why begin this diary today rather than ten years ago when I arrived in Paris, when full of enthusiasm, curious to see everything, to know everything, I still had illusions about great men, about sentiments, about glory! Oh! it is that then my life was too full, my hopes too lively, I saw my career (in letters too beautiful), I would not have lost an instant to reflect, what's the use? one had to walk to the happiness, to the successes that awaited me. Today, everything has let me down. I will write each evening my impressions and my acts, not to distract me, that is impossible, but so that this diary (formless document) serves me in my old age (if I grow old) to set down the confession of my life. It will be the only novel I can well write and which will be worth the trouble of being read. In all the works of this genre that I have tried to write, I know that the breath of truth has been lacking. It is not courage and frankness that I lacked to describe sentiments and events, such as I felt them or observed them in life, it was the courage of the demanding heart which refused to step down from the ideal to reality. I give an example of this, the last novel (or rather short story) that I wrote or will ever write, it is still unfinished at the moment, it is *Eudoxie Mallet*. I wrote these pages on the empire of sentiment that I wished to paint there, a sentiment in reality so incomplete, so beneath the love of Frédéric and Diane that my heart suffered a thousand tortures while I forced my tale to express not what I expressed at XXX but what I would have wanted it to be for me. To write the truth of my weakness and my disappointments to deliver them to the public in literary form was above my strength, it was quite bitter to experience that.

Paris, Colet published her poems, winning a 2,000-franc prize from the Académie française. She went on to win three further prizes from that institution. Her literary salon was frequented by Hugo, Musset, Vigny, Baudelaire, and many painters and politicians. In 1840, the journalist Alphonse Karr attributed the paternity of her coming child to Victor Cousin. Furious, Colet attacked him with a knife. Karr, who escaped with a small wound, decided not to press charges, to the great relief of Cousin.[2] In 1844, Colet published a translation of selected works by Tommaso Campanella. In the 1840s and 1850s, she won more prizes; she also met Gustave Flaubert, a young unknown, in the sculptor James Pradier's studio in 1846. He was twenty-five, she was thirty-six. They became lovers, though the liaison did not last. She left her husband in 1847, writing at speed to meet her financial needs and maintain her independence. Several Fourierists frequented her salon, such as Leconte de Lisle. She died in 1876 and was buried in Verneuil-sur-Avre. In 2016, her tomb stood abandoned: despite fame and multiple awards in her lifetime, Colet had vanished from history in the ensuing century except as an appendage of Flaubert. Flaubert took it upon himself to attack her work after their breakup, in distinction to Victor Hugo who admired it. Reeditions since 2014 have belatedly changed this situation.

In 1845, year of this first memento by Colet, she was a prize-winning author in her mid-thirties, friend of Cousin, known enough in Paris for Karr to slander her in the press, and still a year away from her encounter with the unknown Flaubert, eleven years her junior. She had one prize under her belt from the Académie française, with three more yet to be awarded to her, alongside a prix Lambert from the Institut in 1857, the year *Madame Bovary* was published. Colet was literally a writer of distinction. How then did she come to be so forgotten that her gravesite was abandoned in 2016? The answer may partly lie in her relationship with Flaubert, who was unsparing after their breakup.

Possibly the most striking aspect of this extract is its apparent lack of confidence. Why did she not begin ten years ago, she opens, when she was full of enthusiasm? "Aujourd'hui," she writes, "tout m'a fait défaut." She wonders whether she will grow old; she remarks that in all her writing, "le souffle de vérité a manqué." What she lacked, she notes,

---

[2] Francine du Plessix Gray, *Rage and Fire. A Life of Louise Colet Pioneer Feminist, Literary Star, Flaubert's Muse* (New York: Simon & Schuster, 1994), pp. 79–84.

was "le courage du cœur exigeant;" she finds that lack in what she calls 'the last novel she will ever write.' This is deeply depressing reading, from a young writer already honored by the Académie française. The extract ends thus: "Ecrire la vérité de ma faiblesse et de mes déceptions pour les livrer au public sous une forme littéraire était au-dessus de mes forces." History has remembered Colet as Flaubert's muse; it might be equally fair, if not more so, to say that Flaubert was the older (and far better-known) Colet's muse, and an extremely unfortunate one at that. His reputation visibly did not suffer; hers most assuredly did. It might be interesting to return to her novel *Lui* (1860) and to their correspondence with this viewpoint in mind.

Works

Colet, Louise, *Mementos*, ed. Joëlle Gardes (Paris: Kimé, 2018)

Fleurs du midi (Paris: Dumont, 1836)

Penserosa (Paris: Delloye, 1840)

Le Musée de Versailles (Paris: Vve Dondey-Dupré, 1839)

La Jeunesse de Goethe (Paris: Vve Dondey-Dupré, s.d. [1839])

Les Funérailles de Napoléon (Paris: Garnier, 1840)

La Jeunesse de Mirabeau (Paris: Dumont, 1841)

Les Cœurs brisés (Paris: Berquet & Pétion, 1843)

Le Monument de Molière (Paris: Paulin, 1843)

Deux femmes célèbres, Madame du Châtelet et Madame Hoffmann-Tanska, 2 vols (Coulommiers: Moussin, 1846)

Enfances célèbres (Paris: Hachette, 1854)

La Colonie de Mettray (Paris: Librairie nouvelle, 1852)

L'Acropole d'Athènes (Paris: Librairie nouvelle, 1854)

Une histoire de soldat (Paris: Cadot, 1856)

Un drame dans la rue de Rivoli (Brussels: Office de publicité, 1857)

Lui (Paris: Librairie nouvelle, 1860)

L'Italie des Italiens, 4 volumes (Paris: Dentu, 1862–1864)

Les Derniers Marquis followed by *Deux mois aux Pyrénées* (Paris: Dentu, 1866)

La Vérité sur l'anarchie des esprits en France (Milan: Legros, 1873)

Edgar Quinet, l'esprit nouveau (Paris: Ardemment, 2022) [1875]

Campanella, Tommaso, *Œuvres choisies*, trans. Louise Colet (Paris: Lavigne, 1844)

Sources

Bellet, Roger, ed., *Femmes de lettres au XIXe siècle. Autour de Louise Colet* (Lyon: Presses universitaires de Lyon, 1982)

Bood, Micheline and Grand, Serge, *L'Indomptable Louise Colet* (Paris: P. Horay, 1986)

Clébert, Jean-Paul, *Louise Colet: la Muse* (Paris: Presses de la Renaissance, 1986)

Finch, Alison, *Women's Writing in Nineteenth-Century France* (Cambridge: Cambridge University Press, 2006)

Gray, Francine du Plessix, *Rage and Fire: Life of Louise Colet — Pioneer Feminist, Literary Star, Flaubert's Muse* (New York, NY: Simon & Schuster, 1994)

Poyet, Thierry, ed., *Louise Colet ou L'éclectisme littéraire: une écrivaine parmi des hommes* (Paris: Lettres modernes Minard, 2020)

Stampacchia, Aruta, *Louise Colet e l'Italia* (Genève: Slatkine, 1990)

Index

abolitionism 41
Abrantès, Laure Junot d' 139
Académie française 119, 153, 169, 170
Adelson, Robert G. xiii, 84, 86
Agoult, Charles Louis Constant, comte d' 157
Agoult, Marie Catherine Sophie de Flavigny, comtesse d' [Daniel Stern] x, 126, 145, 147, 155, 156, 157, 158
Aix-la Chapelle 97
Alembert, Jean Le Rond d' 3, 15, 19, 20, 21, 22, 25
Alexander I, Tsar 71
Allan, Stacie 105
Allart de Méritens, Hortense Thérèse Sigismonde Sophie Alexandrine 99, 123, 124, 125, 126
Ambrière, Francis 120
Amsterdam 25
Antilles 35
Aragon, Louis 119
Aragon, Marie-Christine d' 22
Arnold-Tétard, Madeleine 67
Assemblée constituante 88, 89
Assemblée nationale 88, 90
Auraix-Jonchière, Pascale 148
Austerlitz 104
Austria 52, 71

Badinter, Élisabeth 14, 17
Baelen, Jean 134
Balayé, Simone vii, 76, 79, 80

Balzac, Honoré de 98, 114, 119, 139, 140, 145, 157
Bara, Joseph 85
Barbier, Jean-Pierre 118, 163, 165
Barère, Bertrand 35
Barnave, Antoine 35
Barthélémy, Jacques G. 37
Bastille 47, 77, 78
bataille d'Hernani 127
Baudelaire, Charles 119, 169
Beauharnais, Hortense de 60
Beauharnais, Joséphine de 104, 109, 110
Beaumarchais, Pierre-Augustin Caron de 65, 118
Beauvau, Marie-Charlotte de 2, 3, 4, 104, 147
Beccaria, Cesare Bonesana di 65, 78
Bellet, Roger 47, 171
Bensaïd, Daniel 44
Béranger, Pierre-Jean de 132
Bergès, Sandrine 67
Berlin 52, 71
Berlioz, Hector xiii, 153, 154
Berly, Cécile xii, 55
Bern 31
Bernard-Griffiths, Simone 148
Bernardin de Saint-Pierre, Jacques-Henri 25, 35, 70, 72, 133
Bernier, Marc André 64, 66, 67
Berry, Marie Caroline Ferdinande Louise de Bourbon, duchesse de 89
Bertelà, Maddalena 127

Bertin, Louise Angélique 151, 152, 153, 154
Bertrand, Marc 120
Bessire, François 37
Bible, the 47
Bied, Robert 86
Billy, André 126, 127
Blake, William 104
Blanc, Louis 132, 146
Blanc, Olivier 44
Bloch-Dano, Évelyne 134, 147
Bluteau, Jeanne 22
Bochenek, Valérie 134
Boggio, Maricla 44
Boigne, Adélaïde Charlotte Louise Éléonore, comtesse de 111, 112, 113, 114, 115
Boissel, Thierry 67
Bolívar, Simón 131, 133
Bolster, Richard 159
Bonaparte, Napoleon 71, 78, 84, 99, 104, 109, 110, 113, 114, 115, 125, 140
Bonaparte, Pauline 97
Bondy, François 141
Boneau, Denise Lynn 154
Bood, Micheline 171
Boon, Sonja 27
Bordeaux 21, 92, 131, 132
Bory, Robert 159
Bossuet, Jacques-Bénigne 47
Bostic, Heidi xiii, 11
Boswell, James 31
Bott, François 22
Bouchardeau, Huguette 148
Boufflers, Stanislas Jean de, marquis de Remiencourt 4, 97, 104
Bouissounouse, Janine 22
Boulenger, Jacques 120
bourgeoisie 9, 10
Boutin, Aimée 121
Bredin, Jean-Denis 27, 80
Brem, Anne-Marie de 148
Breton, André 132
Brissot, Jacques Pierre 47
Broglie, Gabriel de 37

Broglie, Victor, duc de 79, 97, 113
Brookes, Barbara 67
Brown, Karin 67
Brussels 118
Buffon, Georges-Louis de 25, 35, 77
Burke, Edmund 72
Burnand, Léonard 80
Byron, George Gordon, Lord 53, 78

Cabanis, Pierre Jean Georges 66
Call, Michael J. 94
Calonne, Charles-Alexandre de 53, 54
Camus, Albert 60
Canavaggio, Pierre 148
Caors, Marielle 148, 149
Carpenter, Kirsty 61
Casillo, Robert 80
Cavallucci, Giacomo 121
Charles X 53, 114
Charrière, Isabelle Agnès Élisabeth de ix, xii, 25, 29, 30, 31, 32
Charton, Ariane 127, 159
Chartres, duc de. *See* Philippe Égalité [Louis Philippe, duc d'Orléans]
Chartres, Louise-Marie-Adélaïde de Bourbon, duchesse de 35
Chateaubriand, François-René, vicomte de 48, 71, 72, 97, 103, 104, 115, 126, 157
Chaumont, Jean-Philippe 61
Chauvel, Geneviève 55, 149
Chazal, André 131, 132
Chénier, André 99
Choderlos de Laclos, Pierre 9
Choiseul, Étienne François, Marquis de Stainville, duc de 97
Choiseul, Louise Honorine Crozat du Châtel, duchesse de 1
Chopin, Frédéric 145, 146, 157
Ciureanu, Petre 128
Clancier, Georges-Emmanuel 121
Clébert, Jean-Paul 171
Clésinger, Auguste 146
Cole, John R. 44
Colet, Louise ix, xii, 163, 167, 168, 169, 170

Colet, Mouriès Hippolyte Raymond 168
Colombo, Laura 159
Comédie-Française 41, 98
Comédie italienne 8
Condillac, Étienne Bonnot de 21, 66
Condorcet, Marie Jean Antoine Nicolas de Caritat, marquis de 65
Condorcet, Sophie de Grouchy or Sophie de 19, 21, 22, 48, 60, 63, 64, 65, 66, 67
Congress of Vienna 104
Considérant, Victor 132
Constant, Benjamin 31, 71, 78, 97, 103, 115
Consulate 65
convent 3, 8, 14, 15, 16, 35, 47, 53, 59, 103, 145, 157, 163
Convention xi, 86
Copenhagen 70, 71, 72
Coppet 25, 78
Corbaz, André 27
Corbi Sáez, María Isabel xiii, 5
Corneille, Pierre 9, 34
Cossy, Valérie 32
Cottin, Marie Sophie Risteau x, 91, 92, 93, 94
Coüasnon, Marguerite de 32, 37
Court-Perez, Françoise 141
Cousin, Victor 169
Craveri, Benedetta 3, 5
Crichfield, Grant 105
Cross, Máire Fedelma 134
Custine, Delphine, marquise de 97

D'Alessandro, Maurizio 159
Danton, Georges Jacques 42, 47
Daunais, Isabelle 149
Dauphin, Noëlle 149
David, Jacques-Louis xi, 21, 35, 60, 85
David, Odette 17
Dawson, Deidre 64, 66, 67
Debré, Jean-Louis 134
Decreus, Juliette 128
Delacroix, Eugène 145
Demay, Andrée 11
Denmark 60, 70, 71
De Poortere, Machteld 37, 80

Desanti, Dominique 134, 159
Desbordes, Lucie 121
Desbordes-Valmore, Marceline Félicité Josèphe x, 117, 118, 119, 120, 132, 139, 153
Descaves, Lucien 121
Deschamps, Émile 139
Deschanel, Paul 17
Deshayes, Olivier 37
Desmoulins, Camille 48, 49
Destouches, Camille 159
Diaz, Brigitte 149
Diderot, Denis 8, 15, 21, 25
Didier, Béatrice 149
Directoire 78, 89, 93
divorce 23, 24, 25, 26, 42, 53, 65, 71, 84, 133
Domenech, Jacques 17
Dorval, Marie 118, 145
Doucette, Wendy Carvalho 11
Drouet, Juliette. *See* Gauvin, Julienne Joséphine [Juliette Drouet]
Dubeau, Catherine 27
Dubé, Pierre H. 80
du Châtelet, Émilie ix, 4, 66
du Deffand, Jean-Baptiste de La Lande, marquis 3
du Deffand, Marie de Vichy-Chamrond, marquise ix, xi, xii, 1, 3, 4, 5, 9, 21, 25
Dudevant, Amantine Lucile Aurore Dupin, baronne [George Sand] vii, ix, x, xi, xii, 126, 132, 139, 143, 144, 145, 146, 147, 148, 157, 158
Dudevant, François Casimir 145
Duflot, Marianne 121
Dufour, Hortense 149
Duhamel, Yvonne 121
Dumas, Alexandre, ***fils*** 146
Dumas, Alexandre, ***père*** 85, 98, 139
Dupaty, Louis Emmanuel 97
Dupêchez, Charles 128, 156, 159
Duras, Claire Louisa Rose Bonne, duchesse de 4, 71, 79, 97, 99, 101, 102, 103, 104, 147

Effertz, Julia xiii, 121

Emerson, Ralph Waldo 78
emigration 35, 53, 54, 113, 131, 156
Encyclopédie 21
Engels, Friedrich 132
Enghien, Louis-Antoine-Henri de Bourbon-Condé, duc d' 107, 108, 109, 110
England 9, 10, 26, 30, 31, 35, 42, 53, 65, 66, 78, 93, 112, 113, 114
Enlightenment ix, x, xiii, 10, 31
Épinay, Denis-Joseph Lalive, marquis d' 15
Épinay, Louise Florence Pétronille Tardieu d'Esclavelles, marquise d' x, xii, 13, 14, 15, 16, 17, 21, 22
Estates General 70, 89
Europe vii, x, xiii, 9, 10, 22, 25, 30, 31, 53, 72, 78, 79, 103, 109, 130, 131, 133
exile 54, 60, 78, 89, 112, 163

Fairweather, Maria 80
Faucheux, Michel 44
Fauriel, Charles-Claude 65
Favre, Madline 27
Fielding, Henry 9
Finch, Alison xiii, 141, 171
Flaubert, Gustave 145, 146, 163, 164, 169, 170
Fontana, Biancamaria 80
Fontenelle, Bernard Le Bouyer de 3
Fouché, Joseph 109
Fouquier-Tinville, Antoine 42, 93
Fourier, François Marie Charles 133
France vii, ix, x, xi, xii, xiii, xiv, 9, 10, 16, 21, 25, 26, 30, 31, 35, 36, 42, 43, 48, 49, 51, 52, 53, 54, 60, 66, 70, 72, 77, 78, 79, 85, 88, 89, 93, 98, 101, 102, 103, 104, 110, 112, 113, 114, 115, 118, 119, 120, 125, 132, 133, 145, 146, 147, 153, 156, 157, 163
Frankfurt-am-Main 156
Franklin, Benjamin 21, 98
Frederick the Great 25
French Revolution ix, xi, xiii, 9, 48, 53, 54, 60, 67, 79, 86, 89, 118, 125, 127, 131, 156

Friang, Michèle 153, 154
Galiani, Ferdinando 15
Garibaldi, Giuseppe 133
Garry-Boussel, Claire 80
Gaudefroy, Olivier 134
Gauguin, Paul 131
Gautier, Théophile 120, 139, 141, 146
Gauvin, Julienne Joséphine [Juliette Drouet] x, xi, xii, 9, 161, 162, 163, 164
Gay, Marie Françoise Sophie x, xi, 95, 96, 97, 98, 99, 125
Genand, Stéphanie vii, 80
Geneva 25, 26, 71, 77, 78
Genlis, Stéphanie Félicité, marquise de Sillery, comtesse de xi, 33, 34, 35, 36, 93, 126
Geoffrin, Marie Thérèse ix, 25
Gérard, François Pascal Simon 98
Gérard, Rosemonde 37
Gerhard, Leo 134
Germain, Pierrette 153, 154
Germany xiii, 9, 25, 30, 31, 70, 72, 85, 156, 157
Ghervas, Stella 72
Giacchetti, Claudine 141
Gibbon, Edward 25, 77
Girardin, Delphine Gay de [Vicomte de Launay] xii, 99, 137, 138
Girardin, Émile de 139
Girodet-Trioson, Anne-Louis 98
Girondins 42, 46, 47, 48, 49, 65, 102
Godet, Philippe 32
Goethe, Johann Wolfgang von xiii, 22, 156, 157
Goldoni, Carlo 10
Goncourt brothers [Edmond and Jules de] 146
Goodden, Angelica 81
Gouze, Marie Olympe [Olympe de Gouges] xi, xii, xiv, 39, 40, 41, 42, 43, 47, 48, 65, 79, 133
Graffigny, Françoise de ix, 78
Gramont, Béatrix de Choiseul-Stainville, duchesse de 1

Grand, Serge 171
Grangé, Jérémie 17
Gray, Francine du Plessix 169, 171
Gray, Tim 134
Greece 71
Grégoire, Henri Jean-Baptiste, abbé 41
Greilsamer, Claire and Laurent 149
Grétry, André-Ernest-Modeste 98, 118
Greuze, Jean Baptiste 53
Grimm, Friedrich Melchior von 15, 25, 77
Guadeloupe 118
Guggenheim, Suzanne 159
Guibert, Jacques-Antoine-Hippolyte, comte de 21
guillotine xi, 35, 42, 43, 47, 48, 49, 60, 79, 109, 133
Guizot, François Pierre Guillaume 113
Gustav III of Sweden 77

Hamburg 60
Hamilton, Emma, Lady 53
Harmand, Jean 37
Haroche-Bouzinac, Geneviève 54, 55
Hart, Kathleen xiii, 134
Harvey, Cynthia 149
Hegel, Georg Wilhelm Friedrich 155, 156, 157, 158
Heine, Heinrich 145, 157
Helvétius 3, 8
Herman, Jan 11
Herold, J. Christopher 81
Hilger, Stephanie M. xiii, 73
Hobbes, Thomas 66
Hofmann, Étienne 81
Holbach, Paul-Henri, baron d' 8, 15, 60
Hollstein Hansen, Helynne 128
Holy Alliance 71
Holy Roman Empire 109
Hoog-Naginski, Isabelle 149
Houdetot, Sophie d' 15
Huas, Jeanine 165
Hugo, Victor x, xiv, 9, 35, 98, 99, 104, 133, 139, 145, 153, 157, 158, 161, 162, 163, 164, 169

Hume, David 8, 66
Hundred Days 99, 109, 114
Hutcheson, Francis 66

Industrial Revolution xiii
Iribarne González, María de la Macarena 135
Isabey, Jean-Baptiste 95, 98, 111
Italy 20, 21, 22, 30, 53, 65, 89, 93, 97, 98, 133, 145, 153, 157

Jack, Belinda Elizabeth 149
Jacobins 47, 52, 54, 65, 107, 108
James, Henry 149
Janin, Jules 98, 139
Jasenas, Éliane 121
Jefferson, Thomas 21, 65
Johnston, Joyce Ann Carlton xii, 100, 141
Jouy 97
July 1830 98, 145
July Monarchy 113, 139, 140, 146
Jung-Stilling, Johann Heinrich 71

Kadish, Doris Y. 105
Kale, Steven xiii, 67
Kaplan, Marijn S. 11
Karénine, Wladimir 149
Karr, Alphonse 169
Keats, John 22
Kertanguy, Inès de 55
Klopstock, Friedrich Gottlieb 72
Knapton, Ernest John 73
Kock, Paul de 132
Kohler, Pierre 81
Krief, Huguette xiii, 94
Krüdener, Beate Barbara Juliane, Freifrau von ix, 69, 70, 71, 72
Krulic, Brigitte 135

Labé, Louise 119
Lacour, Léopold 41, 44
Lacouture, Jean 22
Lafargue, Pascale 165
La Fayette, Gilbert du Motier, marquis de 41, 42
La Harpe, Jean-François de 25, 77

Lamartine, Alphonse de 47, 49, 98, 120, 131, 139, 157
Lamennais, Félicité de 133, 145, 146
Lameth, Alexandre de 35, 97
Lameth, Mme Alexandre de 88
Lang, André 81
Laplace, Pierre-Simon, marquis de 66
Laporte, Dominique 149
La Rochefoucauld, François, duc de 66
Lassère, Madeleine 90, 141
Latin 30, 47
Latouche, Henri de 103, 118, 139, 145
La Tour-du-Pin, Frédéric Séraphin, comte de Gouvernet, marquis de 88
La Tour-du-Pin Gouvernet, Henriette Lucy Dillon, marquise de 87, 88, 89, 90
Lausanne 24, 25, 26, 29, 30
Lauzon, Martine 86
Lavoisier, Antoine-Laurent de 60
La Vopa, Anthony J. xiii, 27
Lebrun, Jean Baptiste Pierre 53
Leconte de Lisle, Charles Marie René 169
Ledru-Rollin, Alexandre Auguste 145
Léger, Charles 68
Leipzig 71
Lemercier, Népomucène 97
Leopardi, Giacomo 78
Leprince de Beaumont, Jeanne Marie 97
Leprohon, Pierre 135
Leroux, Pierre 146
Lespinasse, Julie Jeanne Éléonore de 3, 19, 20, 21, 22, 164
Lessing, Gotthold Ephraim 9
Letzter, Jacqueline xiii, 84, 86
Ley, Francis 71, 73
liberalism 113, 114, 127
Liszt, Franz 139, 145, 153, 157
Llorca Tonda, María Ángeles xiii, 5
London 59, 60, 78, 87, 103, 113, 157
Lorusso, Silvia 94
Lotterie, Florence vii
Louis Philippe 1er, roi des Français 119, 140

Louis XIV 15, 16, 31
Louis XV 59
Louis XVI 16, 25, 48, 53, 54, 77, 113, 114
Louis XVII 114
Louis XVIII 53, 99, 112, 113, 114
Louvre 53, 59
Lubin, Georges 148, 149
Luynes, Marie Brûlart de La Borde, duchesse de 3
Lyon 21

Mackintosh, James 67
Mademoiselle Mars [Anne-Françoise-Hippolyte Boutet] 118
Maillebois, Yves Marie Desmarets, comte de 8, 9
Mallet, Paul Henri 71, 168
Malo, Henri 100, 103, 141
Manecy, Jules 100, 141
Mann, Thomas 25
Manzanera López, Laura 44
Marat, Jean-Paul xi, 42, 48, 85
Margerie, Diane de 149
Maricourt, André de 61
Marie Amélie de Bourbon, reine des Français 113
Marie Antoinette xi, 48
Mariéton, Paul 121
Marivaux, Pierre de 3, 8, 9, 15
Marmontel, Jean-François 15, 25, 35, 60, 77
Martin-Dehaye, Sophie 149
Martinique 102, 104
Marx, Karl 132, 134, 146
Maugras, Gaston 17
Maurois, André 149
McNiven Hine, Ellen 86
Méhul, Étienne Nicolas 97
Mellor, Anne K. vii, xiv
Menou, Jean-Claude 159
Mensel, Isabelle 44
Mérimée, Prosper 113, 145
Métais-Thoreau, Odile 105
Michaud, Stéphane 132, 135
Mickiewicz, Adam 145

Milan 125
Mirabeau, Honoré Gabriel Riqueti, comte de 42, 88, 89
Mohr, Annette 17
Molière [Jean-Baptiste Poquelin] 24
Monod, Marie Octave 159
Montagnards 42, 49
Montespan, Françoise de Rochechouart de Mortemart, marquise de 3
Montesquieu, Charles Louis de Secondat, Baron de La Brède et de 47, 78
Montpellier 87, 88
Mooij, Anne Louis Anton xiii, 62
Moorehead, Caroline 90
Moravian Brethren 71
Morgan, Sydney, Lady 93
Morris, Gouverneur 60
Moscow ix, xiv, 78, 104, 113
Moulin, Jeanine 121
Mousset, Sophie 44
Mozart, Wolfgang Amadeus 4, 15, 98
Mühlenbeck, Eugène 73
Munich 70
Muse française, La 118, 139
music 4, 31, 84, 85, 97, 119, 120, 154, 157
Musset, Alfred de 139, 145, 169

Naginski, Isabelle vii, 149
Nantes 84
Naples 52, 54, 109, 113
Naples, Kingdom of 52
Napoleonic Empire xi, xii, 60, 65, 113
Napoléon III 60, 140, 145, 146, 147
Narbonne-Lara, Louis Marie Jacques Amalric, comte de 25, 26, 77, 79
nationalism 54
Naugrette, Florence 165
Navarro, Pascale 37
Necker de Saussure, Albertine 81
Necker, Jacques 25, 77
Necker, Suzanne 23, 24, 25, 77
Nerval, Gérard de [Gérard Labrunie] 85
Netherlands, the 25, 31, 89
Neuchâtel 30

Newton, Isaac 32, 66
Nikliborc, Anna 37
nobility (aristocracy) 9, 16, 30, 31, 35, 48, 89, 92, 112, 113, 131, 133, 156
Nodier, Charles 139
Novarino, Albine 165

Odéon 98, 118
Old Regime xii, xiii, 16, 25, 48, 98
Ollivier, Daniel 159
opera xiii, 30, 98, 138, 153
Opéra-Comique 118, 139
Ossian 72

Pailhès, Gabriel 105
Paine, Thomas 65
Paliyenko, Adrianna M. xiii, 121
Paris vii, xiv, 1, 2, 3, 8, 15, 16, 21, 25, 26, 30, 31, 36, 41, 46, 47, 52, 53, 54, 59, 60, 65, 70, 71, 72, 77, 78, 79, 84, 85, 86, 87, 88, 92, 93, 97, 98, 103, 104, 109, 110, 112, 113, 114, 118, 130, 131, 132, 137, 138, 139, 140, 144, 145, 147, 152, 155, 156, 157, 162, 163, 167, 168, 169
Pascal, Jean-Noël 86
Paul, Tsar 71
Pays de Vaud 24, 25, 31
Peeters, Kris 11
Pelckmans, Paul 11
Perdiguier, Agricol 132
Père Lachaise Cemetery 60, 93, 157
Perey, Lucien 5, 17
Perrot, Michelle xii, 44, 135
Perroud, Claude 47, 49
Peru 78, 130, 131, 132, 133
Pétion de Villeneuve, Jérôme 47
Peylet, Anne-Louise 44
Philippe Égalité [Louis Philippe, duc d'Orléans] 35
philosophes 24, 65, 89
Pitt-Rivers, Françoise 55
Pitt, William, the Younger 77
Piva, Franco 159
Plagnol-Diéval, Marie-Emmanuelle 37
Planté, Christine 121
Plutarch 47, 48

Poisson, Guillaume 80
Pompadour, Jeanne Antoinette 59
Pope, Alexander 4
Portugal 60, 125, 137, 138, 139
Pouchain, Gérard 165
Pouget-Brunereau, Jeanne xiii, 86
Powell, David 149
Poyet, Thierry 171
Pradier, James 163, 169
prisons 2, 3, 4, 35, 46, 47, 48, 49, 65, 78, 104, 114, 132, 133
Protestantism 26, 156
Proudhon, Pierre-Joseph 132
Proust, Marcel 113
Prussia 25, 30, 71, 113
Puech, Jules-L. 135
Pushkin, Alexander 78

Rain, Henriette 159
Rastoueix-Guinot, Brigitte 149
Ravera, Chiara 44
Raynal, Guillaume Thomas, abbé 15, 25, 77
Récamier, Juliette 35, 71, 97, 113
Regency 3
Reid, Martine 37, 149
Rémusat, Claire Élisabeth Jeanne, comtesse de ix, 107, 108, 109, 110, 113
Renan, Joseph Ernest 146
republic 26, 48, 104, 109, 138, 139, 146, 147
republicanism 21, 42, 46, 78, 85, 86, 109, 145, 146, 147, 157
Restoration xii, 52, 89, 98, 103
Reynolds, Siân 49
Riccoboni, Antoine François 8
Riccoboni, Marie Jeanne xiii, 7, 8, 9, 10
Richardson, Samuel 8, 9, 10
Riga 70, 71
Rivarol, Antoine 71
Robb, Bonnie Arden 38
Robb Jr., David M. 55
Robespierre, Maximilien xi, 42, 47, 48, 88, 89, 90, 93, 109
rococo 21

Rohan Chabot, Alix de 90
Roland de La Platière, Jean Marie 47
Roland de la Platière, Marie Jeanne 'Manon' 45, 46, 48, 49
Romanticism vii, ix, xii, xiii, xiv, 4, 9, 22, 36, 46, 48, 72, 78, 93, 94, 99, 103, 113, 119, 120, 126, 127, 133
Rome 52, 133, 139, 157
Rosen, Julia von 81
Rossard, Janine 73
Rossi, Henri xiii, 90, 110
Rousseau, Jean-Jacques 9, 10, 15, 16, 25, 34, 35, 36, 43, 47, 66, 72, 77, 93, 98, 123, 124, 125, 126, 127, 131, 157
royalism (legitimism) 35, 52, 54, 98, 109, 112, 113, 114, 140
Russia 71, 113

Sabourin, Robert 165
Sade, Donatien Alphonse François, marquis de 47
Saint Bris, Gonzague 159
Saint-Lambert, Jean François de 15
Saint Petersburg 53, 71
Saint-Simon, Claude-Henri de Rouvroy, comte de 133
Salm, Constance Marie Pipelet or Constance, princesse de 83, 84, 85, 86
salons 3, 4, 8, 9, 10, 21, 25, 35, 41, 47, 60, 65, 77, 78, 85, 89, 97, 98, 99, 102, 103, 108, 109, 113, 139, 145, 157, 169
Sanchez, Luis Alberto 135
Sandeau, Jules 139, 145, 147
Sand, George. *See* Dudevant, Amantine Lucile Aurore Dupin, baronne [George Sand]
sans-culottes 49, 53, 79
Savary, Anne Jean Marie René 108, 109, 110
Schlegel, A.W. 78
Schliesser, Eric 67
Scribe, Augustin Eugène 153
Séché, Léon 128, 141
Second Empire ix, 140, 146, 157, 163
Second Republic 104, 146

Ségur, Joseph-Alexandre Pierre, vicomte de 5, 97
Senegal 4, 102, 103, 104
September Massacres 42, 47, 48, 78
Sesma, Manuel Garcia 121
Seth, Catriona 86
Shakespeare, William 70, 72, 98
Sherman, Carol Lynn 44
Sirvent Ramos, Ángeles xiii, 5
Sismondi, Jean Charles Léonard de 78
slavery 4, 78, 102, 103, 104
Smart, Annie K. xiii, 44
Smith, Adam 8, 65, 66, 67
Solte-Gresser, Christiane 32
Sommella, Vincenzo 135
Souchon, Paul 165
Soulié, Melchior Frédéric 98
Soumet, Alexandre 98, 139
Souza-Botelho, Adélaïde Marie Émilie de 57, 58, 59
Spain 21, 131, 138, 139
Spencer, Samia xiii, 17
Spenser, Edmund 60
Staël-Holstein, Anne Louise Germaine, baronne de vii, ix, xi, xii, 10, 25, 26, 36, 47, 53, 60, 65, 66, 72, 75, 76, 77, 78, 79, 97, 103, 104, 109, 113, 114, 123, 124, 125, 126, 131, 139
Staël von Holstein, Erik Magnus, baron 77
Stampacchia, Aruta 171
Steegmuller, Francis 18
Stendhal [Henri Beyle] 85
Sterne, Laurence 31
Stock-Morton, Phyllis 159
Strasbourg 71, 163
Suard, Jean Baptiste Antoine 15, 60, 93
Sue, Eugène 98, 132
Sweden 70, 72, 77
Switzerland 25, 30, 31, 60, 71, 98, 103

Taine, Hippolyte Adolphe 146
Talleyrand-Périgord, Charles-Maurice de 35, 60, 61, 89, 109
Tallien, Thérésa Cabarrus, Madame 89
Talma, François-Joseph 97, 118

Thérenty, Marie-Ève 141
Thiers, Marie Joseph Louis Adolphe 113
Tieck, Ludwig 72
Tolstoy, Leo 25
Toussaint Louverture, François-Dominique 104
Tristán y Moscoso, Flore Célestine Thérèse Henriette [Flora Tristan] xii, 26, 129, 130, 131, 132, 133
Trousson, Raymond 32
Troyat, Henri 73, 165
Tuileries 47, 53, 109, 138, 139, 140
Tulard, Jean and Marie-José xiii, 49
Turgot, Anna Robert Jacques 21, 65

Ultras 114
United States 89, 103

Valentino, Henri 18, 68
Vanderboegh, David S. 115
Van Luttervelt, Remmet 32
Vanoflen, Laurence xiii, 5
Venice 70
Vergennes, Charles Gravier, comte de 97, 108, 109
Verlaine, Paul 119
Vernet, Horace 53, 98
Versailles 16, 31, 47, 87, 88, 89, 98, 112, 114
Vial, Eugène 121
Vienna 52, 53, 104
Vier, Jacques Albert 128, 159
Vigée Le Brun, Marie Louise Élisabeth xii, 51, 52, 53, 54, 60, 89
Vigny, Alfred de 98, 139, 157, 169
Volney, Constantin François de Chassebœuf, comte de 72
Voltaire [François-Marie Arouet] xiv, 3, 4, 15, 22, 35, 47, 78, 97, 99

Wagener, Françoise 113, 115
Wagner, Richard 157
Wallenborn, Melitta 81
Waller, Margaret 104
Walpole, Horace 3
Walton, Whitney xii, 128
Waterloo 99, 114

Wellington, Arthur Wellesley, Duke of 114
West, Benjamin 53
wet nurse 47, 53
Wilberforce, William 104
Winegarten, Renee 81
Wollstonecraft, Mary 42
Wordsworth, William 9, 94, 164
Württemberg 71
Wyndham, Violet 38

Zavatti, Giovanna 159
Zweig, Stefan 121

About the Team

Alessandra Tosi was the managing editor for this book.

Emma Carter and Melissa Purkiss performed the copy-editing and proofreading. Melissa indexed the work.

Melissa Purkiss typeset the book in InDesign and produced the paperback and hardback editions. The text font is Tex Gyre Pagella; the heading font is Californian FB.

Jeevanjot Kaur Nagpal designed the cover. The cover was produced in InDesign using the Fontin font.

Cameron Craig produced the EPUB, PDF and XML editions. The conversion was made with open-source software such as pandoc (https://pandoc.org/), created by John MacFarlane, and other tools freely available on our GitHub page (https://github.com/OpenBookPublishers).

Ross Higman produced the HTML edition.

This book has been anonymously peer-reviewed by experts in their field. We thank them for their invaluable help.

This book need not end here...

Share

All our books — including the one you have just read — are free to access online so that students, researchers and members of the public who can't afford a printed edition will have access to the same ideas. This title will be accessed online by hundreds of readers each month across the globe: why not share the link so that someone you know is one of them?

This book and additional content is available at:

https://doi.org/10.11647/OBP.0346

Donate

Open Book Publishers is an award-winning, scholar-led, not-for-profit press making knowledge freely available one book at a time. We don't charge authors to publish with us: instead, our work is supported by our library members and by donations from people who believe that research shouldn't be locked behind paywalls.

Why not join them in freeing knowledge by supporting us:

https://www.openbookpublishers.com/support-us

Follow @OpenBookPublish

Read more at the Open Book Publishers BLOG

You may also be interested in:

An Outline of Romanticism in the West
John Claiborne Isbell

https://doi.org/10.11647/obp.0302

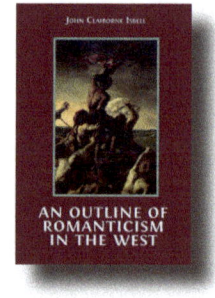

Romanticism and Time
Literary Temporalities
Sophie Laniel-Musitelli and Céline Sabiron (eds)

https://doi.org/10.11647/obp.0232

The Classic Short Story, 1870–1925
Theory of a Genre
Florence Goyet and Yvonne Freccero (trans.)

https://doi.org/10.11647/obp.0039

www.ingramcontent.com/pod-product-compliance
Lightning Source LLC
Chambersburg PA
CBHW042043240426
43667CB00048B/2972